Tonga

a travel survival kit

Deanna Swaney

Tonga - a travel survival kit
1st edition

Published by
Lonely Planet Publications
Head Office: PO Box 617, Hawthorn, Vic 3122, Australia
US Office: PO Box 2001A, Berkeley, CA 94702, USA

Printed by
Colorcraft Ltd, Hong Kong

Photographs by
Deanna Swaney (DS)
Front cover: Tafahi volcano seen from Niuatoputapu Island (DS)

Published
March 1990

Although the author and publisher have tried to make the information as accurate as possible, they accept no responsibility for any loss, injury or inconvenience sustained by any person using this book

National Library of Australia Cataloguing in Publication Data

Swaney, Deanna.
 Tonga, a travel survival kit.

 1st ed.
 Includes index.
 ISBN 0 86442 077 3.

 1. Tonga – Description and travel – Guide-books.
 1. Title

919.61204

Deanna Swaney

After graduating from university, Deanna Swaney made the obligatory European tour and has been addicted to travel ever since. Between wanders around six relatively dry continents, she's enjoyed frequent forays into Oceania, the liquid continent. The universal appeal of the many Pacific 'paradises' she found there resulted in this book and also Lonely Planet's *The Samoas – a travel survival kit*.

When she's not traipsing irresponsibly around the world, Deanna makes her home in Alaska, where she spends her time traipsing irresponsibly around mountains, restaurants, polar bars and shopping malls. She finances this slack behaviour by writing funny coded messages to a Basic IV 8000 mini-computer in the vibrant heart of mid-town Anchorage and writing funny guidebooks for travellers the world over.

Last we heard, she made a wrong turn between Melbourne and the Arctic Circle and wound up in Iceland and Greenland researching our new guide to Arctic island paradises.

Lonely Planet Credits

Editor	Michelle de Kretser
Maps	Vicki Beale
	Valerie Tellini
Cover design, design & illustrations	Chris Lee Ack
Typesetting	Tricia Giles

Thanks also to: Sharan Kaur for proofing, Sharon Wertheim for the index, Ann Jeffree for additional typesetting and Glenn Beanland for map corrections.

From the Author

Special thanks go to Tevita and Katri Va'aivaka (Ha'ateiho, Tongatapu) for their advice and hospitality. Also to Tom and Jan Ginder of somewhere around Perth, Nhulunbuy and Airlie Beach (Australia), for introducing me to the real Mauritius 45' (sic). Marilyn and Roy Staines (alias 'Mom and Dad') of the Keleti Beach Resort (Tongatapu) were extremely helpful and provided a home away from home for me. Tevity Helu and I Futa Helu, both of Nuku'alofa, provided invaluable insights into Tonga and its culture. I'd especially like to thank Remo Finger and Monika Uhrig, formerly of West & East Germany respectively, and Soni Kaifoto (Ha'apai), who shared their wonderful personalities and some good times with me in the most paradisiacal bit of the Kingdom of Tonga. Also, thanks to Peter Shorer for his irreverent nature and for enduring with me the interminable prayer meetings, the maritime crash landings and the abusive surf of Niuafo'ou on our rollicking odyssey to the nethermost regions of Tonga.

The following people also shared their experiences, homes, knowledge and friendship during the researching of this book: Mark Colomb (France), Brad (of the *Iwa*), Mark Scott (USA), Colin and

Margaret Cargill (Australia), Greg Dardis (USA), Greg, Leo and all the Peace Corps gang (Longomapu, Vava'u), Hans and Sela Schmeiser (Neiafu, Vava'u), Langilangi (Pangai, Ha'apai), Bill Afeaki (Tongatapu), Len, Jean and Stephen Smith (Australia), Hugo Brackenbury (UK), Eric Wikman (USA), Andrew Bridgeford (Australia), Dagmar Wanke (West Germany), Seema Sharma (Australia), Carolyn Mata'aho (Niuatoputapu), Paula Lolo (Niuafo'ou), Bruce and Sandy Revington (New Zealand), Joy and Buddy White (USA), Keith Russell (Vanuatu), Peter Leonard Bailey (Canada), Stephen and Christine Peacock (Canada) and Mark Delanney, Dave Dault and Christy Audette, all of Anchorage, Alaska.

Thanks also to the Lonely Planet staff who worked on this book.

Dedication: To Tom, who deserves to find a paradise like Tonga.

A Warning & a Request

Things change – prices go up, schedules change, good places go bad and bad places go bankrupt – nothing stays the same. So if you find things better or worse, recently opened or long since closed, please write and tell us and help make the next edition better!

Your letters will be used to help update future editions and, where possible, important changes will also be included as a Stop Press section in reprints.

All information is greatly appreciated and the best letters will receive a free copy of the next edition, or any other Lonely Planet book of your choice.

Contents

Introduction

Spread across 362,000 square km of the South Pacific Ocean, the Kingdom of Tonga consists of 170 or so remarkably diverse islands which all told occupy only 688 square km of dry land. Despite the country's far-flung nature, the Tongan people, who inhabit only a smattering of their islands – less than 40 – are a nearly homogeneous group and speak a uniform language with only minor local variations. In addition, nearly all Tongans speak some English as a second language and visitors will not need a working knowledge of Tongan in order to communicate with the islanders.

The country consists mainly of four island groups: Tongatapu, Ha'apai, Vava'u and the Niuas. Anyone who wants relative luxury and organised activities

with a South Seas flavour will especially enjoy the main islands of Tongatapu and Vava'u. Divers and snorkellers will find the coral gardens of Vava'u and the countless reefs of Ha'apai irresistible. Bushwalkers will be surprised to find rugged and pristine wilderness on the islands of 'Eua and the Niuas and nearly everyone will be enchanted by the clean turquoise water, the endless deserted white sand beaches, the delicious and bountiful traditional foods, the haunting dances and legends of the islands and the friendly and carefree attitude of their inhabitants.

Tonga is the only South Pacific country which has never been colonised by a European power. One of the consequences of this is that it has pretty much been left

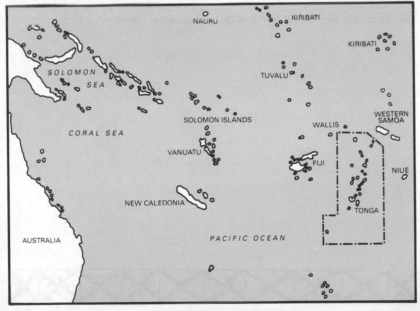

alone by tourists, a fact which the Tonga Visitors' Bureau is desperately trying to change. Without reliable transportation networks, self-contained luxury resort complexes, or extensive advertising abroad, Tonga will be a long time awaiting the kind of high-powered tourism that it is courting; the kind that has drastically altered more traditional destinations such as Tahiti, Fiji and Hawaii. The plus side of this is, of course, that anyone with a little spunk who arrives with a travel-poster dream of old Polynesia will not be disappointed with Tonga.

Those foreigners who somehow 'wash up' on these islands will find themselves on the receiving end of some of the most sincere and unconditional hospitality to be found anywhere on earth. Nowhere else I know of will a traveller feel so little like an outsider and so much like a personal guest of nearly everyone encountered. In his journal, Captain James Cook, who visited Tonga three times in his voyages, wrote of it:

This group I have named the Friendly Archipelago as a lasting friendship seems to subsist among the inhabitants and their courtesy to strangers entitles them to that name.

Since Cook's day, few visitors to the Friendly Islands have failed to respond to their relaxed atmosphere. A popular T-shirt sold in the capital city of Nuku'alofa reads: 'Do it the Tongan way – Tomorrow!'. That fairly sums up the work ethic of the islanders. Some call the syndrome 'Polynesian Paralysis', perhaps the one malady that should be welcomed in a world racked with stress. The best part is that it's contagious. Although there's plenty to see and do in Tonga, there's also plenty not to see and do. There's no television for instance (although videos have caught on to some extent), a negligible crime rate, no deadlines, few hassles, hurries or headaches. . .You get the picture. Add to all that one of the pleasantest climates around and you've got all the elements of the gentle paradise that awaits discovery in Tonga.

Facts about the Country

HISTORY
Prehistory

One legend tells us that the Tongan Islands were fished out of the sea by the mighty Polynesian god Tangaloa, whose tortoiseshell and whalebone fish hook had become entangled around an opening in the island of Nuapapu in the Vava'u Group. The islands emerged originally as a single land mass but, unfortunately, the fishing line broke at a most inopportune moment and bits of land sank back into the sea, leaving only those islands which break the surface today.

Another story has the demigod Maui, a temperamental hero well known throughout the Pacific Islands, doing the fishing. Using a hook borrowed from an old man named Tonga, he yanked up the islands one by one and graciously named the largest one after the man who had made the successful hook.

Archaeologists and anthropologists have placed the date of the initial colonisation of the Tongan group at about 3000 BC, but the earliest date actually confirmed by radiocarbon dating is around 1100 BC.

The Tongan people are Polynesians. The area called Polynesia, meaning 'many islands', consists of a triangle with its corners at Hawaii, Easter Island (off the west coast of South America) and New Zealand, with outliers scattered through Fiji and the East Indies. It is presumed that the Polynesian peoples entered the Pacific from the west – the East Indies or the Philippine islands. Due to the fact that *lapita* pottery similar to that found in the Bismarck Archipelago and New Caledonia has also been found in Tonga and Samoa and that the use of pottery was not in evidence at the time of European contact in the 17th century, it seems likely that they were the first Polynesian areas settled. The discontinuance of the use of pottery is attributed to the lack of suitable clay in the islands and the availability of alternative materials such as coconut shells and sea shells.

The theory put forth by an unconventional Norwegian scientist, Thor Heyerdahl, to the effect that the Polynesians migrated not from Asia but from the Americas is based primarily on the presence of the *kumala* or *kumara*, the sweet potato, in the Pacific and South America but not in Asia. Interestingly enough, the Mormons, ubiquitous throughout the Pacific, also tell a tale of colonisation of the islands by South American mainlanders. The greater part of the scientific community, however, has never taken the idea very seriously.

Early Royalty

Ironically, the legend explaining the origins of Tongan royalty is similar to that of the Incas; both groups profess that their

Tu'i Tonga

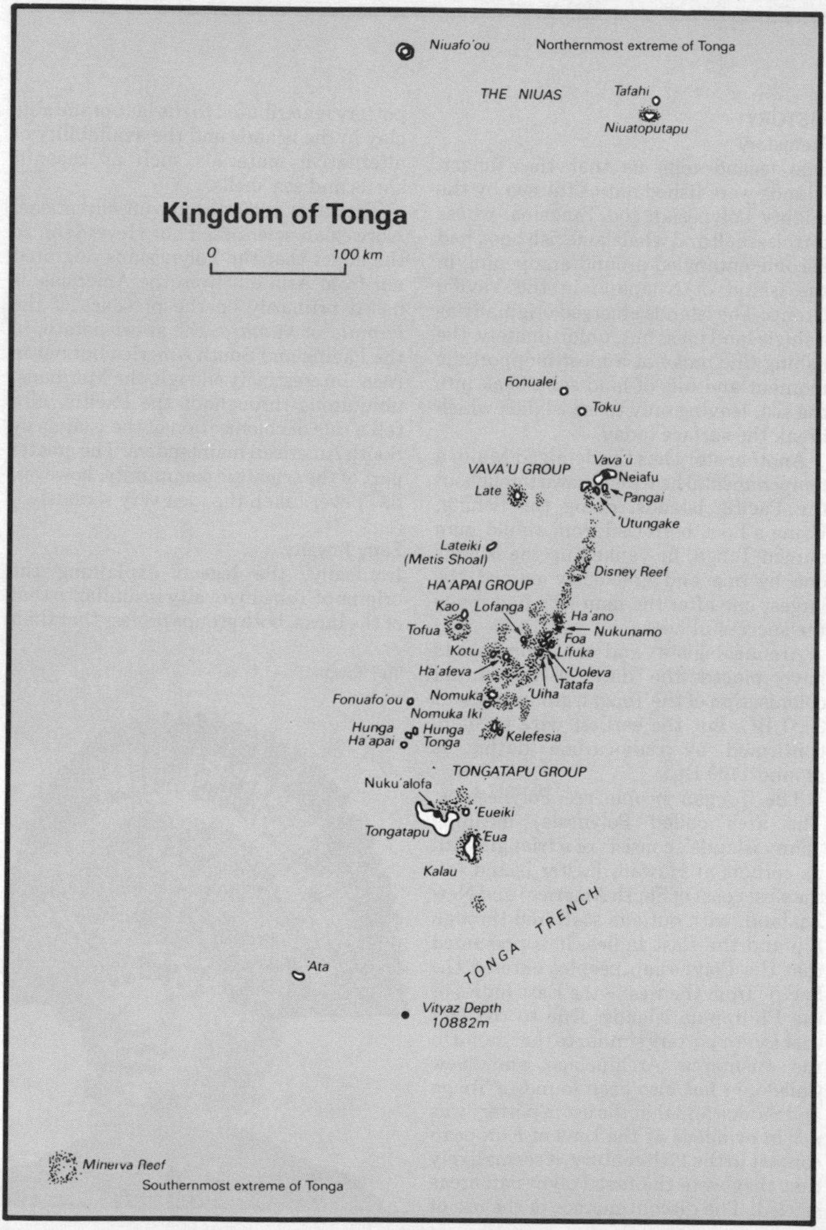
Kingdom of Tonga
0
100 km
Niuafo'ou
Northernmost extreme of Tonga
THE NIUAS
Tafahi
Niuatoputapu
Fonualei
Toku
VAVA'U GROUP
Vava'u
Neiafu
Late
Pangai
'Utungake
Lateiki
(Metis Shoal)
Disney Reef
HA'APAI GROUP
Kao
Lofanga
Ha'ano
Nukunamo
Tofua
Foa
Kotu
Lifuka
Ha'afeva
'Uoleva
Tatafa
Nomuka
'Uiha
Fonuafo'ou
Nomuka Iki
Hunga Ha'apai
Hunga Tonga
Kelefesia
TONGATAPU GROUP
Nuku'alofa
'Eueiki
Tongatapu
'Eua
Kalau
TONGA TRENCH
'Ata
Vityaz Depth
10882m
Minerva Reef
Southernmost extreme of Tonga

first sovereign came to earth as the direct offspring of a solar deity. According to the Tongans, the first Tu'i Tonga (royal title given to a Tongan ruler) was the product of a union between the sun god Tangaloa and a beautiful young earthling named 'Ilaheva. The girl was caught shellfishing one day by the amorous god on a small island near Tongatapu. Nine months later, 'Aho'eitu, who was to become the first in a long line of Tu'is, was born. Thanks to a wealth of oral history at the time of European contact, the date for this event has been placed at 950 AD.

With the title of Tu'i Tonga, of course, came a great deal of respect from the commoners. Distinctive ceremonies evolved concerning the Tu'i Tonga's marriage, burial and mourning. He was addressed in a manner previously reserved for the gods and he was not permitted to be either tattooed or circumcised. His responsibilities encompassed both governmental and religious matters and he was expected to preside over the festival of 'inasi, an agricultural fair in which the biggest and best produce was presented to the gods in order to appease their wrath.

Over the following 400 years or so, the Tongans subscribed to the Fijian attitude that war and strife were activities pursued by noble and worthy men and that peace-loving fellows could only be considered cowardly and effeminate. Accordingly, Tongan warriors embarked in huge catamarans called kalia and set about wreaking all sorts of mischief throughout Fiji and western Polynesia. In this manner they were able to extend the Tu'i Tonga's empire, so that it included territory from parts of Fiji, and stretched eastward to Niue and northward as far as the Samoas and Tokelau.

The title was hereditary, passed from father to son, or to the title-bearer's brother if there was no direct heir to accept it. The 24th Tu'i Tonga, however, created a new position which would take over the temporal responsibilities of his office. It carried the title Tu'i Ha'atakalaua

Wooden war club

and its first bearer was the Tu'i Tonga's brother.

Sometime during the mid-17th century, yet another title emerged and the power associated with it quickly surpassed the other two. At the time of European contact, the newly installed Tu'i Kanokupolu was the most powerful figure in Tonga.

Cannibalism

Cannibalism was practised in Tonga until the missionaries came and explained that in polite society one doesn't roast and eat one's fellows, even if they are considered enemies. A few missionaries ended up in the stewpot while trying to get their point across but it's been well over 100 years since the last guest of honour became the main course. Cannibalism was associated with absorbing the power and cleverness of one's adversaries, and was not a necessary answer to a lack of protein.

European Contact

The first known contact between Europeans and the Tongans occurred in 1616 when a couple of bumbling Dutchmen, an entrepreneur named Jacob Lemaire and his navigator, Willem Cornelius Schouten, passed through the Niuas en route to the East Indies in their ships Eendracht and Hoorn. Although they never landed, they had a brief encounter with a Tongan sailing canoe and as a result at least one Tongan was killed and several were taken captive. However, the Europeans managed to trade a few trinkets for foodstuffs and, like all good explorers, saw fit to rename their 'discoveries': the islands of Niuatoputapu, Tafahi and Niuafo'ou became the Dutch equivalents of Traitor's Island, Coconut Island and Good Hope Island respectively.

Abel Tasman

The next visitor happened to be another Dutchman, Abel Janszoon Tasman, who passed through the southernmost Tongan islands in 1643 with his ships *Heemskerck* and *Zeehan*. A bit more social than his countrymen Schouten and Lemaire, Tasman carried on trade with the natives of 'Ata, 'Eua and Tongatapu (which he named Pylstaart, Middleburgh and Amsterdam); he took on water from the freshwater lake on the island of Nomuka (surprise – this one he named Rotterdam!) in the Ha'apai Group.

Over a century later in 1767, the Englishman Captain Samuel Wallis, who was credited with the discovery of Otaheite (Tahiti), arrived in his ship *Dolphin* in search of the fabled southern continent, Ptolemy's *terra australis incognita*. He spent several days trading in the Niuas and renamed Niuatoputapu and Tafahi (er – Traitor's and Coconut) Keppel and Boscawen, respectively.

Just seven years later on his second Pacific expedition, the second Englishman to set foot on the Tongan Islands landed at 'Eua. This one was Captain James Cook, the most peripatetic of all European

explorers of the day; the man who said of himself, '. . .ambition leads me not only farther than any other man has been before me, but as far as I think it possible for man to go'. He had had instructions from King George III to 'observe the genius, temper, disposition and number of the natives or inhabitants, if there be any and endeavour by all proper means to cultivate a friendship and alliance with them. . .'

During the course of his trip he stopped twice, both times briefly, in Tonga. In October 1773, he spent two days visiting 'Eua and five days on Tongatapu. Upon his arrival in the former, Tongans swarmed his ship. Smiling, friendly and ready to trade (they undoubtedly had heard legends about Tasman's visit), they offered Cook and his men tapa (mulberry bark cloth) and women in exchange for iron. Cook's men performed musical numbers on the bagpipes, the Tongan women sang and danced for the visitors and food and kava (a drink made from the root of the pepper shrub) were served. The kava was prepared by chewing the root, spitting the pulp into a bowl and adding water. Among the Europeans, only Cook himself had the nerve to partake of it.

Cook was also particularly impressed with the friendly and verdant island of Tongatapu, which he compared to the most beautiful and fertile plains of Europe.

Eight months later, on his return voyage, he spent four days trading and taking on water at Nomuka. On his third voyage, however, he spent over two months (April to July 1777) in the Tongan Islands. At his first landfall, at Nomuka, the chief of Ha'apai, Finau, told him of a wealthier island (Lifuka), where supplies would be available. While visiting Lifuka, Cook and his men were treated to lavish feasting and entertainment, a spellbinding display the likes of which the Englishmen had never before witnessed. Needless to say, the foreigners were impressed, and Cook dubbed the Ha'apai Group the

Friendly Archipelago after the apparent disposition of its inhabitants.

Thirty years later, it was learned that the exhibition had been part of a conspiracy on the part of the Tongans to raid the ships *Resolution* and *Discovery* for their plainly visible wealth. The entertainment had been planned in order to gather the Englishmen into a convenient place, so that they could be quickly dispatched and their ships looted. There was, however, a dispute between Finau and his nobles over whether the attack would occur by day or under cover of night. Having previously agreed to follow the chief's plan to take action during the afternoon, the nobles failed to do so at the appointed time. Finau was so incensed at such a defiance of his orders that the operation was abandoned altogether and the Englishmen never learned how narrowly they had escaped.

When Finau announced that he was setting out to visit the Vava'u Group to the north and Cook expressed interest in accompanying him, the chief assured him that the islands contained no suitable anchorage or landing place for ships such as Cook's and that such a trip would be foolhardy. Instead of opting for such adventure, the Englishmen sailed southward through the convoluted reefs and shoals of the southern Ha'apai Group. Upon landing at Tongatapu, Cook learned that he had been deceived: the Vava'u Group contained perhaps the finest anchorages in the entire archipelago.

While visiting in Tongatapu, Cook became friends with Fatafehi Paulaho, the 30th Tu'i Tonga, and was amazed at the reverence and ceremony which surrounded this person: 'I was quite charmed at the decorum. . .I had nowhere seen the like. . .not even amongst more civilised nations.' Out of respect and affection, Cook presented the Tu'i Tonga with a fully grown tortoise. Later given the title Tu'i Malila, the creature lived for nearly 200 years longer. At the time of its death, in 1966, when it bore the scars of many traumatic experiences (among them encounters with a truck and a bushfire), Tu'i Malila enjoyed a seat at the royal kava circle and the run of the palace gardens. The tortoise's remains may be seen today at the Tonga National Centre near Nuku'alofa.

Although Cook had been aware of the existence of the Vava'u Group, he'd never actually visited it and its 'discovery' was left to the Spaniard Don Francisco Antonio Mourelle of the ship *Princesa*, who ran across it en route to Spanish America in 1781. Low on supplies and fair winds, Mourelle was overjoyed to see the island of Fonualei on the horizon, but as he approached he realised it was barren and uninhabited. Accordingly, he named it Amargura, or 'bitterness'. An unfavourable wind prevented his landing at the more promising island of Late, so when he finally made landfall at Vava'u, he named its harbour Puerto de Refugio, which means 'port of refuge', and claimed the entire group for Spain. (The harbour still bears the name Port of Refuge in commemoration of Mourelle's relief at finding it.) After quickly taking on supplies, Mourelle set off southward in search of a fair wind to Mexico.

In 1787, en route from Siberia to the English colonies at New South Wales, the French explorer Jean de la Pérouse spent a short time passing through Tonga while recovering from the famous massacre his expedition had met with on Tutuila, in Samoa. La Pérouse arrived in New South Wales, but after leaving he disappeared, never to be seen again. (The wreckage of both his ships were subsequently discovered off Vanikolo Island in the Solomons.) Antoine d'Entrecasteaux, who set out in search of La Pérouse, arrived in Tongatapu in 1793. His ship's botanist wrote an account of the visit, but little else came out of the French connection in Tonga.

In April 1789, Tonga by chance experienced a historical event the tale of which would be told and retold around the world for hundreds of years to come. Off the volcanic island of Tofua in the Ha'apai Group, Captain William Bligh and 18 crewmen of the HMS *Bounty* were involuntarily relieved of their duties and set adrift in an open boat with a minimum of supplies. They landed at Tofua briefly hoping to secure provisions but local unrest forced them to cast off after loading only the most meagre of rations. Quartermaster John Norton was attacked and killed by islanders and the other Englishmen escaped narrowly. They reached Timor in the Dutch East Indies on 14 June, having survived the longest ever voyage in an open boat. The year 1791 brought Captain Edward Edwards of the HMS *Pandora* to the Tongan archipelago searching for the *Bounty* mutineers, who by this time had settled in comfortably on Pitcairn Island.

Mourelle's raving accounts of the Vava'u Group and his claim to the islands created some excitement back in Spain and, in 1793, Captain Alessandro Malaspina was sent chasing all over the Pacific – to Peru, Alaska, the Philippines, New Zealand and Vava'u (I'd like to do that trip at government expense!!) – to make observations and surveys as well as investigate the feasibility of occupying Vava'u. He placed a decree of Spanish ownership in a bottle and buried it somewhere on the main island. It was never to be found again but that wasn't much of an issue – with numerous concerns in the Americas, Spain lost interest in the project, anyway.

The first permanent European settlers in Tonga were six deserters from the American ship *Otter*, who landed at 'Eua and Ha'apai in 1796. The following year, 10 lay missionaries of the London Missionary Society arrived at Tongatapu on the ship *Duff*. Three were murdered in a local scuffle, six escaped to Australia and one, George Vason, renounced Christianity. He married a Tongan woman and remained among the islanders until 1804. During this time, the chief of Ha'apai, Finau 'Ulukalala, forcefully gained control of all the major island groups and the three royal titles began to fall into disuse.

William Mariner

Thanks to a series of serendipitous incidents, the world has been provided with an extensive account of the customs, language, religion and government of the Tongans before the arrival of Christianity put those things awry.

As a well-educated English lad of 15, William Charles Mariner, the son of a sea captain, went to sea on the privateer *Port-au-Prince* in February 1805. The voyage of plunder and pillage took the ship across the Atlantic, around the Horn, up the west coast of South America, to the Sandwich (Hawaiian) Islands and finally into the Ha'apai Group of Tonga. On 29 November 1806, the crew anchored at the northern end of Lifuka and were immediately welcomed with yams and barbecued pork. Initially, their reception seemed friendly enough, but the following day, the crew became increasingly aware that some sort of plot was afoot and that appropriate caution should be exercised in dealing with the Tongans.

Captain Brown, the whaling master who had assumed command upon the death of the original skipper several months earlier, was convinced that the threat was imagined and he unfortunately chose to deny and ignore it. On 1 December the attack was launched while 300 hostile Tongans were aboard the ship. The British, being sorely outnumbered, chose to destroy the ship, its crew and its attackers rather than allow it to be taken. Young Mariner had gone to procure the explosives when he met with several locals, who escorted him ashore past the fallen bodies of his shipmates.

Mariner was subjected to much persecution by the Tongans until he was summoned by Finau 'Ulukalala I, still the reigning chief of Ha'apai. The king had assumed that Mr Mariner was the captain's son or at least a young chief in his own country and had given orders that the young man's life be preserved.

Meanwhile, the *Port-au-Prince*, which hadn't been destroyed, was dragged ashore, raided and burned. The conflagration heated the cannons sufficiently to cause them to fire, causing a general panic among the Tongans. Calmly accepting his fate, Mariner pantomimed an explanation of the phenomena and thus initiated a sort of rapport with the Tongans that would carry him through the following four years. Although a few other crew members of the *Port-au-Prince* were spared, Mariner was the only one taken so completely under the wing of Finau and he was therefore privy to most of the goings-on in Tongan politics. He learned the language well and travelled about the island groups with the chief, observing and absorbing the finer points of ceremony and protocol among the people. He was given the name Toki 'Ukamea, meaning 'iron axe', and, in a moment of compassion, Finau appointed one of his royal wives, Mafi Hape, to be Mariner's adoptive mother, as he was sure that the young man's real mother at home must be extremely worried about his condition.

After the death of Finau, his son permitted young William to leave Tonga on a passing English vessel. Were it not for a chance meeting in a London restaurant with an amateur anthropologist named Dr John Martin, his unique experiences might forever have been lost to the world. Martin, fascinated with Mariner's tale, suggested collaboration on a book and the result, *An Account of the Natives of the Tonga Islands*, is a masterpiece of Pacific literature.

Christian Influences

After the London Missionary Society fled Tonga for its health in 1799, the kingdom was more or less free of Bible-bashers, until 1822 brought a Wesleyan minister, Reverend Walter Lawry, to Tongatapu. Resistance to his ideas, however, sent him packing back to Australia after only a year. After he left, a Tongan chief became interested in Christianity and when the Wesleyans returned to the islands several years later, they enjoyed much more success. By the time the French Catholic missionaries arrived the Wesleyans had already succeeded in converting the nephew of the Tu'i Kanokupolu and the course of Tongan history was suddenly sent in a new direction.

This young man, Taufa'ahau, had become the ruler of his native Ha'apai in 1820 and had forcefully attained the title of Tu'i Tonga from its heir apparent, Laufilitonga. Upon his baptism in 1831, he took the Christian name Siaosi, or George, after the king of England, and adopted the surname Tupou. His wife, who had previously been the wife of poor Laufilitonga, was baptised Salote, after Queen Charlotte.

Under George's influence, all of Ha'apai converted to Christianity and, shortly thereafter, thanks to the conversion of George's cousin, King 'Ulukalala III of Vava'u, that group followed suit. Upon the death of 'Ulukalala, George assumed his cousin's title too.

In Tongatapu the Wesleyans were already having quite a few successes, including the conversion of George's great-uncle, the Tu'i Kanokupolu. Upon the death of that influential man in 1845, George Tupou assumed his title, thus becoming the most powerful man in a united Tonga under the name King George Tupou I.

The House of Tupou

After uniting Tonga and ascending to its throne, King George found that his troubles were only beginning. On one side, he had the Wesleyan missionaries battling the encroachment of the Catholics who had succeeded in converting several influential chiefs. On the other, he had the traditional chiefs and nobles who were accustomed to wielding the power of life and death over their subservient subjects. As early as 1838, quite a while before his

King George Tupou I

power over all Tonga became a foregone conclusion, King George saw the need for a uniform set of laws to govern the country. His first effort was the Vava'u Code, which forbade worship of the old gods and also prevented those in power from forcefully acquiring the means of the commoners. In 1853, the king made a visit to Australia and, upon learning that not all foreigners were as ignorant as the Wesleyan missionaries, he decided to seek help there in drafting a revision of the code.

The rift between the king and the Wesleyans grew until Reverend Shirley Baker appeared on the scene as a member of the Tongan Mission. George immediately took a liking to Baker and together they began working on governmental revisions. The main result was the perpetual prohibition of serfdom in the kingdom. In addition, it was stipulated that no land in the kingdom could be sold to a foreigner (and this many years before the king could have imagined what was to happen to his fellow Polynesian kingdom of Hawaii!). Lastly, the revised code mandated the distribution of land to male subjects over 16 years of age. Every man was to receive

a village lot and an 'api (plantation of 3.34 hectares) for an annual fee of T$3.20.

The missionaries, jealous of Baker's preferential treatment, made an effort to have him expelled from the church and the kingdom on charges of adultery; but they failed and Baker continued on his course of statesmanship. Together, he and the king came up with a national flag, a state seal and a national anthem, then embarked on the drafting of a constitution. It included a bill of rights, a format for legislative and judicial procedures and a section on land tenure. It also contained laws of succession to the throne. The new constitution was passed on 4 November 1875.

In 1879 the church removed Shirley Baker from association with their mission. The king responded by cancelling Wesleyan leases and appointing Shirley Baker prime minister of Tonga, much to the dismay of nearly everyone but the king himself. In 1885, Baker created the Free Church of Tonga and the king urged all his subjects to abandon the Wesleyans and join the new church. A small-scale 'holy war' ensued. An attempted assassination of the prime minister resulted in the execution of six Wesleyans and exile for four others. Most of the handful of Wesleyans remaining in Tonga emigrated to Fiji.

The strife caught the attention of Britain, which saw Tonga's moment of weakness as an opportunity to gain influence in the country. Assuming that the 89-year-old king had gone a bit senile and that Baker had turned the situation to his own advantage, the British sent an investigatory committee to Tonga to ascertain the stability of the situation there. While they learned that the king's mental health was sound, they forcefully convinced him that religious freedom was necessary in Tonga and eventually deported Baker.

Upon King George's death in 1893 at the age of 96, his great-grandson assumed the throne and took the name George Tupou II. He was by no means a statesman and lacked the flare and character of his predecessor. The British, fearing loss of control under such an administration, coerced him into signing a treaty which placed Tonga under British protection in the field of foreign affairs. King George Tupou II died at the age of 45 in 1918, upon which his 18-year-old daughter Salote became queen.

Queen Salote's primary concerns for her country were not squabbling churches and greedy chiefs but medicine and education. With intelligence, compassion and a naturally regal stature and attitude, she made friends for Tonga throughout the world and was greatly loved by her subjects and by foreigners alike. The tale of her attendance at Queen Elizabeth II's coronation in 1953 has been told and retold. Tongan tradition does not allow imitation of those whom one holds in great respect, so while Elizabeth rode in a covered carriage through pouring rain to Westminster Abbey, the Tongan queen refused to allow her own carriage to be covered. When she died in 1965 the world mourned her, and Tonga regarded itself as a child that had lost its mother.

Queen Salote's son, King Taufa'ahau Tupou IV, is currently the ruler of Tonga. Although he is known worldwide primarily for his ample girth, he has brought about quite a few notable accomplishments. They include the re-establishment of full sovereignty for Tonga on 4 June 1970 and admission to the Commonwealth of Nations shortly thereafter. In 1976, realising that his nation was being largely ignored by the western powers, the king attracted their attention by establishing diplomatic relations with the Soviet Union. New Zealand, the USA and Australia immediately began taking notice of his awakening kingdom in the South Pacific.

In late 1988 the Tongan government became involved in extremely controversial negotiations with the USA concerning nuclear waste disposal. Greenpeace lobbied the government, and the Tongan

King Taufa'ahau Tupou IV

people themselves weren't keen on their country becoming a nuclear dumping ground; consequently, nothing came of the negotiating.

GEOGRAPHY

The Kingdom of Tonga is composed of four major island groups, which are, from south to north, Tongatapu, Ha'apai, Vava'u and the Niuas. Altogether the four groups include some 170 individual islands and a land area of 688 square km.

The Tongatapu Group is the largest in area. It includes the main island of Tongatapu as well as 'Eua, 'Ata, 'Eueiki, Kalau and numerous small islands encompassed within the barrier reef north of the main island. Minerva Reef, 350 km to the south-west of Tongatapu, is Tonga's southernmost extreme.

A hundred km north of Tongatapu is the Ha'apai Group, a cluster of 36 major islands and numerous submerged reefs. The main inhabited islands include Lifuka, Ha'ano, Foa, 'Uiha, Ha'afeva and Nomuka. Tonga's highest point is found on Kao, whose perfect volcanic cone rises to 1109 metres. Kao's sister island, Tofua, is an active, spewing volcano. The 'sometimes island' of Fonuafo'ou is also found in the Ha'apai Group.

Moving another 100 km to the north, one encounters the 34 islands of the Vava'u Group. The largest of these is the main island of Vava'u. The smaller ones are merely peaks rising out of drowned valleys of the same landmass – Hunga, Nuapapu, 'Ovaka, Pangai, 'Utungake, Koloa, Kapa, 'Ofu and Vakaeitu. Volcanic outliers include Toku, Fonualei, Late and Late'iki.

The furthest reaches of the kingdom are found in the three small islands of the Niuas Group, nearly 400 km to the north of Vava'u. Niuatoputapu is a reef-encircled eroded volcano, while its near neighbour Tafahi is a perfect cone 656 metres high. Niuafo'ou is a doughnut-shaped island, the remnant of an enormous cone which collapsed violently and has been destructively active as recently as 1946.

At the Tonga Trench, which reaches a depth of 10,882 metres at Vityaz Deep, the Pacific plate is being swallowed by the Indo-Australian plate. Just west of the trench lie the four island groups of Tonga in two parallel north-south trending lines.

At the zone of subduction which currently lies beneath the western chain, the materials which constitute the Pacific plate are being melted and recombined deep in the earth's mantle. This process, needless to say, is accompanied by a great deal of seismic activity; earthquakes and vulcanism are the results apparent on the surface.

According to the University of North Carolina, Tonga is moving toward Samoa at a rate of 10 cm per year, the most dramatic drift on earth.

Most of Tonga's high islands were created by geologically recent activity. As was mentioned previously, Tafahi, Late and Kao form nearly perfect cones, and Niuafo'ou and Tofua remain active. Fonualei and 'Ata are well eroded but their fiery origins remain obvious, and the two very recently formed islands of Fonuafo'ou (also known as Falcon Island) and Late'iki (Metis Shoal) evidence one of the world's most bizarre geological phenomena. In the words of one articulate Tongan, 'Yes, they come and they go'. . .These oddities will be explained in more detail in the respective sections on the two islands.

The eastern line of islands is the result of the sagging weight of the new crust along the zone of vulcanism to the west, centred on Kao and Tofua. The islands have been squeezed up in much the same way toothpaste is squeezed out of a tube. The islands of 'Eua, Tongatapu and Vava'u are the best examples of tilted blocks of crust. Their respective west, south and north coasts consist of high, abrupt cliffs, while their respective east, north and south coastlines are submerging. In the case of Vava'u and Tongatapu, this is evidenced by mazes of islands, reefs and mangrove-choked lagoons on the Ha'apai side of each.

The main body of the Ha'apai Group consists of two large and eroding coral atolls, the Nomuka and Lulunga groups, and a raised barrier reef (the Lifuka Group). The Ha'apai Group contains several *motus* (coral islets) and countless shoals and barrier reefs, all sustained by coral polyps.

CLIMATE

Despite its great latitudinal variation, Tonga does not experience diverse climatic conditions. The Vava'u and Niua groups receive more precipitation and slightly higher average temperatures than the more southerly islands, but even this is not dramatic.

Tonga is far enough from the equator, as far as Hawaii or the southern Cooks, to enjoy a mild and more comfortable climate than the Samoas or the Solomons. Winter (July to September) temperatures are pleasantly cool, 17°C to 22°C or so, but certain weather patterns such as southerly winds and strong south-east trades can create less than idyllic conditions. At this time of the year come prepared for some chilly days.

Summer (December to April) temperatures vary from 25°C to 33°C, but even then cooler nights are not unusual. Extreme humidity is normally tempered by a light breeze. During early summer, Tonga experiences one of the world's most ideal climates. Later in the season, however, the islands receive most of their annual rainfall and things can get positively messy.

Tonga lies squarely within the South Pacific's notorious cyclone/typhoon belt and has experienced quite a few devastating blows over the years. Yachties, therefore, should try to clear out and head for New Zealand or the Solomons by at least the end of November. The only marginal hurricane shelter for yachts in the islands is Vava'u's Port of Refuge, but winds over 50 knots render it potentially hazardous. Other travellers can be assured that there will be sufficient warning to enable them to move inland before the situation grows too threatening. A really severe typhoon may occur about every 20 years, while milder ones occur on an average of every three or four years.

About 60% of the time the winds are south-easterly, while north-easterly and southerly winds each occur about 10% of the time. Westerly and north-westerly winds bring the worst weather, but it rarely lasts for more than 24 hours.

Average annual precipitation at Nuku'alofa is 1500 mm and measurable rainfall occurs on 35% of the days. Vava'u is the wettest of all the island groups with up to 2500 mm of rain falling annually.

FLORA & FAUNA

Although Tonga isn't particularly known for its flora and fauna, it was the first South Pacific nation to set aside national parks and reserves in order to protect its resources, particularly the numerous coral reefs north of Tongatapu.

Over 100 species of colourful tropical fish, including the tiny but brilliant blue damselfish, brightly coloured clownfish and parrotfish, and a host of others, are readily observed by snorkellers and divers. The reefs themselves form beautiful gardens of shapes and colours. Black coral is common around Tonga and is carved into jewellery and artistic pieces. The beaches and reefs are also home to numerous species of crabs, shellfish, starfish and crustaceans.

Porpoises and migrating humpback whales may also be seen in the waters around Tonga.

Flying fox

The only land mammal native to Tonga is the flying fox, an extremely large bat with a wingspan of up to one metre. Around Kolovai in western Tongatapu, there is a reserve dedicated to their protection. Thousands upon thousands may be seen snoozing upside down in casuarina trees there, an impressive (and, for the squeamish, frightening) sight. Although technically protected, the royal family is allowed to hunt them for sport. Reptiles, in the form of several species of small lizards, are also found in abundance.

Tonga has surprisingly few birds, but of interest are the blue-crowned lory and musk parrot of 'Eua, the tropicbirds that nest on cliffs throughout the islands and the incubator bird or megapode, found only on the island of Niuafo'ou.

Although most of the land in Tonga has been converted into either 'api or town tracts, large areas of natural rainforest and bushland occur on the Niuas and 'Eua as well as on the uninhabited volcanic islands. The upland areas of 'Eua contain a relatively large forest reserve, which is probably the last significant stand of first-growth rainforest in the country.

After you've been there a while you may notice that Tongans have a rather propagandist way of referring to their flora and fauna. Fleas and body crabs are called *kuto fisi* and *kuto ha'amoa* or 'Fijian bugs' and 'Samoan bugs' respectively. Likewise, poisonous kava plants are called *kava fisi* while good drinking kava is *kava tonga*. Large tuna are called *valu tonga* while the smaller variety are *valu ha'amoa*.

GOVERNMENT

Technically, Tonga is a constitutional monarchy based on the British parliamentary system. However, the current king, Taufa'ahau Tupou IV, may be the world's most powerful (as well as largest!) reigning monarch. The constitution was

Royal crest

drawn up and ratified in the mid-1870s by King George Tupou I and Shirley Baker, who later became Tonga's first prime minister. Since its original draft, it has undergone relatively little amendment.

The system provides for a sovereign and a privy council. The king or queen is the head of state and government. His or her cabinet consists of the prime minister (a post currently occupied by the king's ailing brother, Prince Tu'ipelehake) and ministers of the crown. All these positions are appointed by the monarch, and the occupants remain in office until voluntary retirement or death. Also members of the cabinet are the governors of Ha'apai and Vava'u. When presided over by the monarch, the cabinet is called the privy council.

The legislature is unicameral and is composed of an appointed speaker, the cabinet, seven nobles elected by 33 hereditary nobles and seven representatives elected by literate taxpayers over the age of 21. Elections are held every three years.

The highest judicial assembly in the land is the court of appeal, which is made up of the privy council and the chief justice. Below it is the supreme court, the land court (also presided over by the chief justice) and the magistrates court. In criminal law, the accused may opt for trial by jury or by a judge alone.

Local governments consist of town and district officers, who respectively preside over villages and groups of villages.

Education is compulsory for children between the ages of six and 14. It's free in state schools, but the vast majority of Tongans receive their primary and secondary education at one of the numerous Christian institutions. Tertiary education is only available at the University of the South Pacific extension and the private 'Atenisi Institute, both on Tongatapu.

The Tongan Defence Forces are composed of three branches: an infantry, royal guards and maritime forces.

ECONOMY

The vast majority of Tongans are involved in a subsistence life style. Recognising this fact, the government has done its level best to provide all male citizens with a plot of land on which to raise food and other commodities. This is achieved by a unique system of land tenure which, in theory, works as follows:

All the land in the kingdom is the property of the crown but it is divided up into estates assigned either to the king or to one of the nobles. At the age of 16, any male subject wanting to be involved in agriculture is given an 'api of 3.34 hectares for an annual rental fee of T$3.20. In addition, he is allocated a town lot on which to build a home free of charge. The noble in charge of the land received may dispute the assignment, in which case that individual's 'api is taken from royal estates. Every allotment holder must plant at least 200 coconut trees on his parcel within the first 12 months and maintain it as agricultural land or risk losing it.

Foreigners in Tonga may only acquire land by lease, and no more than 5% of the total land area may be controlled by noncitizens.

The obvious problem with this system is shortage of land. Tonga is a small country, and, with a population density of 145 per square km and only 66% of total land area available for habitation or agriculture, it is apparent that not every eligible Tongan has access to such benefits.

Staple subsistence-level agricultural products include pineapples, papayas, kava, taro, watermelons, bananas, manioc, yams, sweet potatoes and, of course, coconuts. In addition, most households have breadfruit and mango trees and keep horses, pigs, and chickens. Many supplement their diet with reef fish caught in a net, or with a line and reel (the reel is usually a glass bottle).

Leading agricultural exports are coconut oil, desiccated coconut and vanilla. On a smaller scale, Tonga also produces peppers, tomatoes, watermelons, limes and kava.

In order to encourage overseas investments and new business, the Tongan government offers five-year tax holidays and quite a few small industries have taken advantage of this and the inexpensive labour situation. Businesses in Tonga, however, may not be more than 49% foreign controlled. A Small Industries Centre exists in the Maufanga suburb of Nuku'alofa; it has been successful in producing knitwear, paper products and furniture. A coconut oil processing plant in the same vicinity has been extremely lucrative, exporting up to 15,000 tonnes annually.

The fishing industry provides minimal income from tuna exports. A sawmill at Ha'atu'a on 'Eua Island prepares native forestry products for local use and export.

Currently, the star on Tonga's economic horizon is tourism. With political strife in nearby Fiji, Vanuatu, New Caledonia and Tahiti, Tonga is hoping to cash in on Australian, North American, and European markets as a new paradisiacal destination. As yet, tourist amenities and infrastructure are minimal, and most takers seem to be those more impecunious foreigners who like things that way. They do manage to cart off a fair number of postage stamps and handicrafts, however, both of which are superb in Tonga.

POPULATION & PEOPLE

Tongans are a fairly homogeneous Polynesian group. The current population stands at about 100,000 and is growing at a staggering annual rate of 3% due to the status and honour that large families traditionally command. The population density stands at about 145 per square km, but the problem of overcrowding is not as serious as these figures would suggest, as widespread emigration relieves a bit of the pressure on the limited territory and resources of the islands.

You'd be hard pressed to find a Tongan without relatives in New Zealand, Australia, or the USA and possibly in a combination of the three.

It's interesting to note that many Tongans who have migrated abroad in search of greener pastures discover that they cannot cope with the hectic pace of life there and ultimately return to Tonga. Their native country may well be the easiest place in the world to live in with a minimum of effort, and Tongans invariably notice that to thrive abroad (except for a very privileged few) requires a rigid schedule dominated by work.

The 'brain drain' created by those skilled or well-educated individuals who do remain outside the country does not present as significant a problem to the Tongan economy as it would initially seem. In Tongan tradition, food, clothing, homes, money and all material goods are communally owned by the extended family and, therefore, any member in need is considered welcome to and deserving of the means of any other member, including those of relatives living overseas. A great deal of money earned by Tongans living and working around the world eventually finds its way back to Tonga and, to a great extent, the nation depends on this income as a vital economic asset.

This system allows Tongan life to continue at a suitably Polynesian pace, while the cash economy and all its associated headaches are contained elsewhere. As would be expected, it often does put some strain on the non-Polynesian spouses of overseas Tongans who have been reared in more materialistic cultures. Countless marriages between Tongans and *palangis* (foreigners) have failed because of the economic drain that the Tongan family represents. Justifiably, families in Tonga are concerned that the second overseas generation, reared in a foreign culture, won't be so generous toward the folks back in the 'old country', relatives they may never have met.

CULTURE

Despite the fact that Tongans are an open and extremely hospitable people, travellers throughout the Pacific (including myself) become confused at their behaviour and come to sense that they are not being let in on some very significant details of the Tongan life style.

Christianity is legislated and professed loudly but the old ways and superstitions quietly remain. Warm and generous adults invite foreigners into their homes and lavish gifts and food on them, yet they seem to regard their own children coldly and without affection. Honest and upstanding individuals will openly rummage through the pockets of an unconscious drunk and help themselves to his money.

How can it all be explained? Conversely, how would you go about explaining to a Tongan why an Australian may address his best friend as 'ratbag' or 'shit-for-brains', why an outwardly friendly palangi puts up a fence to keep his neighbours away, or why Europeans on holiday to 'get away from it all' always seem to be in a hurry.

One foreigner living in Tonga likened *faka tonga*, or the 'Tongan way', to an onion: as soon as he feels that he's finally grasped the essence of the place – the real Tonga, if you will – he finds that it peels off easily to reveal another, deeper, layer. It would be quite safe to say that few outsiders, if any, will ever come to understand all the underlying nuances of any Polynesian culture. Ritual and custom may be easily observed and recounted, but to grasp the meaning of it all is another issue, indeed. I wish it were possible to describe the significance of such things – an innocently raised eyebrow, a formal kava ceremony, the gestures and expressions of a *matapule*, or talking chief, ritually accepting a gift for royalty – but I realise that any explanation I, a non-Tongan, can offer will be quite superficial. Tonga, like other little-known places on earth, challenges visitors to observe and discover, and it greatly rewards those who do.

Social Hierarchy

With the advent of Christianity as the state religion, all Tongans became theoretically equal 'under God' and social ranking lost a great deal of its importance. The constitution of 1875 abolished the traditional feudal system of subservience and serfdom for the commoners, and the chiefs and nobles were denied the privilege of indiscriminate pillage to which they'd been previously accustomed. Old habits die hard, however, and remnants of the traditional system may still be seen today.

Although caste is not as rigid and elaborate as it was before European contact, there remains a two-tier system which determines privilege among individuals and in which no upward mobility is possible. The royal family and the 33 hereditary nobles of the realm and their families enjoy the highest rank in the society. All other Tongans are commoners. Nobles may not marry commoners without risk of losing their titles. A commoner who marries a noble can never attain noble status.

In a sense, a third class does exist: it is composed of expatriates of European descent who, by virtue of their relative wealth (in most cases) and education, receive deferential treatment. Unfortunately, this is usually motivated by fear of the unpredictable dispositions of foreigners.

Social Protocol

In most cases, visitors will not be expected to participate in or even be aware of Tongan codes of behaviour, but those who do are likely to be more casually accepted by the people.

Respect for those considered superior to one's self, whether they really are or not, is a principal motivation in Tongan behaviour. In the presence of royalty, nobles, high commissioners, politicians, religious leaders or what have you, Tongans

become more guarded and deliberate. As a foreigner, you are likely to be regarded in a similar fashion, hence the 'arm's length' feeling many people get when dealing with hospitable locals.

In extreme cases, such as when dealing with royalty and nobles, 'respect' translates into veneration. In the presence of such people Tongan commoners wear ta'ovala, woven mats tied around the waist with coconut sennit, as a sign of respect. To be without one would be the social equivalent of a European male presenting himself to the president or prime minister without a coat and necktie.

In addition, Tongan commoners physically lower themselves in front of a royal who is standing up, in order to demonstrate willing subservience, and in no way imitate their actions (remember the tale of Queen Salote at Queen Elizabeth's coronation). At any gathering at which royalty is to be present, everyone else must be seated before the guests of honour arrive. Once royalty is seated, no other commoners may be admitted or seated (in this one case, western-style punctuality is absolutely necessary). For those who are privileged enough to actually address royalty, there is a special level of the Tongan language which must be used, the equivalent of the King James English reserved for addressing God. The death of a monarch sets off a legislated six-month period of mourning during which, in effect, the entire country shuts down.

One practice, which is in no way unique to Tonga but is ubiquitous there, is gift giving. Gifts are given as a matter of course to new friends, especially if they are foreigners. Gifts are presented to kings and nobles by a family in which there has been a birth, death, marriage or university or high school graduation, in honour or memory of the family member. Tongans leaving on a visit abroad are laden with gifts to be presented to their family members and to the family members of any friends and acquaintances living at their destination. They are also likely to return laden with reciprocal gifts.

Among commoners, gifts will most often come in the form of agricultural produce. Foreigners are often presented with prepared food and handicrafts. Family members abroad get tinned corned beef and kava. New parents, newly married couples and royalty receive the finest agricultural produce, pigs, intricately designed fine mats and immense rolls of tapa.

Gifts are given ceremoniously and accepted graciously. A gift will most often be prefaced by verbal self-abasement, such as 'We are a poor family and our gift is therefore very humble and insufficient to convey the honour you deserve but please be so kind as to accept it as it represents the best that we are capable of producing'. This pap will not be about a mere ballpoint pen but will often refer to a mat which represents hundreds or thousands (yes, thousands!) of hours of work.

Shame and loss of face are not taken lightly in Tonga. An individual who has been seriously shamed or caught (or even suspected of) doing something considered socially unacceptable endures untold measures of self-imposed personal agony. In extreme cases, suicides are not uncommon. In their dealings with Tongans, foreigners should be especially sensitive to this point. If a travel agent botches a reservation, a waitress delivers the wrong plate, or a person on the street admits he does not know where a particular point of interest is (it requires fortitude to do this), a foreigner who becomes outwardly upset in most cases inspires feelings of shame that go deeper than is immediately visible. A *laissez-faire* attitude will go a long way towards preserving a traveller's mental health as well.

Fakaleiti

By traditional definition, a *fakaleiti* is a male child brought up as a female due to a shortage of helping hands around the house. The word translated means simply 'like a lady', but one senses that there's more to the custom than that. Such men dress as females, play female roles and get away with promiscuity on a scale forbidden to biological females.

Although many Tongan teenagers make real sport of teasing and tormenting them, there is no social stigma attached to their open flaunting of sexual preference or transvestitism. Therefore, it is difficult not to suspect that many are simply homosexuals sheltering behind the title fakaleiti in order to be readily accepted in society. Some fakaleiti revert to traditional male roles upon reaching adulthood.

Dress

Although their attire is growing increasingly western, Tongans are by law required to dress modestly in keeping with strict fundamentalist Christian ideals.

Men experience fewer restrictions than women but they are required to wear a shirt at all times when in public (except when on the beach). Failure to do so will result in a fine; this applies to foreigners too, so be warned.

Women must cover their shoulders and chests completely as well as covering their legs at least to the knees. A Tongan woman who doesn't comply with this guideline risks being regarded as very disreputable. Very few Tongans have bathing costumes – they just hop into the sea in whatever they happen to be wearing at the time.

The distinctive pandanus mats which are worn all the time by older people and

Tonga the Friendly Isles

DISCOVERY OF VAVA'U 1781

by younger people to work or on formal occasions are called ta'ovala; they are secured around the waist with a cord of coconut sennit called a *kafa*. The older and tattier they appear, the more they are prized, since they are handed down through several generations as valued heirlooms. In place of a ta'ovala, women sometimes wear a *kiekie*, a decorative band secured about the waist. Men will often wear a wrap-around skirt known as a *tupenu* which extends to the knees, and women an ankle-length *vala* skirt and *kofu* or tunic.

When mourning a relative or friend, Tongans dress in black. During the obligatory mourning for a member of the royal family, all Tongans are required to wear black.

Fishing

Tongans may well be the world's laziest fishermen, but although their methods are nearly effortless, who's to argue with success? They start with a baited hook and line which they tie around a Coke bottle. The hook is thrown into the sea and the bottle buried in the sand or lodged behind a bush and left. A few hours later, the fisherman returns to see what's on the line.

You'll probably notice that they sometimes use a lure in the shape of a rat. Of course this is for a good reason.

Tongan legend tells a story of a crab, a rat and some birds that set out in a canoe for *moana*, the deep sea beyond the reef, leaving a kingfisher behind. The kingfisher got angry at being left, so he flew out to the canoe and pecked a hole in it. Of course, the craft sank. While the crab could swim away and the birds could fly, the rat had to hitch a ride on the head of an octopus, but, unfortunately, he was so shaken up about the whole incident that he inadvertently shat on the octopus' head. To this day, octopi hate rats and try to eat them whenever possible. Therefore, the Tongans have a lot of luck catching octopi by

employing this method. Again, you can't argue with success. . .

Dance

Unlike the vibrant *tamure* of Tahiti and the erotic hula of Hawaii, Tongan dances for females are subtle, artistic and require the dancer to convey meaning with an economy of motion.

The most frequently performed traditional dance in Tonga is called the *lakalaka*. The dancers, most often women but occasionally including men, stand in rows, dressed in similar costumes that are decorated with leaves, shells, flowers and pandanus. They sway, sing, smile broadly and tell stories with their hand movements. One person of high rank, called the *vahenga*, performs apart from the other dancers and is dressed differently. A female vahenga will perform the female part of the dance and a male will follow the male dancers.

The *ma'ulu'ulu* is a dance performed at feasts, on holidays, and at special state functions. Its movements, known as *haka*, are choreographed by an artist, the *punake*, who is always a man of high rank. He also composes the song it is meant to illustrate. The dancers are always women; they seat themselves in rows and use only hand movements to convey the story.

The female solo dance, the most beautiful and graceful of all Tongan dances, is called the *tau'olunga*. The qualifications for a dancer are rather strict. The ideal candidate would be fair with long black hair, shapely but not thin (big is beautiful in Tonga), with attractive face and legs and a flawless complexion. The dancer performs wearing a flowing knee-length dress with bare shoulders, and with flowers in her hair and on her wrists and ankles. Her body is covered with coconut oil in order to draw attention to her skin. The dancer must always smile genuinely and keep her knees together. The tau'olunga is performed at government and village functions, on the birthdays of influential people and for visits by dignitaries. A girl will also perform it at her own wedding, a suitable occasion to display the 'merchandise'.

While the female dances are gentle and accompanied by music, the male dances are meant to convey the fierce warrior spirit of Tongan tradition. The most popular is the *kailao*, the war dance, which is meant to be reminiscent of the days when canoes full of Tongan men set out on raiding missions to neighbouring islands. The rapid movements re-enact violent attacks and are accompanied by loud, ominous drumming, fierce cries, beating feet and the pounding of *pate*, or spearlike *pales*, which represent war clubs.

The fire dance, perhaps the most dramatic Tongan dance, is also the favourite of most visitors. One or two dancers gyrate, leap and spin while juggling flaming torches to the time of a rapid drumbeat.

The *fakapale* is a curious custom associated with Tongan dancing. The word means literally 'to award a prize'. Originally, the prizes consisted of fine mats and tapa heaped before a dancer as gifts given in recognition of ability. Today, handicrafts have been replaced with money: notes are plastered onto the oiled bodies of the dancers during the performance by admiring spectators. As might be expected, Tongan performances make excellent fundraisers.

RELIGION

Tongans take their religion seriously, or at least that's what they'd have you believe. Since the constitution of the nation was outlined by a missionary, Shirley Baker, it's not surprising that national adherence to Christian principles was written into it. Sundays in Tonga are to be used for nothing but eating, sleeping, and going to church. Since they attend two or three worship services each Sunday (in addition to choir practice), the Tongans have little time left over for eating and sleeping.

Tongan law states that the Sabbath Day (read 'Sunday') is to be considered forever sacred; a Sunday stroll in Tonga will give a visitor the eerie feeling that someone has finally dropped the bomb. Taxis don't operate, all businesses are closed, sports events are prohibited,

Basilica of St Anthony of Padua, Nuku'alofa

planes may not land and even driving a car requires special clearance. Any Tongan caught swimming at the beach or guilty of any other breach of the Sabbath is subject to a T$10 fine or three months hard labour. Some yachtie friends of mine ran up on a reef one Sunday and the Tongan harbour personnel refused to respond to their Mayday on the grounds that it was Sunday!

Foreigners are, of course, exempt from the swimming and driving restrictions and some recent relaxations of the law have actually sanctioned the Sunday opening of three tourist restaurants on or near Tongatapu. Many travellers take the 'if you can't beat 'em, join 'em' attitude and attend church on Sundays, only to find that Tongans have astonishing musical ability and that their rendition of traditional hymns is consistently magnificent.

Although Tonga technically promotes religious freedom, anyone practising anything other than Christianity had best keep it to themselves. Even unconventional Christian (or partially so) sects such as the Mormons and Bahai have been experiencing close scrutiny by the state. In late 1988, Tonga began refusing tourist visas to Fijian Indians. Ostensibly, it was feared that illegal immigration by these people would take jobs from Tongans; one suspects, however, that the encroachment of Hinduism was feared even more.

The Free Wesleyan Church claims the largest number of adherents, followed by the (Methodist) Free Church of Tonga, the Church of England, the Roman Catholics, Seventh Day Adventists and the Mormons. All these sects operate educational facilities, and the majority of Tongan children receive their education from one or the other. The royal family worships at the Free Wesleyan Church's Centenary Chapel in Nuku'alofa.

And no discussion of religion in Tonga would be complete without mentioning the often-related anecdote about the Seventh Day Adventists. Normally, they celebrate their Sabbath on Saturday, of course, but in Tonga they accept Sunday as their holy day. Why? Because the International Dateline bends out of its path in order to include Tonga and, were it not for that fact, Sunday in Tonga would actually be Saturday!

Despite the fact that Tongans appear to be highly religious, are required to dress conservatively and abhor any sort of physical contact between men and women in public, they have never adopted the strict sexual code that is traditionally prescribed by orthodox Christianity. In fact, many young Tongans cohabitate before marriage and quite a few married men openly keep mistresses and court foreign women. Young Tongan women don't seem to have many hang-ups, either.

Tongan cemeteries provide the ultimate examples of postmortem kitsch. Non-Catholic burials (Catholics use monuments) consist of sandy mounds topped with artificial flowers beneath inverted goldfish bowls, plastic images or photos of Jesus Christ, ribbons, banners, shells, and beer bottles and cans.

With all this hoopla over Christianity, one would assume that the pre-European religious beliefs had been totally abandoned. But there are still quite a few Tongans who quietly believe in the old spirits, taboos, superstitions, medical charms and Polynesian gods that characterised the well-defined religious traditions before the arrival of the missionaries. For anyone interested in the details of ancient Tongan religious rites and traditions, the second volume of William Mariner & John Martin's book, *An Account of the Natives of the Tonga Islands*, published by Vava'u Press, contains a fascinating and in-depth discussion of pre-missionary beliefs.

FESTIVALS & HOLIDAYS

All Tongan families need as an excuse for a feast is a birthday, a visitor, an academic accomplishment, a birth, a marriage, or just a sunny Sunday. Coronations, university graduations, religious holidays and royal birthdays invite celebration on an even larger scale, often with several days of feasting, dancing, organised entertainment and general lightheartedness. Children and youths detonate home-made bamboo and kerosene bazookas that explode with the same impact as heavy artillery! The king's birthday is accompanied by the *heilala*, a nearly weeklong festival which includes processions, contests and feasting.

Agricultural fairs, which are derived from the ancient 'inasi festivals, take place in all the major island groups around the months of August to October and are presided over by the king.

Public holidays include:

1 January
New Year's Day
March/April
Easter
25 April
Anzac Day
4 May
HRH Crown Prince Tupouto'a's Birthday
4 June
Emancipation Day
4 July
King Taufa'ahau Tupou IV's Birthday
4 November
Constitution Day
4 December
King George I's Birthday
25 December
Christmas Day
26 December
Boxing Day

You begin to get the idea that '4' may be the royal lucky number!

LANGUAGE

Tongan is a Polynesian language, similar to Samoan, Hawaiian, Maori and Tahitian. It is also, incidentally, strikingly similar in both sound and grammar to Malay, forming a basis for the accepted theory that the Polynesian peoples originated in South-East Asia.

Pronunciation

Pronunciation is straightforward. The five vowels may be either long or short depending on whether or not they are stressed, but the actual difference in sound between them is very slight to the unpractised ear. The long sound is simply an extended version of the short vowel, and is conventionally indicated by a superscribed bar. Stress is normally placed on the next to last syllable. A glottal stop, represented by an apostrophe ('), is equivalent to the space between the syllables of 'oh-oh'. Diphthongs, or combinations of vowels, are pronounced by enunciating each of the component sounds individually. They are broken up by the insertion of a glottal stop.

The letters used in the Tongan alphabet are more or less pronounced as follows:

Vowels

a   as in 'and'
e   as in 'end'
i   as in 'pin'
o   as in 'hot'
u   as in 'put'

Consonants

f   as in 'far'
h   as in 'here'
k   as the 'gh' in 'gherkin', unvoiced
l   as in 'love', with a slap of the tongue
m   as in 'may'
n   as in 'now'
ng as in 'singer', not 'finger'
p   midway between 'park' and 'bark', unvoiced
s   as in 'sand', with a slight tendency towards 'sh'
t   midway between 'tip' and 'dip', unvoiced
v   as in 'very'

Some Basic Vocabulary

Since their language is spoken only in Tonga, the Tongans are both pleased and surprised when foreigners make an attempt to use it at all. The following are a

few useful words and phrases to get you
started:

Greetings & Civilities

hello	*malo 'e lelei*
good-bye	*'alu 'a* or *nofo 'a* (in response only)
welcome	*talitali fiefia*
thank you	*malo*
Thank you very much.	*Malo 'aupito.*
How are you?	*Fefe hake?*
Fine, thank you.	*Sai pe, malo.*

Pronouns

I/mine	*koau/'a'aku*
you/yours	*ko koe/'a'au*
you (plural)	*ho moutolu*
we	*'oku mau*
they	*'oku nau*

Some Useful Words

cheap/expensive	*ma'ama'a/mamafa*
good/bad	*lelei/kovi*
pretty	*faka 'ofa 'ofa* (this one is great!)
stop/go	*tu'u/'alu*
yes/no	*'io/'ikai*
foreigner	*palangi* (originally *papalangi*)
Miss/Mrs/Mr	*ta'ahine/fine'eiki/ tangata'eiki*
man/woman	*tangata/fefine*
child	*tamasi'i*
sun/wind/rain	*la'a/matangi/'uha*

Some Useful Phrases

How much?
'Oku fiha?
How many?
Ko 'e me'a 'e fiha?
My name is ....
Ko hoku hingoa ko ....
What is this called?
Ko 'e ha hono hingoa 'o 'e me'a ko 'eni?
I come from ....
Ko 'eku ha'u mei ....
When do you open/close?
Temou 'ava/tapuni he fiha?

Getting Around

Where is the ....?
'Oku tu'u 'i fe 'a 'e ....?
restaurant
falekai
market
maketi
police station
fale polisi
hospital
falemahaki
Where is the boat/plane to ....?
Ko 'e fe ha feitu'u teu ma'u 'ai ha vaka/vakapuna 'oku foalu ki ....?
When does the boat/plane leave?
Ko 'e fiha 'oku folau 'ai 'e vaka/ vakapuna?
Where can I find a place to stay?
Ko 'e fe nai ha feitu'u lava 'o nofo 'ai?
Where is the toilet?
Ko fe 'a 'e fale malolo?
Where can I buy ....?
Teu fakatau mei fe ha ....?
How far is it to ....?
Ko 'e ha hono mama'o 'o .... mei heni?
Turn left/right.
'Afe to'omata'u/to'ohena.
Go straight ahead.
'Alu hangatonu

Numbers

1	*taha*
2	*'ua*
3	*tolu*
4	*fa*
5	*nima*
6	*'ono*
7	*fitu*
8	*valu*
9	*hiva*
10	*hongofulu*
11	*hongofulumataha*
12	*hongofuluma'ua*
20	*'uafulu*
21	*'uafulumataha*
30	*tolungofulu*
31	*tolungofulumataha*
40	*fangofulu*
50	*nimangofulu*

60	*'onongofulu*	10,000	*tahamano*	
70	*fitungofulu*	11,000	*manoma'afe*	
80	*valungofulu*	12,000	*manoma'ua'afe*	
90	*hivangofulu*	20,000	*'uamano*	
100	*teau*	100,000	*tahakilu*	
101	*teaumataha*	200,000	*'uakilu*	
110	*teaumahongofulu*	1,000,000	*tahamiliona*	
200	*'uangeau*	5,672	*nima'afe'onongeau*	
300	*tolungeau*		*fitungofuluma'ua*	
1000	*taha'afe*			
1001	*taha'afemataha*			

Facts for the Visitor

VISAS & DOCUMENTS

Customs and immigration in Tonga could well be, for the average visitor, the most hassle-free system in the world. At the moment, Tonga admits all tourists except Fijian passport holders of Indian descent. You'll need only a valid passport and an onward ticket (no exceptions!) in order to be admitted for a stay of 30 days. Your stay can be extended for up to six months at any immigration office (each island group has one), where you'll be met with a smile and few questions.

If you're entering from an infected area, usually interpreted as sub-Saharan Africa or Latin America, you'll need proof that you've had a yellow fever vaccination.

Ports of entry for cruising yachts are Nuku'alofa (Tongatapu), Neiafu (Vava'u) and Falehau (Niuatoputapu). In order to clear in, yachties must pull up alongside the wharf with their yellow quarantine flag raised. Customs and immigration officials will board, ask the usual questions about food and health, and request passports and a passenger list. Checking in on Sunday is currently out of the question.

There is a monthly charge, based on the length of the yacht, for anchoring anywhere in Tongan waters. The average charge is about T$20 to T$40 for a month or portion thereof.

Embassies & Consulates

Tonga has diplomatic representation in the UK. The Tonga High Commission is in New Zealand House, Haymarket, London SW1Y 4TQ.

There are honorary consuls in Hong Kong, the USA (San Francisco) and Japan. There is an honorary consul in Australia (Sydney) as well: Tongan Consulate-General (tel (02) 929 8794), 158 Pacific Highway, North Sydney.

Long-Term Visits

If you're planning to settle down in Tonga as a refugee from the chaos of some western home country, be warned that immigration to Tonga is not easy. Short of marrying a Tongan citizen, noncorporate immigration is nigh unto impossible. You might be able to volunteer your services as an English teacher in a village. (Classes are in Tongan until sixth year, when the students learn English; after sixth year, all classes are conducted in English). Persons with exceptional skills such as medical professionals or secondary school teachers willing to work voluntarily may have a chance, and Peace Corps or Australian Volunteers Abroad get two-year stints, but beyond that, the situation is pretty hopeless.

Business immigrants will normally be permitted to remain only as long as they retain their jobs and those intent upon setting up a business will nearly always be required to place controlling interest in the hands of a Tongan partner. For more information on business investments in Tonga, write to the Ministry of Labour, Commerce & Industries, P O Box 110, Nuku'alofa, Kingdom of Tonga.

MONEY

In the early 1800s, when young William Mariner explained the monetary system used by Europeans to the Tongan chief Finau, the latter understood it perfectly and immediately grasped the advantages it had over the traditional system of barter used in the Tonga Islands. In his innocent intelligence, however, he also surmised the potential drawback of such a system and determined it unsuitable for use in his country. From Mariner's book:

If [money] were made of iron and could be converted into knives, axes and chisels there would be some sense in placing a value on it; but as it is, I see none. If a man has more yams than he wants, let him exchange some of them away for pork. . .Certainly money is much handier and more convenient but then, as it will not spoil by being kept, people will store it up instead of sharing it out as a chief ought to do, and thus become selfish. . .I understand now very well what it is that makes the *papalangis* so selfish – it is this money!

During the initial raid of the *Port-au-Prince*, Finau had been disappointed to find very little of value to him. Unlike Captain Cook's ships, which had carried all sorts of valuable trade baubles, Mariner's ship had contained only whale oil, bits of iron and, for some inexplicable reason, 10,000 pieces of metal reminiscent of the beanlike *pa'anga*, playing pieces the Tongans used in a game called *lofo*. Finau had taken them for worthless objects and assumed that the ship had belonged to a very poor man indeed – perhaps to King George's cook (a cook being the lowest rank in Tongan society at the time). It was with regret that he realised he had burned the ship of an extremely rich man without first securing all his 'pa'anga'. Not surprisingly, the Tongan unit of currency is now called the pa'anga!

The pa'anga is on par with the Australian dollar. At the time of writing it was equivalent to:

A$ 1	=	T$1
US$ 1	=	T$1.32
UK£1	=	T$2.11
NZ$ 1	=	T$0.77
FFr 1	=	T$0.21
DM 1	=	T$0.72
Y100	=	T$0.94

Bills come in denominations of T$1, T$2, T$5, T$10, T$20 and T$50. Coins come in denominations of 1, 2, 5, 10, 20 and 50 seniti. Older T$1 and T$2 coins will sometimes turn up in change, especially in the Ha'apai Group. The T$2 coin is huge, and there is one kind of T$1 coin

available that is rectangular in shape. If you get one of the latter, hold onto it (a friend of mine got one in change in Ha'apai) – collectors have been known to pay up to A$400 for one in good condition!

Changing Money

Currency exchange is fairly straightforward. US, New Zealand, and Australian dollars, and pounds sterling seem to be the most easily exchanged, but Deutschmark, yen and francs are also acceptable, as are Fijian dollars and Samoan tala. The best rates can be had at the Bank of Tonga, which has offices in Nuku'alofa, 'Eua, Pangai (Ha'apai), Neiafu (Vava'u) and Hihifo (Niuatoputapu). Banks are open from 9 am to 4 pm weekdays; the sub-office of the Bank of Tonga in Nuku'alofa is open on Saturdays as well, until 12 noon. At the main branch of the Bank of Tonga in the capital, there are special tellers who do currency exchange, thus eliminating a long wait in a very long queue.

The International Dateline Hotel in Nuku'alofa and the Paradise International Resort in Vava'u both do currency exchange, but at a lower rate than the banks.

All brands of travellers' cheques are acceptable, and fetch 4% to 5% more than cash.

Credit Cards

Credit cards are only accepted at major tourist facilities: the Dateline and Ramanlal hotels in Nuku'alofa, Friendly Island Airways, a few handicraft shops, the Seaview and Alisi & André restaurants (both of which are also in the capital city), and the Paradise International Resort on Vava'u Island.

Visa, American Express, Australian Bankcard and MasterCharge are the most frequently accepted cards.

COSTS

For imported goods such as electronics

Top: Traditional cart near Ha'akame, Tongatapu Island
Bottom: Fine mats & tapa being presented to 'Atenisi Institute, Nuku'alofa

Top: Flea Market, Nuku'alofa
Left: 'Revenge of the blue cans', cemetery, Mu'a, Tongatapu Island
Right: Woodcarver, Niutoua Tongatapu Island

equipment, film and packaged foods, prices in Tonga are much higher than those in the USA and Europe, slightly higher than in Australia and about on par with New Zealand. Prices for automobiles and their components are far beyond the bounds of reason and, consequently, transport is fairly dear with respect to distances travelled. Basic food and accommodation are generally more reasonable than they are in other South Pacific countries – slightly higher than in Samoa and Fiji but considerably lower than in the Cooks, Vanuatu and (especially) French Polynesia. At the present time, an individual can get by quite comfortably in Tonga on T$20 per day and can live austerely for half that.

Duty-free shopping is available at the International Dateline Hotel and at Fua'amotu International Airport.

TIPPING

Tipping is not practised at all in Tonga. It would be unacceptable and unthinkable to receive a gift if one were denied the opportunity to reciprocate.

TOURIST INFORMATION
Local Tourist Offices

There are tourist information offices in both Nuku'alofa and Vava'u, but don't expect too much from them in the way of up-to-date answers to specific questions. They will provide some nice brochures and advertisements as well as a variety of simple maps and town plans. The key is not to rely too heavily on anything they tell you, since in most cases it is months or even years out of date and the maps bear little resemblance to reality. For what it's worth, their head office address is Tonga Visitors' Bureau, Vuna Rd, Nuku'alofa, Kingdom of Tonga.

The most up-to-date information you'll find is at the Keleti Beach on Tongatapu and at the Hilltop Guest House on Vava'u, where the managers actively keep up on current events and new developments in order to be able to pass them on to visitors and guests. Other travellers will also prove to be a valuable source of current information.

Sketchy maps are available at the Friendly Islands Bookshop, but don't rely too heavily on their accuracy. Topographic sheets can be bought at the Department of Lands & Survey, which is in the four-storey concrete block on Vuna Rd in Nuku'alofa.

Overseas Reps

If you're in Australia, try contacting the Tonga Visitors' Bureau (tel (02) 29 8041), 5th floor, 35 Clarence St, Sydney, or the Tongan Island Tourist Centre, 20 Loftus St, Sydney.

In New Zealand, contact the Tonga Visitors' Bureau Promotional Agent (tel 676 205), 15 Flavia Place, Lynfield, Auckland, New Zealand.

For tourist information in the UK, contact the Tonga High Commission, New Zealand House, Haymarket, London, SW1Y 4TQ.

GENERAL INFORMATION
Post

Postage stamps in Tonga are unusual and very collectable. They often come in odd fruity shapes, vibrant colours and envelope-swallowing sizes. They depict colourful shells, birds and Tongan scenes or commemorate events such as royal birthdays, exhibitions and visits to foreign heads of state. The island of Niuafo'ou uses its own stamps and these

are also diverse and colourful representations of that island's uniqueness. Old and unusual stamps may be purchased at the Philatelic Bureau and the Langa Fonua Handicraft Centre (which is in the same building as Friendly Islands Airways) in Nuku'alofa, and at the shop on Pangai Island (Tongatapu Group).

There is a post office on every major island but, if possible, avoid posting anything from the Niuas, particularly Niuafo'ou, since communications there are very limited and several months can pass without a ship to carry mail. The service to Europe, Australasia and North America is quite good.

Currently, a letter to Australasia costs 32 seniti and one to Europe or North America costs 57 seniti.

Telecommunications

Although most villages have conspicuous telephone boxes, they have long since ceased to function, so don't bother with them. There are Cable & Wireless offices in Nuku'alofa, Pangai (Ha'apai), Neiafu (Vava'u), 'Ohonua ('Eua) and Hihifo (Niuatoputapu). International calls, telegrams, telex and fax services are available. The office on Salote Rd, in Nuku'alofa, is open 24 hours a day seven days a week. Reverse charge calls to

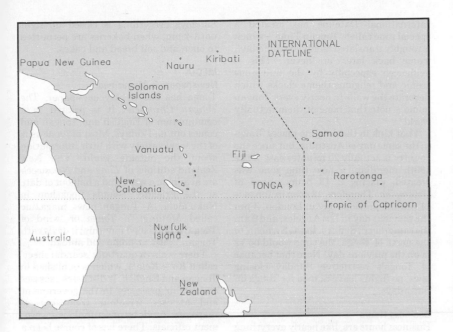

certain destinations are accepted as are telephone credit cards from some international systems – ask in advance which cards may be used.

The emergency phone number, as in North America, is 911. The international operator is 913, the inter-island operator is 910 and directory assistance is 919 (the last is useful because telephone directories are, for practical purposes, nonexistent. 'You should know your friends' telephone numbers. . .Why do you need a directory?'). Local calls from public phones cost 10 seniti.

Coconut Telephone You will probably notice another means of communication in use throughout the islands: the 'coconut telephone'. Through an amazing system unknown to western technology, people all over the island know what's going on in government, what foreigners are up to (they're watching you!), who is

sleeping with whom, what the king is doing at the moment, and so on, while it's happening or immediately thereafter. I've honestly never before seen anything like it!

Electricity

As in Australia and New Zealand, electricity is 240 volts AC, 50 Hz. To operate North American appliances carry an adapter and be prepared to mutilate the plug in order to fit it into the outlets.

Time

The king likes to think of his country as the 'land where time begins', since Tonga (along with far eastern Siberia) is the first place to see a new day. The land 'where time begins' is also the place where the local way of doing things is 'tomorrow', where roosters seem to have no idea what time it is, and where an odd kink in the

International Dateline has created a special zone called 'Tongan Time' – which is roughly translated as 'maybe someday', 'come back later' or 'never'. This is evidenced especially by the numerous scenic and religious theme clocks which decorate the walls in nearly every Tongan home – note that none of them actually work!

That kink in the dateline places Tonga in the same day as Australia, but since the country is actually 20 minutes east of the 180th meridian, a new time zone was created, placing it 13 hours ahead of Greenwich! Therefore, 12 noon in Tonga is 11 pm the previous day in London, 3 pm the previous day in Los Angeles, and 9 am the same day in Sydney. In the Samoas, to the north of Tonga, the time would be 12 noon the previous day! Note that because of Tonga's restrictive Sunday closing laws, no flights leave Samoa for Tonga on Saturdays.

Business Hours

Business hours are, like nearly everything in Tonga, flexible. As a general rule, banks are open between 9 am and 4 pm, government offices from 9 am to 12.30 pm and 1.30 to 4.30 pm. Shops remain open from 8 am to 1 pm and 2 to 5 pm, while restaurants and takeaway shops operate between 8 am and 4 pm, if they serve breakfast and lunch, or from 6 to 10 pm if they serve only the evening meal. Saturday shopping hours are 8 am to 12 noon. The markets normally get under way by about 6 am and close at 4 pm. On Sundays everything is closed up tight until 4 pm, when bakeries are permitted to open and sell bread and cakes.

MEDIA

Newspapers & Magazines

Tonga has one weekly newspaper, *The Tongan Chronicle*. It is printed in a combination of English and Tongan and comes out on Fridays. Most of its news is of the local variety with little information about the outside world. The New Zealand editions of *Time* and *Newsweek* are available a week and a half out of date at the Friendly Islands Bookshop in Nuku'alofa. A Tongan news magazine called *Matangi 'a Tonga* or 'wind of Tonga' is published monthly; it deals with Tongan issues at home and abroad.

There is also a quarterly 'scandal sheet' called *Ko 'e Kele'a*, which is published in Tongan and English. It discusses excesses and unfair practices in the government and exposes frivolous treatment of taxpayers' funds by unscrupulous government officials. There has of course been a movement to suppress it, but its continued existence is a tribute to tolerance in Tonga.

Radio & Television

The government owned Radio Tonga, A3Z, broadcasts a variety of things including traditional Tongan music, rock music from Europe, the USA and Australia, and worldwide news. The Voice of America is broadcast at 1.15 pm daily except Sundays; the BBC broadcasts

The Tonga Chronicle

15 Seniti.

Where Time Begins

Volume XXV, No. 23.　　　Nuku'alofa, TONGA　　　Thursday, November 3, 1988.

three times, at 7 am, 1 pm and 8 pm, from Monday to Saturday, and at 8 pm only on Sundays.

Tonga has no television station, but in the Niuas it is possible to pick up American Samoan broadcasting on very clear days.

HEALTH

There are few health risks in Tonga that require great concern. You probably won't encounter anything more serious than 'Polynesian paralysis', which seems to affect everyone including Tongans. Those who spend too much time feasting, relaxing in the shade and napping on sandy white beaches will begin to notice the classic symptoms of this incapacitating disease: lack of motivation, excessive weight gain, increased appetite and general lethargy. The only cure is evacuation to a stressed-out industrial country combined with massive doses of noise, work, traffic and television.

However, if problems do arise the following notes will help. If the symptoms persist, or if you come up against any serious health problem, you should, of course, seek trained medical assistance. And remember that you should always see your doctor before travelling to another country, especially if it's a tropical one.

Travel Health Guides

There are a number of books on travel health:

Staying Healthy in Asia, Africa & Latin America, Volunteers in Asia. Probably the best all-round guide to carry, as it's compact but very detailed and well organised.

Travellers' Health, Dr Richard Dawood, Oxford University Press. Comprehensive, easy to read, authoritative and also highly recommended, although it's rather large to lug around.

Where There is No Doctor, David Werner, Hesperian Foundation. A very detailed guide intended for someone, like a Peace Corps worker, going to work in an undeveloped country, rather than for the average traveller.

Travel with Children, Maureen Wheeler, Lonely Planet Publications. Basic advice on travel health for younger children.

Pre-Departure Preparations

Dental care is all but nonexistent in Tonga. Make sure you get your teeth checked before you set out.

Travel Insurance A travel insurance policy to cover theft, loss and medical problems is a wise idea. There are a wide variety of policies and your travel agent will have recommendations. The international student travel policies handled by STA or other student travel organisations are usually good value. Some policies offer lower and higher medical expenses options but the higher one is chiefly for countries with extremely high medical costs.

Check the small print. Some policies specifically exclude 'dangerous activities', which can include scuba diving, motor cycling, even trekking. If these activities are on your agenda you don't want that sort of policy.

Also, you may prefer a policy which pays doctors or hospitals direct rather than you having to pay now and claim later. If you have to claim later make sure you keep all documentation. Some policies ask you to call back (reverse charges) to a centre in your home country where an immediate assessment of your problem is made.

Finally, check if the policy covers ambulances or an emergency flight home. If you have to stretch out you will need two seats and somebody has to pay for it!

Medical Kit A small, straightforward medical kit is a wise thing to carry. Talk to your doctor before you leave home for advice on medications to carry with you. A course of antibiotics might come in handy, though ideally antibiotics should be administered only under medical supervision and should never be taken indiscriminately. The overuse of antibiotics can weaken your body's ability to deal with infections naturally and can reduce the drug's efficacy on a future occasion. Take only the recommended dose at the prescribed intervals and continue using the antibiotic for the prescribed period, even if the illness seems to be cured earlier. Antibiotics are quite specific to the infections they can treat; stop immediately if there are any serious reactions and don't use them at all if you are unsure if you have the correct one.

Be careful of buying drugs in developing countries, particularly where the expiry date may have passed or correct storage conditions not followed. In many such countries drugs which are no longer recommended, or have even been banned, in the west may be being dispensed.

If you intend to do some island-hopping, you might want to ask your doctor for a remedy for seasickness (see the Ferry section in the Getting Around chapter).

Other items that may prove useful in you medical kit are Band-aids, a sterilised gauze bandage, Elastoplast, cotton balls, a thermometer, tweezers, scissors, antibiotic cream, rubbing alcohol or peroxide, a high-protection sunblock, insect repellent, contraceptives, iodine-based water sterilisation tablets and multivitamins. For pain and fever, you could carry paracetemol (called acetominaphen in North America).

Immunisations If you want to enter Tonga from an area infected with yellow fever (which is usually taken to mean sub-Saharan Africa or South America), you'll need proof that you've had a yellow fever vaccination.

Food & Water
The most common complaint of visitors is called 'Tonga Tummy', which is just a South Seas variation of 'Montezuma's Revenge'. The bacteria found naturally in food and water will be different from those you are accustomed to at home. Your stomach will probably notice this, and discomfort and diarrhoea may be its response to the problem.

A few rushed toilet trips with no other symptoms is not indicative of a serious problem. Moderate diarrhoea, involving half-a-dozen loose movements in a day, is more of a nuisance. Dehydration is the main danger with any diarrhoea, particularly for children, so fluid replenishment is the number one treatment. Weak black tea with a little sugar, soda water, or soft drinks allowed to go flat and diluted 50% with water are good. With severe diarrhoea a rehydrating solution is necessary to replace minerals and salts. You should stick to a bland diet as you recover.

Lomotil or Imodium can be used to bring relief from the symptoms, although they do not actually cure diarrhoea. Only use these drugs if absolutely necessary – if you *must* travel, for example. For children Imodium is preferable, but do not use these drugs if the patient has a high fever or is severely dehydrated. Antibiotics can be very useful in treating severe diarrhoea, especially if it is accompanied by nausea, vomiting, stomach cramps or mild fever. Three days treatment should be sufficient and an improvement should occur within 24 hours.

In order to prevent more serious stomach ailments, wash vegetables and fruits with rainwater and boil any questionable drinking water before use. The water that emerges from Tongan taps tastes foul and briny but it is safe to drink. Most people, however, prefer rainwater, which is collected in tanks and is available almost everywhere.

Food poisoning is a very real problem; I encountered numerous tourists who had been down with it. Symptoms include fever, vomiting, a solid but tender abdominal area and loss of appetite, possibly accompanied by urgent dashes to the toilet. Treat the problem with rest, and lots of water or juice. The problem should pass in two to three days; if not, seek medical help immediately.

Climatic Considerations

Sunburn In tropical countries such as Tonga the rays of the sun are more direct than in temperate countries and therefore their burning capacity is much greater – twice as great, for instance, as in Sydney or Los Angeles. A good strong sunblock and possibly even a dab or two of zinc oxide will prevent a painful and potentially dangerous burn. A sunblock with a protection factor of at least 15 is normally recommended under such conditions. A hat provides extra protection. Calamine lotion is good for mild sunburn.

Prickly Heat Prickly heat is an itchy rash caused by excessive perspiration trapped under the skin. It usually strikes people who have just arrived in a hot climate and whose pores have not yet opened sufficiently to cope with greater sweating. Keeping cool, bathing often, using a mild talcum powder or even resorting to air-conditioning may help until you acclimatise.

Heat Exhaustion Dehydration or salt deficiency can cause heat exhaustion. Take time to acclimatise to high temperatures and make sure you get sufficient liquids. Salt deficiency is characterised by fatigue, lethargy, headaches, giddiness and muscle cramps and in this case salt tablets may help. Vomiting or diarrhoea can deplete your liquid and salt levels. Anhydrotic heat exhaustion, caused by an inability to sweat, is quite rare; unlike the other forms of heat exhaustion it is likely to strike people who have been in a hot climate for some time rather than newcomers.

Heat Stroke This serious, sometimes fatal, condition can occur if the body's heat-regulating mechanism breaks down and the body temperature rises to dangerous levels. Long, continuous periods of exposure to high temperatures can leave you vulnerable to heat stroke, and you should avoid excessive alcohol or strenuous activity when you first arrive in a hot climate.

The symptoms are feeling unwell, not sweating very much or at all, and high body temperature (39°C to 41°C). Where sweating has ceased, the skin becomes flushed and red. Severe, throbbing headaches and lack of coordination will also occur and the sufferer may be confused or aggressive. Eventually the victim will become delirious or convulse. Hospitalisation is essential, but meanwhile get the patient out of the sun, remove clothing, cover them with a wet sheet or towel and then fan continually.

Fungal Infections Hot weather fungal infections are most likely to occur on the scalp, between the toes or fingers (athlete's foot), in the groin (jock itch or crotch rot) and on the body (ringworm). You get ringworm (which is a fungus infection, not a worm) from infected animals or by walking on damp surfaces, like shower floors.

To prevent fungal infections wear loose, comfortable clothes, avoid artificial fibres, wash frequently and dry carefully. If you do get an infection, wash the infected area daily with a disinfectant or medicated soap and water, and rinse and dry well. Apply an antifungal powder such as Tinaderm. Try to expose the infected area to air or sunlight as much as possible, wash all towels and underwear in hot water and change them often.

Animal & Insect-Borne Diseases

The good news is that Tonga is free of both malaria and rabies at the present time. Buzzing mosquitoes may drive you to insanity at night and the fierce barking dogs may appear threatening but they are not carriers of insidious diseases. However, before leaving home you should check that the situation hasn't changed.

Take repellent or nets for the mosquitoes, while a supply of large stones may be used to keep aggressive dogs at bay. If you are bitten by a dog, you should have a tetanus vaccine within a few hours (if you haven't had a booster shot in the past 10 years).

Marine Dangers

There are some marine hazards which you should be aware of. Coral is sharp and can cause nasty cuts which may become infected. Skin punctures can easily become infected in hot climates and may be difficult to heal. Treat any cut with an antiseptic solution and mercurochrome. Where possible avoid bandages and Band-aids, which can keep wounds wet. Coral cuts are notoriously slow to heal, as the coral injects a weak venom into the wound. Avoid coral cuts by wearing shoes when walking on reefs and clean any cut thoroughly.

Several species of jellyfish deliver an excruciating sting, and stings from the inhabitants of cone shells can be deadly. Learn which ones are dangerous before collecting them and handle them with the greatest of care. Local advice is the best way of avoiding contact with these undesirables.

The agony caused by the poison of the stonefish is legendary and, although they are not common, utmost care should be taken to avoid accidentally treading on one. Always wear reef shoes or sneakers while walking through the water and don't touch anything unfamiliar while snorkelling.

Since the waters around Tonga are full of staphylococcus bacteria, it is best not to swim with an open wound. Staph infections are miserable and are very difficult to treat. Sadly, many villagers in Tonga die of such infections that have ulcerated and spread to vital organs.

Your immune system cannot fight such an infection once it has taken hold. If you have a painfully infected or ulcerated cut or boil accompanied by fever and/or headache, seek medical assistance at once. The variety of staph found in Tonga reacts to an artificial penicillin called

flucloxicillin; one cycle of this drug is normally not enough to prevent the infection returning later, so it's important that you have medical advice about treatment. If it does return, it will be in a stronger form and consequently even more dangerous and difficult to treat.

Sexually Transmitted Diseases

Sexual contact with an infected sexual partner spreads these diseases. While abstinence is the only 100% preventative, using condoms is also effective; remember to bring some with you. Gonorrhoea and syphilis are the most common sexually transmitted diseases; sores, blisters or rashes around the genitals, and discharges or pain when urinating are common symptoms. Symptoms may be less marked or not observed at all in women. The symptoms of syphilis eventually disappear completely but the disease continues and can cause severe problems in later years. Treatment of gonorrhoea and syphilis is by antibiotics.

There are numerous other sexually transmitted diseases, for most of which effective treatment is available. However, there is no cure for herpes and there is also currently no cure for AIDS. Using condoms is, to date, the most effective preventative.

AIDS can also be spread through infected blood transfusions; most developing countries cannot afford to screen blood for transfusions. It can also be spread by dirty needles – vaccinations, acupuncture and tattooing can potentially be as dangerous as intravenous drug use if the equipment is not clean. If you do need an injection it may be a good idea to buy a new syringe from a pharmacy and ask the doctor to use it.

All visitors to Tonga receive a warning brochure about AIDS upon arrival, and warnings against promiscuity are posted all over the kingdom. Fortunately, AIDS has not yet arrived in Tonga and the Tongans, with their fairly relaxed sexual attitudes, are terrified of it. Due to the emergence of AIDS, prostitution in Tonga has nearly disappeared.

Women's Health

Gynaecological Problems Poor diet, lowered resistance due to the use of antibiotics for stomach upsets and even contraceptive pills can lead to vaginal infections when travelling in hot climates. Keeping the genital area clean, and wearing skirts or loose-fitting trousers and cotton underwear will help to prevent infections.

Yeast infections, characterised by a rash, itch and discharge, can be treated with a vinegar or even lemon juice douche or with yoghurt. Nystatin suppositories are the usual medical prescription. Trichomonas is a more serious infection, with a discharge and a burning sensation when urinating. Male sexual partners must also be treated, and if a vinegar-water douche is not effective medical attention should be sought. Flagyl is the prescribed drug.

Pregnancy Most miscarriages occur during the first three months of pregnancy, so this is the most risky time to travel. The last three months should also be spent within reasonable distance of good medical care, as quite serious problems can develop at this time. Pregnant women should avoid all unnecessary medication, but vaccinations and malarial prophylactics should still be taken where possible. Additional care should be taken to prevent illness and particular attention should be paid to diet and nutrition.

Medical Care in Tonga

Not surprisingly, medical care is limited in Tonga. There are hospitals in Vaiola (Tongatapu), Hihifo (Ha'apai) and Neiafu (Vava'u) which are competent with very minor ailments and will dispense medicines, but serious medical problems should be taken to Pago Pago (American Samoa), Hawaii, Australia, or New Zealand. An entire day should be set aside for a visit to hospital clinics. A charge of $2 will be made. Medicines are free for Tongans and foreigners pay only a token fee.

There are several competent private physicians in Nuku'alofa; they charge T$5 to T$15, depending upon the length of the consultation, and are probably your best bet in the long run. I highly recommend Dr Helga Shafer-Durst at the German clinic (Kliniki Siamane) in Nuku'alofa. Minor complaints may also be treated at the Nuku'alofa Clinic, which is behind the post office.

WOMEN TRAVELLERS

Thanks to western videos, which are extremely popular in Tonga, foreign women have got the reputation for easy availability whether or not they profess 'occupied' status. The polite refusal of sexual favours on the part of a foreign woman is taken as 'keep trying' by hopeful Tongan men, and their patience and persistence in the matter is astounding. The word 'ikai ('no') shouted 50 times in rapid succession may begin to seep in. While this will be annoying, sober Tongans are unlikely to physically force the issue.

To avoid some measure of the attention a lone foreign woman is likely to attract, modest dress works well. Look at how young Tongan women dress and do likewise. Don't turn up at a pub or disco alone unless you're expecting advances and ignore the inane remarks of adolescents who'll try to chat you up. Most of all, however, don't be paranoid or you'll miss out on some very pleasant (and platonic, if you'd like) friendships.

DANGERS & ANNOYANCES

Theft is not a problem in Tonga, and you and your belongings are far more secure from violence there than in your home country. 'Borrowing', however, is rife. This is how it works: all property in Tonga is effectively communal. If one person has something another needs, the latter 'borrows' it. Of course, it can be 'borrowed' back if needed, but it will otherwise never again see its rightful owner. Unattended items are considered ripe for 'borrowing', so if you're concerned about your material possessions, keep an eye on them.

The police and government officials in Tonga seem to be friendly and straightforward. I've never heard of a tourist having problems with officials unless they've overstayed in the country or been caught carrying illicit substances.

FILM & PHOTOGRAPHY

It would be a safe bet to say that nowhere else in the world will you find so many willing and photogenic subjects for your camera as in Tonga. Tongans are in no way camera-shy and any chance to be photographed is seized enthusiastically. It's difficult to get a candid shot for this reason and your perfect 'people shot' will soon turn into a crowd scene if you're not quick about snapping it, but a foreigner with a camera will certainly be able to make a lot of friends. . .The 'rich tourist' stigma certainly exists in Tonga but it doesn't cause resentment.

There seem to be no restrictions on photography, either. I once came across a group of soldiers digging in the Royal Tombs on 'Uiha and asked permission to photograph them. One of them laughed saying 'Why do you ask? This is a free country!' On another occasion, I was at the airport when the king was arriving and, again, I asked permission to take photos. 'Of course,' the police officer replied. 'When the plane arrives, just walk out onto the tarmac to get the best view.'

The only drawback to photography in Tonga is the price and scarcity of film. You'll be able to find Kodacolour and Kodachrome 64 as well as instamatic film, but anything more unusual will have to be brought from home. Kodachrome 64 (36 exposures) costs T$14 including processing, while print film costs about half that without processing. Film is available in the Tungi Arcade and Foto-fix on Taufa'ahau Rd in Nuku'alofa, and at

Burns Philp in Neiafu, Vava'u. The shop in Tungi Arcade can also manage minimal camera repairs, and they sell camera batteries and components as well. The prices of camera equipment are beyond all reason in Tonga – bring everything you'll be needing from home!

ACCOMMODATION

As a general rule, don't trust accommodation bookings made by airlines or travel agents, since there are often weak or missing links in the system. Make bookings yourself by post or telephone if you want to be assured of a room upon arrival.

There is a 5% government tax on all accommodation within the country.

Quite often, foreigners will be invited by friendly Tongans to stay in their homes. There could be no better way to learn about the culture and life style of the country than by experiencing it first hand, and the hospitality of the Tongan people is abundant and genuine. Keep in mind, however, that their means are limited, and although most Tongan families would proudly and happily give you their last cent and refuse any compensation, it's of course best not to let things come to that. This is more easily said than done, however, and guests/hosts may have to resort to a battle of wits in order to get the situation onto an even keel. Simple gifts such as kava or alcohol will normally be accepted where cash will not. Gifts for the children will also be welcomed. As disgusting as it sounds, most families are also short of tinned corned beef, which is a staple in the Tongan diet; since it cannot be grown on the family plantation, a gift of this commodity will be greatly appreciated.

Hotels & Resorts

Hotels and beach resorts are slightly upmarket, but don't go there expecting anything like what's available in Hawaii or French Polynesia. Most beach resorts are pleasant, but the 'luxury' hotels are similar in price to those at home while being similar in luxury and service to cheaper motels. Those who are looking for international standards in accommodation should forget about going to Tonga – they'll have a miserable time there. The most plush place to stay in Tonga is the Paradise International in Neiafu (Vava'u), followed pathetically by the International Dateline and Ramanlal in Nuku'alofa.

Guest Houses

Budget accommodation of varying quality may be found throughout the islands, and prices are quite low compared to those in neighbouring countries, with the exception of perhaps Western Samoa and Fiji. In every island group are found comfortable and homey guest houses where travellers can settle in and spend some time savouring the local culture without going broke in the process. Most of them are clean, and meals either can be arranged or are included in the price of the accommodation. Some make cooking facilities available to guests. Plan on T$8 to T$10 per person per night for a bed and on around T$20 if meals are included. Ordinarily, bath and toilet facilities are communal, and only cold showers are available (not a serious problem in this climate).

Camping

Although it is technically not permitted, camping is not only possible but, short of staying with locals, is the only form of accommodation available on some islands. If you plan to stay on islands such as Foa, 'Uiha, Nomuka, Ha'afeva, or Niuafo'ou, it's best to turn up with a tent. That way, if an invitation to stay with a family is not forthcoming, you'll have shelter from the weather. In addition, some islands like 'Eua, the Niuas and all of Ha'apai have lovely bushland or beaches perfect for walking and camping, and those who wish to do some communing with nature will appreciate the option.

FOOD

Visitors will find most Tongan food a delight. The people's diet consists mostly of root vegetables, coconut products, taro, fresh fruit, pork, chicken, corned beef and fish, but the delicious and imaginative recipes derived from these items make good Tongan cuisine a favourite of anyone fortunate enough to try it.

Unfortunately, the situation in Tonga is getting fairly grim foodwise. The health of the people is suffering as junk foods and expensive supermarket items invade and replace the healthy diet to which Tongans have long been accustomed. The ultimate blasphemy is the availability and status attached to the use of such products as tinned vegetables, fish and fruit, and disgusting fare such as white bleached bread, greasy fried *sipi* and artificial snack foods, while traditional items lie rotting on the ground throughout the kingdom.

A quote from the excellent essay *Our Crowded Islands* by 'Epeli Hau'ofa sums up the trend: 'We are losing the best in us while adopting the cheapest, the most superficial and often dangerous, aspects of other civilisations.'

Restaurants

Generally speaking, Tongans are too poor to eat out, so most of the more expensive restaurants feature foreign cuisines – Chinese, Mexican, German, North American, French and so on – which cater to tourists. Most cheaper eating establishments serve only greasy and gristly American or Australian fast food. With a few notable exceptions, these places could prove hazardous to your health. Normally, good Tongan cuisine will be available at feasts, some guest houses and at a couple of restaurants.

Outdoor markets sell a variety of local produce and can be found in Nuku'alofa, Neiafu (Vava'u) and Pangai (Ha'apai). Supermarkets such as Morris Hedstrom and Burns Philp also exist in those places.

Feasts

A Tongan feast is an event which should not be missed. A feast is a matter of pride to the person or group preparing it. In Tonga, feasts are staged in order to commemorate a notable event such as a royal visit, a school graduation, an agricultural fair, a state holiday, or the arrival of a friend or relative from overseas. In 1988, a fair number of cruising yachts visited the island of Niuatoputapu and the friendly residents of that island used each arrival as an excuse to prepare a lavish feast.

In honour of such events as coronations or royal birthdays, whole villages spend days preparing food enough to feed entire islands. A pig is slaughtered and roasted for each invited guest, and after the VIPs have eaten their fill, the villages feast on the ample remains.

Visitors who are not fortunate enough to attend a local feast can still participate in one staged to give tourists an idea of what the Tongan tradition is all about.

A feast normally requires a *'umu*, an underground oven used to bake the food. Dishes traditionally served will include roasted suckling pig, chicken, *'ika* (fish), *fingota* (shellfish), *'ota 'ika* (raw fish dish similar to Mexican or Chilean *ceviche*), *lu pulu* (corned beef and boiled taro in coconut cream), *feke* (octopus), *manioke* (cassava), *kumala* (sweet potato), *lu* and *talo* (taro leaves and roots), *'ufi* (yams), curries and delicious *faikakai* (breadfruit pudding). An array of fresh fruits and juices will also be served.

Making & Using a 'Umu

A 'umu is a very effective underground oven used throughout Polynesia and Melanesia. Those who attend a Tongan feast are likely to see one in the form of wafting smoke being emitted from a small sandy mound.

The 'umu is quite easy to make. First, dig a hole in the ground 25 cm or so deep and a metre in diameter. Collect enough coral or volcanic rocks (each seven cm or so in diameter) to fill the bottom of the pit. Then collect wood, coconut husks and other flammable natural materials and start a bonfire in the pit. Throw the rocks on top, and when they're glowing hot, remove the remnants of wood and cover the rocks with split banana tree trunks, banana leaves, or bark.

Now for the food. The root vegetables (talo, 'ufi, manioke and kumala) together with the breadfruit should be spread out evenly on top of the rocks. Cover them with a layer of sticks to ventilate them and then place the meat to be cooked on the sticks. If you're baking an entire animal, of course, it will be necessary to prepare a larger 'umu. It would help, also, to place several of the heated rocks inside the innards of the animal in order to cook it throughout. Over the meat place more sticks, banana leaves and burlap or flour sacks. Fill in with earth and pack tightly.

The less steam that escapes, the more effective the oven. Baking time will depend on the nature of the meat. Whole pigs should bake for up to six hours, while small slices will be ready in two. Once everything's been dug out, you're ready to eat.

Recipes

If you'd like to try some of the best of Tongan cooking, here are several of the recipes very popular at feasts and on special occasions:

Lu Pulu
1 chopped onion
1 cup coconut cream
340 grams corned beef
20 young taro leaves (lu)
1 tsp salt

To make coconut cream, grate the meat of three to four mature coconuts. Add one cup hot water for each two cups of meat, let stand for quarter of an hour or so and pass through cheesecloth or coconut sennit to extract the cream. Next, cut the taro leaves into small pieces and boil with corned beef, coconut cream, onion and salt for

10 to 15 minutes. For a more traditional version, wrap the mixture in a banana leaf, tie with a banana leaf rib and bake in a 'umu for an hour or so.

'Ota 'Ika

1 onion
1 carrot
1 cucumber
1 tomato
1 tsp salt
5 lemons
cream from six mature coconuts (see lu pulu recipe)
½ tsp pepper
1 kg raw fish (snapper, tuna, etc)

Clean and de-bone fish, and cut it into chunklike pieces two cm in width. Extract juice from four lemons, stir in the salt and allow fish to marinate in it for 1½ hours. Chop vegetables into fine pieces. Drain fish mixture, and add coconut cream and unsalted juice from the remaining lemon. When ready to serve, add vegetables and pepper.

Faikakai Topai

2 cups coconut cream (see lu pulu recipe)
2 cups sugar
1 roasted breadfruit

Bake roasted breadfruit (in skin) for one hour. Pound flesh into a paste and cut into small squares. Melt sugar until brown but do not burn. Add coconut cream and boil for about 10 minutes or until mixture thickens into a gooey mass. Pour over breadfruit chunks. At this

point it may be served, or you can wrap the whole mixture in a banana leaf, tie it with a banana leaf rib and bake in a 'umu for up to an hour. It is also possible to use yam or taro in place of the breadfruit, or to add papaya to the sugar mixture. Be creative with this one – it's delicious!

DRINKS
Nonalcoholic Drinks

The most refreshing drink available is the juice of the immature coconut, which is slightly carbonated and quite delicious. Green coconuts are collected by climbing the coconut trees, and Tongans are normally happy to scramble up a tree in order to secure drinking nuts for visitors. Naturally, the visitors are normally impressed! Those who plan to drink coconuts instead of carrying water while bushwalking should be sure to carry a bush knife to hack away the tough green husk. More mature nuts can be opened (with some difficulty) with a pointed stick and a bit of elbow grease. The meat of the green coconut is soft and pliable and many people prefer it to the crunchy meat of the brown nut.

Fruit juices are available everywhere to those willing to extract them. A particularly nice combination is the speciality of Keleti Beach Resort on Tongatapu – the juice of watermelon, pineapple and coconut over ice. Unfortunately, most restaurants inexplicably serve tinned juice.

Sweet and syrupy foreign soft drinks are available almost everywhere. In addition to the ubiquitous Coca-Cola and Fanta, you can buy radioactive GLO, which seems to be exported from New Zealand in an effort to keep the country nuclear-free. Give this stuff a miss! The equally horrid local soft drink is called Slake, and it's so awful and chemical that it shouldn't be given a passing thought.

Alcohol

Alcohol is very popular in Tonga. Particularly on Tongatapu and Vava'u

Breadfruit

Royal beer label

you'll never lack a place to buy a drink (except on Sunday, of course). Technically, a drinking licence is necessary to buy alcohol in Tonga, but palangis are exempt from this rule. Those who want a licence for the novelty of it can buy one for T$1 at the police station in Nuku'alofa. It will outline the amount of alcoholic beverage the licencee is permitted to purchase over the course of a year.

The beer you'll find everywhere is Royal, which is very nice.

Due to the licensing restriction and the high price of alcohol, quite a few Tongans resort to making a yeasty but bearable home brew out of things found around the house. This is highly illegal, of course, and also can be dangerous (ask for a rundown of the ingredients before you drink any), but it's the Tongan response to a perceived need.

Kava

Kava is a drink derived from the root of the pepper plant and it is ubiquitous in Tonga. You'll often hear that it tastes like dishwater – it certainly looks like well-used dishwater – but dishwater probably tastes better, since it may contain a residue of foodstuffs, while kava is just murky and almost tasteless. Its nature, however, belies its popularity. Tongans and other Pacific Islanders drink bucketfuls of the stuff in one sitting. Kava circles are

basic social units and on Friday nights, Tongan men gather and drink kava from late afternoon to the wee hours of the morning.

The ground-up root is mixed with water in a carved four-legged bowl. The men (and, on rare occasions, women) seat themselves in a circle with the bowl at the head. Each man in turn claps and receives a coconut shell full of kava. He'll down it, reserving a bit to sprinkle over his shoulder. Then he'll hurl the shell across the floor back to the server. This procedure continues for hours on end until the men begin to feel very vague and hazy. Kava is not a narcotic, but it does tend to make one feel lethargic or ill when consumed in large quantities (which it usually is).

Friday night kava clubs may be found all over the islands. Some are simply social events, and others are used as fundraisers and include entertainment and music. Visitors who are prepared to participate in the circles are always welcome and any taxi driver will be able to tell you where the nearest one is going on.

The drink is made from the ground root of *piper methysticum* and the active ingredients include 12 or 14 chemicals of an alkaloid nature. It is both anaesthetic and analgesic, high in fibre content, low in calories and serves as a mild tranquilliser, an antibacterial and antifungal agent, a diuretic, an appetite supressant and a soporific. It is legal in North America, Europe and Australia, and Tongans habitually send packages of it to family members overseas who can't seem to be without it.

BOOKS & BOOKSHOPS

Given the price and scarcity of reading material in Tonga, you'd be wise to bring along whatever books you'll be needing there. In response to the shortage of affordable books, a couple of book exchanges have sprung up on Tongatapu (on a two-for-one exchange basis); they are not advertised so you have to know where to find them (I'll tell you where they are in the section on Tongatapu). Other travellers will also be a good source of exchange material.

The only bookshop of any consequence in the country is the Friendly Islands Bookshop on Taufa'ahau Rd in Nuku'alofa, but their prices are inordinately high, especially for pulp paperbacks. They do have a fairly good selection of works on Tonga and related island topics, which are difficult if not impossible to find outside the country, and they are, surprisingly, quite reasonable in most cases. Limited titles are also available at the Visitors' Bureau handicraft centre in Neiafu, Vava'u.

If you'll be in Tonga for a while, you can get a library card for T$2 annually (T$1 for students) and borrow from the limited collection downstairs in the Basilica of St Anthony of Padua in Nuku'alofa.

Due to the brief history of its written language and relatively obscure geographical position, little has been written about Tonga in particular. If you'd like to do a bit of reading up before you go, however, the following list includes titles which should be available in libraries abroad.

History

Tonga Islands: William Mariner's Account, Dr John Martin, Vava'u Press, 4th edition, 1981. Originally published with the title *An Account of the Natives of the Tonga Islands* in 1817, this book is the best work available on the nature of pre-Christian Tonga. It includes references to the religion, language, customs and life style of the people. It also makes very interesting and entertaining reading.

The Tongan Past, Patricia Ledyard, Vava'u Press, 1982. Very light and digestible introduction to Tongan history. However, there's an annoying amount of editorialising in the form of European-style excuses for unique Tongan behaviour.

The Fatal Impact, Alan Moorehead, Penguin, 1968. A critical treatment of the havoc wreaked on the Pacific by early European explorers and fortune-seekers. Although it doesn't deal with Tonga directly, the issues are certainly relevant.

Slavers in Paradise, H E Maude, University of the South Pacific, 1986. A tragic and enlightening account of the kidnapping of Pacific Islanders by the Peruvian slave traders in the early 1860s.

A Dream of Islands, Gavan Dawes, Jacaranda Press, 1980. This book deals with the lives and perspectives of island inspired authors and artists such as Gauguin, Melville and Stevenson.

Voyages to Paradise, William R Grey, National Geographic Society, 1981. A history of the voyages of Captain Cook, including his three visits to Tonga. Classic 'Geographic' style: it's easy reading and there are loads of colour photos.

The Fire Has Jumped, edited by Garth Rogers, Institute of Pacific Studies, 1986. A rather disorganised but interesting account of the volcanic eruptions on Niuafo'ou in the mid-1940s and the subsequent resettlement of its people. There are eyewitness accounts of the disaster in both English and Tongan as well as a discussion of the distinctive features of life on remote Niuafo'ou.

The Mutiny on Board the HMS Bounty, William Bligh, Signet 1961. Bligh's journals during and after his command of the *Bounty*.

The Journals of Captain Cook, edited by J C Beaglehole. A straight-from-the-horse's-mouth account of early exploration in the Pacific and elsewhere.

Travel Guides

Virtually every guidebook company (Fodor's, Frommer's, Sunset, Dollarwise, etc) has an all-inclusive guidebook on the South Pacific, but these cater mostly to the up-market sort of tourism that wants to stuff six South Pacific countries into two weeks' holiday. Some other guides, aimed specifically at less constrained visitors, which should be useful include:

South Pacific Handbook, David Stanley, Moon Publications, 3rd Edition, 1986. A thorough guidebook which covers adequately everything between the Galapagos and the Solomons.

Exploring Tropical Isles & Seas, Frederic Martini, Prentice-Hall, 1984. This book contains only bare-bones information about individual island groups. The real emphasis is on the natural history and environmental aspects of tropical islands in the Atlantic and Pacific. I highly recommend it!

If you'll be wandering beyond Tonga in the Pacific, Lonely Planet also publishes travel survival kits to Samoa, Tahiti, Fiji, the Cook Islands, Micronesia, the Solomon Islands, Papua New Guinea and New Zealand. The Galapagos and Easter Island are covered well in our guides to Ecuador and Chile respectively. A guide to Vanuatu is forthcoming – check with your bookseller.

Language

Tongan Grammar, C M Churchward, Vava'u Press, 1953. A complete study of the Tongan language, but you'll need a fair familiarity with the principles of linguistics in order to get much out of it.

Miscellaneous

Tales of the Tikongs and *Kisses in the Nederends*, 'Epeli Hau'ofa, Penguin. These books are not to be missed by anyone travelling to Tonga! They are tales of the coming of age of a small Pacific island kingdom called Tiko, a thinly disguised Tonga, by that country's most renowned and respected author. Humorous and thought-provoking reading! *Our Crowded Islands*, 'Epeli Hau'ofa, University of the South Pacific, 1977. A very enlightening essay about population growth and outside influences on the island of Tongatapu. Recommended! *Friendly Isles: A Tale of Tonga* and *'Utulei, My Tongan Home*, Patricia Ledyard, Vava'u Press, 1956 & 1974,

respectively. History and anecdotes of Tongan life by an American woman who came to Tonga as a teacher over 40 years ago and never left. Both books are quite entertaining.

Pacific Islands Yearbook, edited by John Carter, Pacific Publications, 14th edition, 1981. Facts and figures in brief.

Pacific Tourism as Islanders See It, University of the South Pacific, 1980. Essays by islanders regarding the increase of tourism and, consequently, outside influences on their cultures and life styles. . .a pertinent moral dilemma.

Tonga, James Siers. A 'coffee table' book of photographs of people and places in the Friendly Islands.

Island Realm: A Pacific Panorama, Ian Todd, Angus & Robertson, 1974. A brief description and history of all Pacific Islands. . .really little more than an overview with some nice photos.

The Niu Idea Cookbook, The Peace Corps. This seems to be available in Tonga only, but it's a very good amateur endeavour to compile a thorough collection of recipes for those delicious and mysterious Tongan dishes visitors to the islands will never forget. It's more of a contribution to island cuisine, I believe, than its authors realise!

THINGS TO BUY

It would be safe to say that Tongan handicrafts, in general, are the finest, most beautiful and most affordable in the Pacific. Despite the skill, care and time required to create the magnificent carvings, weavings, jewellery and tapa, they are surprisingly reasonably priced. If you watch a woodcarver at work, or women singing and laughing together while weaving or making tapa, it becomes obvious that they are caught up in the joy of creation for its own sake, not only for the benefit of tourists (and, hence, their own bank accounts). With the exception of the carvings, Tongans themselves use the products they design and make.

The methods used in producing

Turtle tapa

handicrafts are the same today as they were in ancient times, and only natural materials are used: bone, sandalwood, shells, mulberry bark, pandanus fronds, coconut husks, earthen or vegetable dyes and coral, to name a few.

Tapa

From the cool early hours of the morning until the hour of the evening meal, rural Tonga is filled with the sound of pounding tapa mallets. Tapa has come to be the symbol representing Tonga to the world and it is considered, along with pandanus weavings, to be the *koloa*, the wealth of Tongan families. On the occasion of a wedding, funeral, graduation, or royal event, large amounts of tapa in lengths of 25 to 150 metres are made and exchanged.

Although in English the product is familiarly known as tapa, the Tongan word for it is *ngatu*; it is only called tapa in its undecorated early stage. It is made from *hiapo*, the underbark of the paper mulberry tree (*broussonetia papyrifera*), which grows primarily on the islands of 'Eua and Tongatapu.

The mature trees are cut near their base, which normally measures only three cm or so in diameter, and the bark is removed. After a day or two of drying, the rough outer bark is peeled away leaving the soft, fibrous inner bark. It is then beaten with an ironwood, or *toa* wood, mallet called an *'ike* on a long wooden *tutua* (anvil) to separate and spread the fibres. When it is about 45 cm in width, it is folded with another piece and pounded further. A single length of cloth is known as a *feta'aki*, becoming *langanga* after being pasted into long strips. These strips placed side by side are also pasted together using sticky half-cooked tubers of manioke.

First a *kupesi*, or relief of the pattern, is made. A kupesi has a woven pandanus base, called the *papa*. A design made with coconut fronds (*tui'aniu*) is sewn to the base with coconut sennit. The strips of tapa are placed over the kupesi tablet and rubbed with feta'aki and coconut husk dipped in a ruddy vegetable dye in order to bring out the design.

After the tapa has dried, the stencilled designs are painted by hand in black and rich earthy reds and browns, usually derived from candlenuts and mangrove bark.

Carving

Although most Tongan carvings are skilfully made and quite beautiful, they are not traditional. In the case of carving, Tonga has given in to the tourist market. Tourists expect to find tikis in Polynesia and Tonga happily provides them; never mind that such items did not figure in the pre-tourism scheme of things. Wood-carving provides not only income, but also an avenue of relaxing creativity for Tongan men.

The woods most often used are the mahoganylike *milo* and the similar but heavier *pua-pua*. Sandalwood, from the island of 'Eua, with its distinctly beautiful fragrance is also very popular but is becoming increasingly rare, due to illicit export to the Chinese and other Asian markets.

The most common subjects are of course those that appeal to tourists, such as turtles, tikis, fish, weapons and masks. Some extremely kitschy items like salad bowls, floor lamps, ashtrays, and soap dishes are also available.

Black coral is becoming an increasingly popular medium. At the time of writing it was not endangered in Tonga, but since some countries prohibit its importation, it's best to check before buying. The same goes for materials for which concern is immediately warranted such as whalebone and tortoiseshell. It is claimed that whalebone carved in Tonga is collected by divers, who take it from whales that have died naturally; you'd want to be certain of this before buying.

Jewellery

All Tongan jewellery is made from natural products but, as was mentioned in the section on carving, many of these products are protected or restricted overseas and due concern for the environment as well as import laws should be considered before purchasing such items, particularly if they use tortoiseshell.

Other materials used in the production of every imaginable type of ornament include sharks' teeth, whalebone, coral, cowrie shells, coconut shell, *pueki* shells, *tuitui* (candlenut) and *taku misi* or sea urchin spines. Taku misi are small salmon, peach or orange-coloured shafts which make lovely necklaces when polished. Even more commonly, they are used to make wind chimes, as they emit a very pleasant sound when struck.

Weaving

Like tapa, woven mats are traditionally considered a form of wealth by Tongan families and are therefore exchanged as tokens of esteem on special occasions. Tongan weaving, however, is not limited to mats - hats, clothing, toys, baskets,

belts and trays are also woven of pandanus and put to everyday use. Historically, even the long-distance sailing canoes carried sails of woven pandanus.

The preparation of the pandanus leaf for use is quite involved. First, it is cut, and then stripped of thorns and rough spots. Once this initial process is completed, different methods are used to bring out the unique qualities and colours of each type.

There are four types of pandanus used in Tonga, each with its own texture and colour which suit it to particular uses. They are known as *tofua*, which is nearly white, *pa'ongo*, which is brown, *tapahina*, off-white or light brown, and *kie*, the finest of all, which is creamy white.

Tofua requires the simplest of the four processes. The leaves are bundled, boiled in water for an hour or two and laid in the sun to dry. Pa'ongo and tapahina are derived from leaves which are covered with a mat (pandanus, of course) and turned daily to prevent rot. After a few days they turn a chocolate brown colour and are gathered, braided into plaits called *fakate'ete'epuaka*, bundled up and hung in a dark place to dry.

The soft fibres of the kie leaves are peeled away from the coarser undersides, tied into bunches and blanched by placing them in the sea for up to a fortnight. After being brought ashore, they are carefully washed to remove the salt and dried in the sun. Each leaf is then curled and made softer by pulling it between the fingers and the lip of a clam shell. It is then cut to the desired width, ready to be woven.

The kie fibres, when cut into threadlike strips, become extremely valuable, silklike fine mats called *fihu*, unmatched anywhere in the world. A good *fala fihu* will require thousands of hours of weaving time, and mothers often begin work on one at the birth of a daughter in the hope of finishing in time to present it as part of her dowry.

Other types of mats include the *fala*

tu'i, fala pa'ongo, and *fala tofua*. The first is the most complex – a mat of double thickness, one layer woven of coarse tofua and the other of finer pa'ongo. The fala pa'ongo on its own is dark in colour and is normally presented to those of high status in the society. The fala tofua is of a lighter colour.

The black seen in many pandanus baskets is derived by dyeing the leaves with the juice of *loa 'ano* or *manaui* before weaving. Baskets are stiffened by weaving around ribs of coconut frond. Fibres of *fau* or hibiscus bark are often used along with the pandanus when making baskets or dancing costumes.

WHAT TO BRING

Given the comfortable and relatively consistent climate of the Tonga Islands, clothing can be kept at a minimum. A pair of shorts for men or a cotton skirt for women, light cotton shirts and trousers, a beach towel, a hat, flip-flops (thongs), walking shoes, a swimsuit and a jumper, flannel shirt, or light jacket will be about all anyone will need. This wardrobe can be supplemented as necessary at the flea market in Nuku'alofa, where any type of clothing imaginable, clean and in good condition, can be bought for T\$1 to T\$2.

Note that Tongan law prohibits anyone from appearing in public without a shirt; offenders are fined. This doesn't apply to the beach, of course.

Personal items such as sunblocks, tampons, toothpaste, contraceptives, mosquito repellent and shampoos should probably be brought from home, since the availability and quality as well as the price of such things in Tonga is unpredictable. Film and camera equipment is also best brought from home.

A few paperbacks to read on the beach, a torch for exploring caves, a Swiss army knife, a universal-type drain plug, snorkelling gear and rain gear are also advised.

If you'll be bushwalking or travelling by ferry, a sleeping bag and ground cover will be practically essential, while a tent will allow you the freedom to stay overnight on a particularly appealing beach, forest or mountain.

Getting There

The South Pacific is a relatively expensive place transportwise and some serious route-planning is in order if you don't have unlimited funds to allow you the luxury of whim-to-whim travel. Remember that everyone arriving in Tonga needs either an air ticket out or a guarantee by a yacht owner that you will be departing on the same boat you arrived on.

As a general rule, don't trust airline bookings made in Tonga. They don't have computer booking and they normally screw it up. Given the number of faxes that are sent back and forth between agents and overseas airlines offices, however, it's almost excusable.

AIR

The vast majority of Tonga's visitors arrive on scheduled flights at Fua'amotu International Airport on Tongatapu. While Tonga isn't exactly a remote or obscure destination like Tuvalu or Niue, it isn't as popular as Fiji or Tahiti either and airfares certainly do reflect that situation. From New Zealand, Australia, Fiji, the Samoas and Hawaii, access to Tonga is fairly straightforward. From anywhere else, travelling to Tonga will entail first reaching one of those connecting points. Auckland, Nadi or Suva, and 'Apia seem to be the easiest thanks to the relative reliability of Air New Zealand, Air Pacific and Polynesian Airlines, respectively.

Coming from Pago Pago, Honolulu or direct from Sydney will require travelling on Hawaiian Airlines, which doesn't have quite as reliable a reputation. In fact, anyone in a hurry should also avoid Pago Pago at all costs. Hawaiian has a monopoly there, and one traveller told me a tale of having to arrange to get himself deported in order to get out. Fortunately, he knew someone who worked in the immigration department. . .

Note that because of Tonga's restrictive Sunday closing laws, no flights leave Samoa for Tonga on Saturdays.

From the USA & Canada

The least expensive but probably most time-consuming way to get to Tonga from the US west coast is on Hawaiian Airlines via Honolulu and Pago Pago. They fly from Seattle, Portland, Anchorage, San Francisco, Las Vegas and Los Angeles for a return fare of between US$800 and US$1100 depending upon season. November and December are the dearest and most congested times to travel, while the northern summer, which corresponds to the Tongan winter, is the cheapest and easiest time to get a booking.

Due to the popularity of Australia and New Zealand with North Americans and to the fact that Hawaiian has the lowest fares to the South Pacific, you'd be wise to book well in advance of your trip – at least three months before your intended departure.

Thanks to Alaska Airlines' and Hawaiian Airlines' reciprocal agreement, frequent-flyer kilometrage is interchangeable between the two. Tonga is the farthest afield of any point accessible through this scheme. Lots of the tourists I encountered in Tonga had gone this route so if you do a lot of travelling on either airline, look into it.

North Americans who'd rather avoid Hawaiian have several other options. Good connections can be made at Fiji or Auckland, which are both easily accessible on Qantas and Air New Zealand, but plan on a return fare of between US$1200 and US$1500. There are package deals to Fiji which begin at US$899 for one-week visits including airfare and accommodation, but the price goes up with longer stays. Air Pacific flies to Tonga from Nadi and Suva on Mondays, Wednesdays, Thursdays and Saturdays.

Canadians can take Qantas or Air Pacific direct from Vancouver with an intermediate stop in Honolulu. The Air Pacific Vancouver/Nadi flight on Thursdays and Saturdays at 8.30 pm connects with their flight to Tongatapu.

From Australia & New Zealand
Hawaiian, Air New Zealand and Air Pacific all have return services from Sydney to Tongatapu for A$777. Air New Zealand entails by far the least hassle and Hawaiian by far the most. Air New Zealand flies twice weekly with a connection in Auckland, Air Pacific four times weekly with a change in Nadi and Hawaiian only once a week with at least a three-day stopover in Pago Pago.

The fare from Auckland to Tonga on Air New Zealand currently runs at about NZ$550 but there are specials for as low as NZ$450 return. Hawaiian is the same price but requires a one or two-day stopover in Pago Pago. Polynesian Airlines also does this route twice weekly, and more frequently via 'Apia (Western Samoa).

From the UK & Europe
There is no straightforward way to get from Europe to the South Pacific. Europeans will have to get themselves to the North American west coast, Sydney or Auckland, and work out a routing from there. Given that the South Pacific is Europe's antipodes, a Round-The-World ticket may prove a viable option.

From other Pacific Islands
From Pago Pago, Hawaiian Airlines flies to Tonga twice weekly. The return fare is currently US$280 for the weekend flight and US$200 if you travel during the week – a bit steep for a flight of about one hour! From Nadi and Suva, there are four flights weekly. There is a Polynesian Airlines service twice weekly from 'Apia (Western Samoa). From the Cook Islands,

you'll have to fly via New Zealand, Fiji, or Hawaii and the same goes for French Polynesia.

You can fly to or from Nauru to Tonga via New Caledonia with Air Nauru. Theoretically, Air Nauru could also get you to Tonga from Manila, Taipei, Singapore, Hong Kong, Japan and Micronesia, but don't count on it under any circumstances!!

Special Tickets & Passes
Polypass Polynesian Airlines' Polypass is an extremely popular option open to those who don't mind limited time in a number of South Pacific destinations. It is good for 30 days and includes travel to Tonga, Fiji, Western Samoa and the Cook Islands as well as one return trip to each New Zealand and Australia. The price is US$799 for adults, US$400 for children under 12 and US$80 for children under two years of age. Tahiti may be added for an extra US$100. This is a good way to fill up your passport quickly but see absolutely nothing. However, if you'll be visiting more than one Pacific destination from Australia, the Polypass is cheaper than individual flights.

A much better Polypass option includes one circuit of the classic 'triangle' of Fiji, Tonga and Western Samoa. It is valid for one year and costs only US$383.

Round-The-World Tickets Round-The-World (RTW) tickets have become very popular in the last few years. The RTW tickets offered by airlines are often real bargains, and since Tonga is pretty much at the other side of the world from Europe or North America, it may work out no more expensive or even cheaper to keep going in the same direction right round the world rather than U-turn when you want to return.

The official airline RTW tickets are usually put together by a combination of two airlines, and permit you to fly anywhere you want on their route systems so long as you do not backtrack. Other restrictions are that you (usually) must book the first sector in advance and cancellation penalties then apply. There may be restrictions on how many stops you are permitted, and usually the tickets are valid from 90 days up to a year. Typical prices for these South Pacific RTW tickets are from UK£1400 to UK£1700 or US$2500 to US$3000. An alternative type of RTW ticket is one put together by a travel agent using a combination of discounted tickets. A UK agent like Trailfinders can put together some interesting London-to-London RTW combinations.

See your travel agent for details.

Circle Pacific Tickets Circle Pacific tickets are similar to RTW tickets, and use a combination of airlines to circle the Pacific. As with RTW tickets, there are advance purchase restrictions and limits on how many stopovers you can make. Typically, fares range between US$1500 and US$2000. You may be able to organise such a ticket that takes in Tonga, among many other Pacific destinations. Again, check with your travel agent for details.

CARGO SHIP

Many travellers come to the South Pacific with grandiose dreams of island-hopping aboard cargo ships, but few actually do. The truth of the matter is that the days of working or bumming your way around the world on cargo ships are just about over. All sorts of insurance and freight company restrictions have made such travel difficult.

Those who are serious about trying to go this route should approach the captain of the boat while the ship is in port. On some freight lines, the captain has the option of deciding who goes and who doesn't. The newspapers in Nuku'alofa, Pago Pago, 'Apia, Suva and Honolulu (the most difficult of all!) list the sailing schedules and routes of the various lines up to three months in advance.

YACHT

Between the months of May and October, the harbours of the South Pacific are crowded with cruising yachts from all over the world. Invariably, these yachts are following the favourable winds westward from the Americas.

Routes from the US west coast will invariably include Hawaii and Palmyra before starting on the traditional route through the Samoas, Tonga, Fiji and New Zealand. From the Atlantic and Caribbean, yachties access this area via Venezuela, Panama, the Galapagos, the Marquesas, the Society Islands and Tuamotus, possibly making stops at Suwarrow in the northern Cooks, Rarotonga or Niue en route. Due to the hurricane season which begins in late November, most yachties will want to clear Fiji or Tonga and be on their way to New Zealand or the Solomons (most often the former) by the early part of that month.

Access to Tonga is almost always from American or Western Samoa. Often, yachts anchor for a few days in Niuatoputapu where they check into the country, before crowding into the Port of Refuge, anchoring in front of the Paradise International and proceeding to set up the annual yachtie social colony that is really going strong by the beginning of October. Most of the yachties take day trips around the Vava'u Group before proceeding on to Nuku'alofa, with a possible intermediate visit to the Ha'apai Group.

The significance of all this is that the yachting community is very friendly, especially toward those who display an interest in yachts and other things nautical. Often they are looking for crew, and for those who'd like a bit of low-key adventure, this is the way to go. Most of the time, crew members will only be asked to take a turn on watch – that is, scan the horizon for cargo ships, stray containers and the odd reef – and possibly to cook or clean up the ship. In port, they may be required to dive and scrape the bottom, paint or make repairs. In most cases, sailing experience is not necessary and crew members have the option to learn as they go. Most yachties will charge crew US$10 to US$15 per day for food and supplies.

The best places to secure a passage on a cruising yacht are, naturally, east or north-east of Tonga. The west coast of the USA is a prime hunting ground – San Francisco, Newport Beach, San Diego, and Honolulu are all good. Likewise, it shouldn't be too difficult to crew on in Papeete, Pago Pago, 'Apia, or Rarotonga either.

The best way to make known your availability is to post a notice on the bulletin board of the yacht club in the port. It would also be helpful to visit the docks and ask people if they know anyone setting off on a cruise around the time you'd like to go who might be looking for crew members. It may be a matter of interest that the most successful passage-seekers tend to be young women who are willing to crew on with male 'single-handers' (that is, who sail alone). Naturally, the bounds of the relationship should be fairly well defined before setting out!

For sanity's sake, bear in mind that not everyone is compatible with everyone else and that under the conditions of a long ocean voyage, rivalries and petty distress are magnified many times. Only set out on a long passage with someone you can feel relatively comfortable with and remember that, once aboard, the skipper's judgement is law.

If you'd like to enjoy some relative freedom of movement on a yacht, it's a good idea to try to find one that has wind-vane steering. Nobody likes to spend all day and all night at the wheel staring at a compass, and more often than not such a job is likely to go to the crew members of the lowest status. Comfort is also greatly increased on yachts which have a furling jib, a dodger to keep out the weather, a toilet (head) and a shower. Those which are rigged for racing are generally more manageable than simple live-aboards. As a general rule, about three metres of length for each person aboard affords relatively uncrowded conditions.

For those not interested in cruising, yachties have a mind-boggling store of knowledge about world weather patterns, navigation and maritime geography, and can be considered a good source of information regarding such things.

While they seem to emanate an aura of wealth, most yachties are as impecunious as the average traveller and are always looking for ways to pick up a bit of money. If you're looking for a babysitter or a day charter, just ask around the harbours, particularly in Neiafu and Nuku'alofa. Quite a few skippers are of necessity certified divers also, and those with credentials to teach and certify others will normally be happy to do so. When I was in Tonga, the going rate for scuba certification was US$200 and required a minimum of eight days of instruction. Many will also give classes in celestial navigation and sailing for a reasonable fee.

A particularly good trip you might want to consider is a three-week whale-watching expedition aboard the 22-metre schooner *Wavewalker*. It is commissioned to study whales and dolphins in the Tonga/Samoa area and calls in at remote islands. Participants pay a fee, and join in the sailing and maintenance of the ship. Full details are available from: South Pacific Voyages, PO Box 2235, Auckland 1, New Zealand.

LEAVING TONGA
Departure Tax
There is a departure tax of T$5 for every person flying out of the country, payable at the airport at the time of check-in.

Getting Around

AIR

Travelling by air in Tonga doesn't offer too many choices. The only airline operating domestic flights is Friendly Islands Airways (FIA), Tonga's national airline. Their fares aptly reflect their monopoly status.

With only three planes, a Britten-Norman Islander which does runs to 'Eua and two DeHavilland Otters which do the other runs, their scheduling is quite haphazard. You might have booked and paid for a flight, for instance, but if there's insufficient interest in the run, it will be cancelled. In addition, the Ha'apai Group often gets overflown if there aren't enough passengers to justify landing there. Also, any member of the royal family can effectively commandeer a plane, and

posted timetables go awry. Still, despite all these problems, FIA is still the easiest way to get around Tonga.

Every day, they do three return flights between Tongatapu and 'Eua and two between Tongatapu and Vava'u, with stops in Ha'apai when warranted. 'Every day', of course, means daily except Sunday. Currently, FIA does not have service to the Niuas.

Fares are as follows:

Tongatapu/'Eua	T$18
Tongatapu/Ha'apai	T$62
Tongatapu/Vava'u	T$88
Ha'apai/Vava'u	T$44

FIA allows 10 kg free baggage. For T$3, the FIA bus will fetch you at your hotel, thus

DOMESTIC FLIGHT TICKET 0017425

FRIENDLY ISLANDS AIRWAYS

avoiding a T$10 taxi fare (with four people the taxi would be cheaper than the bus, of course!). Sign up for the bus trip at the time of booking.

BUS
Local buses run on the islands of Tongatapu, 'Eua, and Vava'u, and on Lifuka and Foa in the Ha'apai Group. The fares run from 20 to 40 seniti depending upon the distance travelled. Tongatapu and Vava'u are fairly well covered by bus routes, but on other islands transport is very limited. The biggest problem with travelling by bus is that they operate at the whims of the driver. If he feels like knocking off at 1 pm he does, and passengers counting on bus service are left stranded. Never, under any circumstances, rely on catching a bus after about 3 pm.

In the urban areas of Tongatapu, bus stops are marked with a sign that reads 'Pasi'. Elsewhere, you can flag down a bus by waving your outstretched arm, palm down, as the bus approaches. In Tonga, unlike in other South Pacific countries, you pay as you board the bus.

TAXI
There are taxis on Vava'u and Tongatapu islands.

FERRY
There are several ferries which run between the main island groups as well as between some small islands within those groups. A trip by ferry in Tonga is a cultural experience on a major scale. Cabin space is limited but the price of a cabin will set you back several times the amount of airfare anyway, so you'll probably end up a deck passenger. Indoor spaces are stuffy, cramped and claustrophobic, while outdoor spaces are likely to be wet and/or cold.

Tongans are normally not very good sailors either, and the sight of them puking everywhere as well as the smell, filth, cockroaches and rubbish all over the ship are bound to have some effect even on those not normally prone to seasickness. You'd be wise to take precautions. The toilets on board the ferries go beyond unspeakable. A pair of hip waders and a gas mask may come in handy, for what it's worth.

Sometimes a 'business' class is available for about 30% more. The purpose of this is racist – it exists to separate Tongans from foreigners. However, on a particularly crowded run, business class or not, it is full of Tongans because there simply isn't any space elsewhere. Videos are shown and food is also available in business class, but very few people actually feel like eating it.

Travellers would be well advised to bring along a ground cover and a sleeping bag if they plan to do any sleeping on the boat. Food and drinks are not normally available on board so bring some goodies too, if you think you'll be able to eat. Especially on trips to the Niuas, which seem to go on and on, a couple of books will also go a long way towards relieving the monotony of the open seas.

The MV 'Olovaha (affectionately known as 'Orange Vomit' or, more pleasantly, 'Olive Oyl' by those who know it well), does weekly runs between Tongatapu, Ha'apai, Vava'u and on occasion, the Niuas (rarely is it able to land at Niuafo'ou). If you'd like further information, go to their office in the middle of the flea market in Nuku'alofa or near the wharf in Vava'u.

The MV Fokololo 'oe Hau (or 'Floating Coffin'!) is a canal boat highly unsuited to the open seas. Nevertheless, it runs between Tongatapu, Ha'apai, Vava'u and the Niuas, landing at Niuafo'ou only when the weather is extremely calm. The schedule is left more or less to the whims of the Walter Line, which operates it. Walter Line's other boat is the MV 'Onga Ha'angana, which operates between Tongatapu and the Ha'apai islands of Lifuka, 'Uiha, Nomuka and Ha'afeva. Between Tuesday and Saturday the MV Ngataluta'ane goes daily from Nuku'alofa to 'Eua and back. The Walter Line office is located in the four-storey building above the video shop on Taufa'ahau Rd.

To get to smaller islands throughout the country, you can hitchhike on private fishing boats and launches. Just ask around port and landing areas for one going your way. Expect to pay about T$1 for a trip of up to an hour. Alternatively, boats can be chartered to various small islands. Charters to out-of-the-way areas cost up to T$300 per day.

MV Ngataluta'ane

Dep	Nuku'alofa	0530	Tues to Sat
Arr	'Eua	0900	Ditto
Dep	'Eua	1100	Ditto
Arr	Nuku'alofa	1330	Ditto

One-way fares are: adults T$4.50; students T$4; chidren aged 4-12 T$3.50.

MV 'Olovaha
Schedules:

Dep	Nuku'alofa	1800	Tues
Arr	Ha'afeva	0100	Wed
Dep	Ha'afeva	0300	Wed
Arr	Pangai	0500	Wed
Dep	Pangai	0700	Wed
Arr	Vava'u	1300	Wed
Dep	Vava'u	2200	Thurs
Arr	Pangai	0500	Fri
Dep	Pangai	0700	Fri
Arr	Ha'afeva	0900	Fri
Dep	Ha'afeva	1130	Fri
Arr	Nuku'alofa	1800	Fri

Fares (one-way in T$):

Route	Cabin	Business	Economy	Student	Under 12
Nuk-Hfv	80	30	16	11	8
Nuk-Pangai	90	36	20	16	10
Nuk-Vava'u	135	52	30	23	15
Nuk-Niuas	270	89	60	45	29
Hfv-Pangai	30	9	8	6	4
Hfv-Vava'u	100	35	23	17	11
Hfv-Niuas	220	84	50	38	25
Pangai-Vava'u	86	28	15	10	8
Pangai-Niuas	190	74	43	33	22
Vava'u-Niuas	140	49	32	24	16
Nf-Ntt	92	35	22	18	11

Nuk = Nuku'alofa   Hfv = Ha'afeva   Nf = Niuafo'ou   Ntt = Niuatoputapu

YACHT

The yachtie route through Tonga begins in Niuatoputapu and runs southward to and through Vava'u, to Ha'apai and thence to Nuku'alofa (Tongatapu). Quite a few of those going to New Zealand stop at Minerva Reef en route. October and November are the best months to go yacht hitchhiking in Tonga. Details about crewing onto a yacht are covered in the Getting There chapter.

Yacht charters with Moorings, Ltd are available in the Vava'u Group. Particulars regarding that option will be detailed in the Vava'u chapter.

DRIVING

Renting a vehicle in Tonga is of limited value, since there isn't exactly a vast

MV Fokololo 'oe Hau & MV 'Onga Ha'angana
Fares (one-way in T$):

Route	Adults	Students	Under 12
Nuk-Hfv	13	8	3
Nuk-Pangai	15	10	7
Nuk-Vava'u	25	18	10
Pangai-Vava'u	13	8	4
Nuk-Ntt	55	35	20
Vava'u-Nf	40	25	15
Ntt-Nf	20	13	8
Nuk-Nf	60	45	30
Nuk-'Uiha	11	7	5
Nuk-Nomuka	8	5	4
Hfv-Pangai	4	2	1
Nomuka-Pangai	6	4	2

network of roads to be explored. A current driving licence is required to operate a car in Tonga. If you take your licence to the central police station in Nuku'alofa you can buy a temporary Tongan licence for T$8. There is no driving exam.

If you happen to be driving in Tonga and see a blue and grey Chevrolet Silverado with the number plate HM1 led by police escort, pull off the road and wait for it to pass. If it is accompanied by a siren, the king is aboard (or the senior royal who's present in the country at the time). If there's only a flashing blue light, it could be the queen, the princess or one of the princes.

Both Avis and Budget Rent-a-Car are available on Tongatapu and there is an independent agency operating on Vava'u. Avis charges from T$32 for a four-door manual transmission Toyota to T$60 for a four-door automatic air-conditioned Toyota Cressida and tacks on a per kilometre rate of 15 to 25 seniti. Unlimited kilometrage rates, with a minimum of two days' hire, range from T$39 to T$85. Insurance is available for T$6 per day with T$1000 deductible.

Budget's rates are almost the same, but they also have a manual transmission 10-passenger van which rents for T$65.

In Vava'u, the situation is a bit better. Half-day (12 hours of your choice!) rentals at the Neiafu Tahi Agency cost only T$20 for a Suzuki 4WD or a Toyota Corolla. Full-day (24-hour) rentals cost T$40.

MOTORCYCLE

On Tongatapu and Vava'u motorcycles may be rented by the day or week. Expect to pay a daily rate of upwards of T$25 for a motorcycle that will carry two people. A Tongan licence is necessary if you want to ride a motorcycle and is available at the central police station in Nuku'alofa for T$2. No driving exam is required. Insurance is available for an extra charge and fuel is the responsibility of the hirer.

BICYCLE

On both Tongatapu and Vava'u bicycles may be rented by the day or week. Flat Tongatapu is ideally suited to travel by pushbike and Vava'u can be negotiated with a bit of effort. It will allow you to see the islands at island pace. Distances are not great in Tonga and the low traffic density is conducive to travel by bike. Expect to pay a daily rate of around T$5 or T$6 for a pushbike.

HORSE

You can either tramp around the island on foot or you can rent the services of a horse. The latter will be available on all inhabited islands: just ask anyone who owns a horse and you're likely to be able to strike up an informal deal. Expect to pay about T$5 per day. Be warned that the horses are usually only available sans saddle, reins and other amenities, so unless you're a very good bareback rider, you could have some problems. Tongan horses also seem to be very adept at shedding unwanted objects that might have climbed onto their backs; this could also be a matter for concern.

WALKING

Very good bushwalking opportunities are available in the Niuas and on 'Eua, but all the islands offer possibilities: plantation tracks, sandy beaches, reefs, rainforests and volcanoes, all invite exploration on foot. Walkers are advised to carry plenty of liquid or a bush knife which can be used to open coconuts. Be sensitive when collecting coconuts – most of the trees belong to a plantation owner and visitors should ask permission before collecting nuts indiscriminately.

LOCAL TRANSPORT
Airport Transport

There is no public bus between the airport and Nuku'alofa, but the Dateline and Ramanlal hotels have private buses which charge T$4 one way. Friendly Islands Airways provides a service to the airport for those booked onto their flights for T$3.

A taxi ride to or from the airport is limited to T$12 by the government and in fact most drivers charge only T$10.

TOURS

Both diving and sightseeing companies run tours to reefs and points of interest on Tongatapu and in the Vava'u Group. For more detailed information, refer to the individual chapters.

All-day taxi tours of Tongatapu Island which include all the traditional 'tourist' sites, go for between T$60 and T$80 for up to four people. Several of the drivers are familiar with the history and legend surrounding the various points of interest, and those who want quick spoon-fed familiarisation with the island should consider this option.

Tongatapu Island

Tongatapu, the 'sacred southern island', along with its capital, Nuku'alofa, the 'abode of love', is the hub of all activity in the kingdom. With a land area of nearly 260 square km, Tongatapu occupies a third of the country's territory. The island's population currently stands at about 64,000 with the majority living in Nuku'alofa and adjoining villages.

The island of Tongatapu is pancake-flat, tilting slightly toward the sagging weight of the Ha'apai volcanoes. Cliffs on the southern shore rise to 30 metres while the northern coast is a drowned maze of islands and reefs.

Due to its prominence as the Tongan capital for at least 600 years, the Lapaha area of Tongatapu contains most of the archaeological sites in Tonga and some of the richest in the Pacific. Networks of moats and *langi*, or tiered tombs, exist throughout the area. A few have been excavated and can be visited today.

Tongatapu also has myriad beaches, caves and quiet villages, all of which invite exploration. On the southern coast are the famous Houma blowholes and a natural sea arch. To the north is a maze of reefs and motus (coral islets), some of which are part of the first national park system in the South Pacific.

Culturally, Tongatapu is a good introduction to the country, and even those planning to set off to the more remote islands would do well to spend at least a couple of days here. All visitors (excluding yachties) arrive on Tongatapu, the place where old and new Tonga collide and sometimes successfully coexist.

History

Thanks to oral tradition, the known history of Tongatapu reads like a long series of Old Testament begats with a bit of editorialising thrown in when one Tu'i Tonga or another did something notable.

The first Tu'i, as you may remember, was the son of the sun god Tangaloa and a lovely Tongan maiden and came to power sometime in the middle of the 10th century. Between that time and the ascent of King George Tupou I, the title had been held by 38 men.

Around the year 1200, the Tu'i Tonga Tu'itatui set about building the only trilithic gate in Oceania. The Ha'amonga 'a Maui, or 'Maui's burden', near the village of Niutoua has been compared to Stonehenge, to which it bears a superficial resemblance. The present king noticed the similarity and suggested that a design on the lintel may represent some astronomical phenomenon. Experiments have just about confirmed that the diagram represents the directions of the rising and setting sun on the solstices.

The legend was, however, that the Tu'i Tonga constructed it originally to remind two quarrelling sons that unity was better than division. After creating a wonderful future tourist attraction for Tonga and Niutoua, he moved his capital to Lapaha, on the calm lagoon near present-day Mu'a.

During the following 100 years or so, war canoes full of Tongan raiding parties set out for neighbouring islands. They created an empire ranging from the Lau Group in Fiji to the west, across to Niue in the east and northward to Futuna and Samoa, all of it ruled by the Tu'i Tonga from his capital on Tongatapu.

Sometime in the 1400s, the Tu'i Tonga Kau'ulufonua delegated some of his power and authority to his brother, thus creating the title Tu'i Ha'atakalaua. About 200 years later, the title Tu'i Kanokupolu was created by the reigning Tu'i Ha'atakalaua, Mo'ungatonga.

All these title-holders struggled against the division of power. The Tu'i Tonga gradually lost influence, and with the death of the last one, Laufilitonga, in 1865, the Tu'i Kanokupolu was the supreme power in the islands.

The first European visitor to the island was Dutchman Abel Janszoon Tasman, who spent a few days trading with islanders and named the island Amsterdam. The next European contact came with Captain James Cook, who became close friends with the 30th Tu'i Tonga, Fatafehi Paulaho, and presented him with Tu'i Malila, the tortoise that was treated as a chief and given the run of the place for nearly 200 years.

Nuku'alofa

Nuku'alofa is Tonga's big smoke. Although it is a very drowsy place by international standards, someone visiting or returning to Nuku'alofa from 'Eua, Ha'apai, or the Niuas will feel like a country child arriving in New York. Nuku'alofa has shops, restaurants, hotels, discos, travel agents. . .all the trappings of a small-scale big city.

These days, the city is expanding and swallowing up surrounding agricultural land and wetlands. As long as the population of Tonga continues to grow, migration from outer islands puts pressure on the capital to absorb the population and some Tongans are growing concerned that their tranquil life style is slipping away before their eyes. Their once-beautiful, mangrove-edged lagoon is now suffering from contamination and over-fishing, leaving it almost devoid of marine life.

Besides being the seat of government and home of the royal family, Nuku'alofa is also the centre of industry, the transport hub and the production and distribution centre for imported goods entering the country. Therefore, the prices and availability of imported goods in Nuku'alofa are a bit more favourable than on the outer islands. Items produced locally such as agricultural goods and handicrafts tend to be a bit higher, although the selection is much greater than in the rest of the country.

Although Nuku'alofa doesn't have any earth-shaking 'must see', there are still a lot of interesting things around the town, all of which are accessible on foot.

History

Nuku'alofa began life as a fortress for the western district of Tongatapu. Will Mariner recounts in depth the sacking of the fort of 'Nioocalofa' by Finau, the chief of Ha'apai.

It seems that attacks on this fort had become a sort of annual event with the Ha'apai raiders, having been faithfully executed for at least 11 years, but this particular visit (in about 1807) was the sacking to end all sacking. Finau and his men fired on the fort with cannons from the *Port-au-Prince* (the British privateer which had brought Mariner to Tonga and had been subsequently destroyed), set fire to it and burned it to the ground.

After their fun, their priests, who claimed to be speaking for the gods, advised them that it would be necessary to reconstruct the fort, which they did. At least it gave them a reason to embark upon their annual holiday of destruction the following year! Unfortunately, a rival chief set it on fire shortly thereafter; Finau was watching from Pangai Island, which prevented him from doing anything about it. He later learned that the other chief, Tarki, had destroyed Finau's building just for the fun of irritating him while he was watching.

Today the city is far less stormy, and the inhabitants are more concerned about living in the 20th century than playing feudal war games. But who would expect the 'abode of love' to be anything but pleasant?

Information

Tourist Office The Tonga Visitors' Bureau

is on Vuna Rd, just west of the International Dateline Hotel.

While the office is architecturally worth a look and the staff are friendly, it's probably best not to get too technical in your questions. However, they do have some informative handouts dealing with various aspects of Tongan life and a town plan of Nuku'alofa.

There is a bulletin board in the Visitors' Bureau listing available housing; if you'll be staying awhile in Nuku'alofa, it may be cheaper to hire a flat rather than pay for nightly accommodation.

Ignore completely the airline schedules posted there, however. In some cases they are more than a year out of date! Travel agents in town will be better equipped to suss out unpredictable airline timetables, anyway.

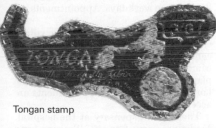

Tongan stamp

Post Tongan postal services are surprisingly reliable. The GPO in Nuku'alofa is on the corner of Taufa'ahau and Wellington roads. The poste restante address is simply Poste Restante, GPO, Nuku'alofa, Tonga Islands. They file letters alphabetically and, since Tongan names are constructed the same way as European names, they don't have any problem picking out the surname and filing it correctly.

To post a letter to anywhere in the South Pacific or Australasia costs 42 seniti. A letter to Europe, the Americas, Asia, or Africa costs 57 seniti. To a destination within Tonga it costs 32 seniti. Postcards go for slightly less.

For stamp collectors, philatelic services are available at the GPO, at the Philatelic Bureau in the Treasury building and at the Langa Fonua Handicraft Centre (which is in the same building as Friendly Islands Airways). The banana stamps for which Tonga is famous, however, are no longer available for use, as they are now used exclusively for government correspondence. You may find some used ones at the Langa Fonua shop. Niuafo'ou stamps are available only at the Philatelic Bureau.

Telecommunications The Cable & Wireless Office is on Salote Rd. They offer telephone, telegraph, telex and fax services 24 hours daily including Sunday. For a charge of T$1, reverse charge calls are accepted to countries having reciprocal agreements with Tonga.

Banks The best rates can be had at the Bank of Tonga, which has offices in Nuku'alofa. Banks are open from 9 am to 4 pm weekdays; the sub-office of the Bank of Tonga in Nuku'alofa is open on Saturdays as well, until 12 noon. At the main branch of the Bank of Tonga there are special tellers who do currency exchange, thus eliminating a long wait in a very long queue.

The International Dateline Hotel also does currency exchange, but at a lower rate than the banks.

Consulates The following is a list of where to find foreign diplomatic representatives in Nuku'alofa:

Australian High Commission
    Salote Rd
British High Commission
    Vuna Rd
Nauru Consulate
    c/o Reichelmann, Vuna Rd
New Zealand High Commission
    Taufa'ahau Rd
Spanish Honorary Consul
    I Futa Helu, 'Atenisi Institute
Swedish Consulate
    Ministry of Labour building, Salote Rd
Taiwan Consulate
    corner Railway & Holomui roads

West German Consulate
Otto G Sanft Store, Taufa'ahau Rd

Airline Offices Following is a list of airline offices in the capital:

Air Nauru
Ramanlal building, Taufa'ahau Rd
(tel 21810)
Air New Zealand
Union Travel, Tungi Arcade (tel 21740)
Air Pacific
Jones Travel (tel 21422)
Friendly Islands Airways
Langa Fonua building (tel 22566)
Hawaiian Airlines
Teta's Tours, Taufa'ahau Rd (tel 21688)
Polynesian Airlines
Salote Rd (tel 21565)

Tour Agencies Several agencies in Nuku'alofa offer a variety of tours to many of the points of interest around the island. If you're in a hurry, this is a way to quickly 'do' the sights. Expect to pay about T$20 for a half day or T$25 to T$30 for a full-day tour.

Union Travel
PO Box 4, Nuku'alofa: tours of eastern and western Tongatapu, town tours (tel 21646)
Teta's Tours
PO Box 215, Nuku'alofa: eastern and western tours, town tours, circle island tours (tel 21688)
Gateway Travel & Tours
full and half-day tours to main Tongatapu sights (tel 21215)

Full-day taxi tours are available for between T$60 and T$80 for up to four people. These tours are done by an incredible Tongan named Tevita Helu, who has travelled throughout the world performing with a traditional Tongan musical group. His tours are both interesting and informative, and you'll certainly get your money's worth in history and hospitality if you opt to go this route! If you'd like more information, contact Tevita at PO Box 957, Nuku'alofa, Kingdom of Tonga, or phone the Keleti

Beach Resort (tel 21179) on Tongatapu to make enquiries.

Health Nuku'alofa has two pharmacies, one in the Nuku'alofa Clinic behind the GPO and the other in the Ministry of Labour building below the Swedish Consulate. There is a doctor at the former who is available for consultation between 9.30 am and 4 pm weekdays and 9.30 am to 12 noon on Saturdays. No appointments are necessary.

If you have a problem you're unsure of dealing with – anything more serious than cuts, scrapes, or diarrhoea – it's probably best to go to the German Clinic (Kliniki Siamane; tel 22736). The German doctor there charges T$5 to T$15 per visit and she is familiar with tropical ailments. The clinic is open from 9 am to 12.30 pm and 2 to 5 pm on weekdays. Appointments are required.

The National Hospital is in the village of Vaiola, a 10-minute bus ride from the central bus terminal at Talamahu Market. Seeing the doctor costs T$2, but plan on spending the day waiting in the horrendous queue. No appointments are accepted.

There is a dispensary at the hospital. Medicines are free to Tongans and foreigners pay only a token fee – 15% or so of the real price.

Another alternative is the Catholic Clinic in the village of Pe'a, where the sisters are pretty good at looking after minor ailments for a standard T$1 charge. To get there, take the Vaini bus from the east bus terminal at the Talamahu Market and ask to be dropped at the clinic.

Laundry Andersen Laundry Service (tel 22296), on Wellington and Railway roads, is open from 8 am to 6 pm Monday to Saturday. They'll do one load of washing for T$2.50 and, for that much again, they'll also dry it for you. Ten pieces ironed costs T$2, and their

Top: Royal Palace, Nuku'alofa
Left: Pigs as guests of honour at feast, Pangai Island, Tongatapu Group
Right: Langi tombs, Mu'a, Tongatapu Island

Top: Port of Refuge, Neiafu, Vava'u Island
Left: Large tapa, Ha'atu'a, 'Eua Island
Right: Cliffs at 'Anokula, 'Eua Island

convenient pick-up and delivery of a wash is an extra T$2.

The house across Railway Rd from the market, with all the clotheslines out front, also has a laundry service; the Dateline Hotel does guests' laundry for an outrageous fee.

Bookshops & Exchanges The only bookshop of any consequence in the country is the Friendly Islands Bookshop on Taufa'ahau Rd, but their prices are inordinately high, especially for pulp paperbacks.

However, they do have a fairly good selection of works on Tonga and related island topics, which are difficult if not impossible to find outside the country, and these are, surprisingly, quite reasonable in most cases.

There is a two-for-one book exchange at a nameless shop across the street from Queen Salote Wharf.

Royal Palace

The Royal Palace on the waterfront has come to be a symbol of Tonga to the world. It is a white, Victorian structure made of timber and surrounded by large lawns and Norfolk Island pines. Although it's certainly not what immediately comes to mind when you think 'royal', it still stands out in Nuku'alofa.

It was prefabricated in New Zealand in 1867 and was transported to Tonga exclusively as a royal residence. In 1882 the upstairs verandah was added and the Royal Chapel was constructed behind the palace. Sunday services used to take place in the chapel before it was damaged in a hurricane. The coronations of King George II, Queen Salote and King Taufa'ahau Tupou IV took place there in 1893, 1918 and 1967, respectively. The coronation chair in the chapel is partially constructed of the *koka* tree on Lifuka (Ha'apai) under which King George I was invested with the title Tu'i Kanokupolu.

The small octagonal gazebolike building in the gardens is called the Palesi and was used as a rest house for visiting chiefs.

The palace grounds are not open to visitors but a good view of the palace itself is available from the waterfront area just to the west. Just beyond it, on the slopes of Mt Zion, is the Sia Ko Veiongo, the 'royal estate'. It was here that the fortress of Nuku'alofa once stood and its ludicrous history of attacks and conflagrations took place. Now the site is occupied by a radio tower and the grave of Captain Croker of the HMS *Favourite*, who was killed attacking the fortress on 24 June 1840.

Tonga Visitors' Bureau

The Tonga Visitors' Bureau is on Vuna Rd, just west of the International Dateline Hotel. It's worth a visit to have a look at the building, whose construction was a community effort. It was commissioned by the king in order to promote the traditional Tongan construction methods and to encourage tourism as a source of revenue after the main island was damaged by a serious earthquake on 23 June 1977. The building costs of T$45,000 were donated by the Australian government as part of an earthquake recovery program.

The posts are made of *tangato* and *tamanu* wood from the island of 'Eua and the framing is of bamboo. The walls are covered with pa'ongo pandanus mats woven in Niuafo'ou. The ceiling and roof are of finely designed, plaited coconut fibre, while the bindings on the ceiling beams depict the Norfolk Island pines which are found in abundance in Nuku'alofa. In addition, there are about 89 square metres of tapa depicting the royal crest, which was designed in 1862 by the grandson of King George Tupou I.

The poles in front of the office are a gift from the people of New Zealand. They represent in wood both ancient and modern patterns used in the designs painted on tapa. Below these are depictions of vines and shells native to Tonga. One pole is considered 'male' and the other 'female'. The male pole portrays a *motoku* (heron), whale, pig, octopus and

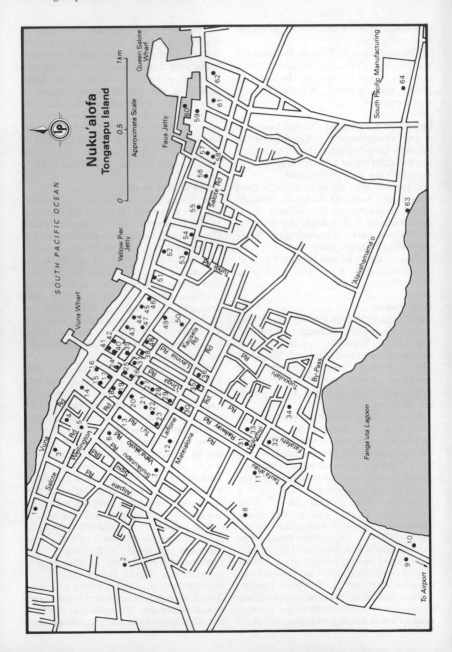

1	Sunrise Guest House	34	Sela's Guest House
2	'Atenisi Institute	35	Church of Tonga
3	Seaview Restaurant	36	Way-Inn Motel
4	British High Commission	37	Morris Hedstrom
5	Mt Zion	38	Burns Philp
6	Centenary Chapel	39	Talamahu Market & Bus Stations
7	Queen Salote College	40	Parliament House
8	Police Training School	41	Shipping Corporation of Polynesia
9	National Hospital, Vaiola	42	Ministry of Lands,
10	Tonga National Centre,		Survey & Natural Resources
	Handicraft & Cultural Centre	43	Tonga Visitors' Bureau
11	Budget Car Rental	44	Fasi-Moe-Afi Guest House
12	Royal Tombs	45	Pangaimotu Office & Bike Rentals,
13	Chez Alisi & André		Hua-Hua Restaurant
14	Royal Palace	46	International Dateline Hotel
15	Nuku'alofa Pharmacy & Clinic	47	Fa'onelua Tropical Gardens
16	Bank of Tonga	48	Cowley's Bread Bin,
17	GPO		Polynesian Airlines
18	Hawaiian Airlines, Teta Tours	49	Ministry of Labour, Fasi Pharmacy,
19	Air Pacific, Gateway Travel & Tours		Swedish Consulate
20	West German Consulate	50	Latter Day Saints
21	Ramanlal Hotel, Avis Car Rental		Mission Centre & Chapel
22	Air New Zealand,	51	Beach House
	Arcade Restaurant	52	Kimiko's Guest House
23	Free Church of Tonga	53	Joe's Tropicana Bar
24	Ministry of Police & Prisons,	54	Cable & Wireless
	Central Police Station	55	Fred's Restaurant
25	Friendly Islands Airways	56	Kilikilihau Shopping Centre
26	Friendly Islands	57	Coralhead Diving
	Marketing Cooperative	58	Oldest Church
27	Fakalato Restaurant	59	Vuna Government Market
28	Foto Fix	60	Inter-Island Ferries
29	Friendly Islands Bookshop	61	Fakafanua Centre,
30	Catholic Basilica of St Anthony		St Mary's Cathedral
	of Padua, Akiko's Restaurant	62	Pacific Forum Line, Warner
31	Seventh Day Adventist Church		Pacific Line, Customs Department
32	Taiwan Consulate	63	Joe's Kahana Lagoon Resort
33	K's Guest House	64	Small Industries Centre

rat. The heron is of a type found in New Zealand and represents the common Polynesian ancestry of the two island groups. On the 'female' pole are a sea turtle, a bat and a dog, the design of which was taken from an ancient Tongan war club.

Vuna Wharf

Vuna Wharf, at the end of Taufa'ahau Rd, was constructed in 1906 and used to serve as the main disembarkation point in the country. It was replaced in 1966 by Queen Salote Wharf several km to the east and then nearly destroyed in the earthquake of 1977. There used to be a railway along Railway Rd – it was used to transport copra to the Vuna Wharf where it was loaded onto steamers for export.

Royal Tombs

The Mala'ekula, the large parklike area across from the basilica, was named after the Katoanga Kula festival, which was held here in the days of King George Tupou I (the *mala'e* part of the name refers to a sacred area). The area is now off limits to the public. Since 1893 it has contained the royal tombs: the graves of all the Tongan sovereigns as well as their husbands, wives and other relatives. It was once used as a golf course, but now the royal cattle are resident there.

'Atenisi Institute

The only private university in Tonga, the 'Atenisi Institute is a unique institution that operates without subsidy from either church or state and therefore without obligation to further the views of either one. It was founded in 1967 by an extraordinary individual, I Futa Helu, to operate under a classic western format in the tradition of Oxford. He writes in the university syllabus:

. . .concern with the classical tradition means the keeping of a traditional core of studies. This is the academic equivalent English attitude that a university which does not teach philosophy as a discipline is a 'mickey-mouse' university. . .all South Sea island communities have created beautiful cultures, but it must be pointed out that in all these cultures criticism as an institution is discouraged, and criticism is the very heart of education.

When I asked Mr Helu what he thought of Christianity and the grasp it has on Tonga, he replied: 'Christianity is the bugbear of every facet of Tongan life, a burden. . .'Atenisi is an island of freethinking and criticism in a rigid and structured society.'

Classes in Tongan language and culture are offered as well as philosophy, sciences and other disciplines. Visitors who'll be spending time in Tonga may want to take advantage of them. Tuition is currently around T$40 per course.

If you're visiting during the month of November, try not to miss 'Atenisi's graduation ceremony, which is unlike any you've ever seen before. There is dancing, entertainment, royal gifting, and feasting; there's also a unique tradition called 'presentation of the *vala*', which sees villages of graduates present the university with gifts of elaborate fine mats and immense pieces of tapa, all of which end up in a heap on the common. Rarely will you ever see so many hours of work and so much artistic expertise treated so casually.

Interesting Buildings

Ovalau Building The Ovalau Building on Vuna Rd, now used as a New Zealand High Commission residence, was built at Levuka on the island of Ovalau, Fiji. This nice old weatherboard structure was shipped to Tonga and reconstructed in the early 1950s.

Nuku'alofa Club The Nuku'alofa Club is the exclusive pub/billiards hall just behind the palace grounds. It was founded as a private club in 1914 and now serves as a meeting place of the 'upper crust' in Tongan business, society and government. It is open to only male members and their male guests, although tourists (male only, of course) are sometimes admitted. I think the atmosphere might be a bit stuffy in there. . .

British High Commissioner's Residence This is on the waterfront, west of the palace. It was given to the government by its original owner in 1901 in exchange for another waterfront lot and was leased to the British government in turn. On the front lawn are four cannon from the British privateer *Port-au-Prince*, ransacked at Lifuka (Ha'apai) in 1806.

Queen Salote College Although it was planned as a tribute to 50 years of Christianity in Tonga as early as 1876 and although King George Tupou I donated £1000 to build a ladies school to be named after his wife, the Queen Salote College project didn't immediately get off the ground. It was finally chartered in 1923 on the site of the Tupou College, ostensibly a boys school, although it had accepted female students as early as 1869. Today the school is on Mateialona Rd.

Tonga High School Next door to Queen Salote College is the Tonga High School. The land for the school was donated by King George Tupou I in 1882. Although the first school was relocated in 1941, a new high school was started here in 1962 by Queen Salote. Today, the English language school (Tonga Side School) and the government kindergarten are housed here. Also on the site is the Queen Salote Tupou III Memorial Hall, which was begun in 1966.

Free Wesleyan Church President's Residence This is found on the corner of Siulikutapu and Wellington roads. It is a rather opulent structure, which was built in 1871 for Reverend Shirley Baker (who would become Tonga's first prime minister).

Prime Minister's Residence On Vuna Rd, not far from the Visitors' Bureau, is the residence of Prince Tu'ipelehake, the current Prime Minister of Tonga. Built in 1953, it previously housed an agricultural store and the Tonga Club, a drinking establishment now found two blocks behind the Dateline Hotel.

Langa Fonua Building This gingerbread-style structure on Taufa'ahau Rd was built by a British ex-pat for his five daughters, who lived in New Zealand and came to Tonga for the winters. It now houses the women's handicraft cooperative founded by Queen Salote in 1953 and the Friendly Islands Airways office.

New Zealand High Commission This is an architecturally pleasant building that sits well on its corner across the street from the GPO. Upstairs is a reading library, a great spot in which to pass a hot afternoon reading. The Australian High Commission behind the immense flame tree on Salote Rd has a similar facility.

Prime Minister's Office The Prime Minister's Office, across Taufa'ahau Rd from the GPO, is where much of the hot air blowing around Tonga originates. It contains numerous government offices. The tower was damaged in the 1977 earthquake but was rebuilt shortly thereafter.

Churches

Nuku'alofa's most distinctive structure is the Basilica of St Anthony of Padua, much of which was built by volunteer labour between May 1977 and January 1980. It looks like something that belongs on the head of a Chinese peasant in an old movie. The interior, however, is quite nice and represents a great deal of artistic accomplishment on the part of the volunteers who produced it.

In the library on the ground floor is intricate shellwork designed by local women; the shells come from all over Tonga. The altar, lectern, baptistry, pews and tables were handcrafted and the Stations of the Cross are made of coconut wood inlaid with mother-of-pearl. At Station XI, a tiny gold coconut tree that belonged to Queen Salote Tupou III is fitted into the hair of Christ.

The large ceiling beams are made of wood imported from New Zealand and the smaller cross-beams came from the Royal Estate on 'Eua. Beam junctures are covered with coconut sennit mats woven locally.

The other Catholic church in town is St Mary's, near Faua Jetty on Vuna Rd. Although it's a more conventional structure, it's worth visiting for its beautiful rose gardens, stained glass and vaulted ceiling.

The Centenary Chapel, where the king and queen attend service, was completed in 1952 and accommodates more than 2000 people. Like the basilica, it was constructed mostly by volunteer labour. Many visitors to Tonga, even devout non-Christians, like to attend church here in order to catch a glimpse of the royal family and hear the magnificent singing voices of the congregation. The Centenary Chapel is on Wellington Rd, behind Mt Zion.

The old Free Wesleyan church was built in 1888 on the present site of the Centenary Chapel, but it was moved in 1949 to its current location near the Royal Tombs. This monumental task (you'll realise how monumental when you see the building!) was transported the 274 metres to its new position in just one day!

The first Wesleyan church built in Nuku'alofa is the ramshackle building on Salote Rd behind Coralhead Diving. The place is loaded with character and the door is always open. The building resembles a *fale* (a traditional thatched house).

Parks

The Pangai area of the waterfront, beside the royal palace, is a public ground used for royal kava ceremonies and feasts. On Saturdays, local teams play football and cricket there. On one corner is a dolphin fountain (which never seems to have any water in it) presented by the British government to commemorate the HMS *Dolphin*, the first British warship to land at Tonga. Right on the waterfront is a line-up of big guns and a flag pole used on ceremonial occasions.

The Town Common is a large lawn area behind the Treasury; it contains a small bandstand and the Tongan War Memorial, which honours Tongans who served in the World Wars. Across the street to the east is the quaint little parliament building, prefabricated in New Zealand, transported to Tonga and reconstructed in 1894. The huge green area is used for sports and picnics.

Near the International Dateline Hotel are the Fa'onelua Tropical Gardens, commonly known as the 'bark' among Tongans (the letters 'b' and 'p' are not distinguished in Tongan). These days there's very little garden and a lot of barren lawn area, infested with coral, shell and woodcarvers trying to intercept

'rich' tourists en route to the Dateline Hotel. But it's a good spot for a picnic or reading a book on a hot afternoon.

Markets

Nuku'alofa's Talamahu Market is the best one in the country. All sorts of agricultural produce is sold and, occasionally, the owners of nearby shops in need of cash will sell off family heirlooms at ridiculously low prices. I certainly wouldn't encourage visitors to take home 70-metre lengths of tapa which may have been in Tongan families for generations, but to do so may also help someone in financial distress. Those looking for high quality fine mats will find this one of the only ways to acquire them.

The Vuna Government Market, across from the Treasury building on the waterfront, used to be the Customs House. It now serves as a meat and fish market.

The flea market, across Vuna Rd from the waterfront, sells just about anything imaginable. The result of charity bazaar donations in the USA, this place is Tonga's answer to Vinnie's discount house. Jewellery, dishes, pots and pans and all sorts of kitsch are shamelessly hawked. Travellers will also discover that it's possible to augment a self-destructing wardrobe very cheaply here. Very acceptable shirts, dresses and trousers can be had for T$1 to T$2 apiece.

Places to Stay – bottom end

Guest houses in Nuku'alofa come and go with the slightest provocation, so undoubtedly some of those mentioned here will have faded away by the time you arrive and others will have surfaced.

Without question, however, the best accommodation in any range available in Nuku'alofa is the *Beach House* on Vuna Rd, 1½ blocks east of the Dateline Hotel. This lovely old tropical building is surrounded by a wide and airy verandah and a nice lawn, and is cooled by an ocean breeze.

The *South Pacific Handbook* states that 'Somerset Maugham would have stayed there', and the *Pacific Islands Yearbook* lists it as 'pure Maugham', so there seems to be a consensus of opinion here.

For an ultra-clean room, hot showers and breakfast they charge T$10 per person. No private baths are available. If they're full when you arrive (which they almost always are) you can ask if the lounge is available. They'll let you sleep in there until a room becomes available. If you'd like to stay here, it would be safest to book in advance by writing to the managers at Beach House, PO Box 18, Nuku'alofa, Kingdom of Tonga.

If Beach House is full, ask them to direct you to *Faupula & Irene's*, the home of a local couple that serves as a sort of overflow for Beach House. Quite a few who've stayed with this charming couple have preferred this place to any more formal accommodation.

Another very good place to stay is *Sela's Guest House*, just off Fatafehi Rd near the lagoon side of the peninsula. Sela originally established the place as an introduction to Tonga for Peace Corps volunteers. She is an excellent cook and her entire family is very friendly and welcoming toward guests. In addition, rooms are clean and the atmosphere is quite homelike. All of Sela's problems seem to be animal related – noisy fighting dogs, sleepless roosters, snorting pigs and an irritating cuckoo clock. All but the last are unfortunately almost unavoidable in Tonga. Sela's is a bit warmer than places nearer the sea, but the place is less 'Maugham' and more typically Tongan than Beach House.

Only cold showers and communal baths are available. Sela charges T$7 single and T$10 double. Meals are T$3 for brekkie, T$4 for lunch and T$5 for dinner. Tea and toast costs only 50 seniti. Even if you're not staying here, you can enjoy Sela's

culinary prowess by arranging meals in advance.

K's Guest House, not far from Sela's, seems to be the cheapest guest house in town. Facilities are minimal, it's grotty and there are no cooking facilities, but those on the barest of budgets will appreciate the T$4 per person price. If two people are travelling together, note that a double room at Sela's is only T$2 more. Alternatively, the *Salvation Army's People's Palace* in the suburb of Longolongo costs only T$3 per night, but it's little more than a place to crash.

The *Fasi-Moe-'Afi Guest House*, which used to be a very nice place to stay for those who could deal with the eccentricities of the infamous Herman the German, has now deteriorated into the sort of place that has nothing going for it. Herman went to manage John's Place, a fast-food joint in the centre, and the folks that took over the guest house don't seem to care much whether they have guests or not. It's a grotty, stuffy place and the Visitors' Bureau accommodation guide lists the fact that it's next door to the Visitors' Bureau as its only amenity. They charge T$8 single and T$15 double, but it's best given a miss.

Kimiko's Guest House, on Vuna Rd near Beach House, is fairly nice and a good alternative if Sela's and Beach House are full. It's clean but offers only cold showers. For a single they charge T$8, while a double room costs T$14.

Places to Stay – middle

Leitolua Motel (tel 23763) on 'Unga Rd is good value. Single rooms cost T$15 and doubles cost T$20. An apartment with a bedroom, lounge, kitchen, hot shower and washing machine costs T$30 for two people and T$5 for each additional person. Transport from the airport can be arranged for T$6 if you phone them when you arrive.

The *Pacific Apartments* on Kitione Rd are also recommended. Two apartments are available, one upstairs and one down.

A bed only in the upstairs unit will cost T$25, while the whole apartment, which has two double rooms, a kitchen, lounge, hot shower and balcony, rents for only T$40. The downstairs unit costs T$20 for a bed or T$35 for the apartment, which has two double bedrooms, a garage, hot shower and verandah. This place is especially good and quite economical if you've got a group.

West of the palace area is the *Sunrise Guest House*, which rents single rooms for T$30. The price includes three meals daily. It's a bit far from the centre but the location is relatively quiet.

The *Way-Inn Motel* on Fatafehi Rd costs T$15 single and T$18 double, but most people who stay here only use the room for a couple of hours.

Places to Stay – top end
Joe's Kahana Lagoon is on the lagoon side of the peninsula and is therefore a bit malodorous. The view is good, anyway, and the rooms are clean, but the service is reportedly hopeless. Kitchen facilities are available and they do airport transfers for T$5. Single rooms rent for T$45, doubles for T$55 and triple units for T$75.

The *Friendly Islander Hotel*, two km east of Queen Salote Wharf, has a disco and pool. Individual rooms offer ceiling fans, balconies, telephones and radios. Single rooms rent for T$42 and doubles for T$50 per night.

In the centre is the *Ramanlal Hotel*, which always seems to be under construction. When I was last there, its advertised pool was a slimy concrete hole in the ground and workers were pounding away all hours of the night. Although this situation was expected to change, check on the progress before booking. Some of the air-conditioners work and each room is equipped with a fridge and telephone. They charge T$46, T$55 and T$60 for singles, doubles and triples.

The *International Dateline Hotel* on Vuna Rd is government-owned and touts itself as *the* place to stay in Nuku'alofa.

The fact is, some of the bottom-end accommodation is nicer and offers better service. Like most government institutions, this place is overstaffed and underattended.

For tourists, they offer a marginally clean pool (nonresidents can use it for T$1.50), a snack bar, lounge, Tongan feasts and dancing, duty-free shopping, day tours, live music in the bar, and airport transfers for T$4. With the exception of the pool, nonresidents can enjoy these things for the same price as guests.

Their rates are T$67 for a single room, T$75 for a double, and T$75 for a triple. A suite costs T$100 per night. Major credit cards are accepted.

Long-Term Accommodation
Houses and flats for rent are posted on the bulletin board at the Tonga Visitors' Bureau. These are good value if you plan to stay in town for a while. It's easy to find something reasonably nice for T$250 to T$300 per month. Elegance will set you back upwards of T$600 per month.

Places to Eat
Budget Eats The most popular lunch time spot in town is *Akiko's Japanese Restaurant* in the basement of the basilica. She has daily specials for T$2, although there are rumours that the price will go up soon. Omo rice, fried rice and other rice dishes are available daily for T$1.50 if you're not keen on the special. Lunch is served from 11 am to 1.45 pm but if you arrive after 1 pm the special will be gone.

Akiko's also serves dinners, which include a variety of Chinese dishes, tempura and hamburgers. Prices range from T$3.50 to T$4.50.

John's Place, on Taufa'ahau Rd in the centre, serves the usual fast-food gamut of greasy fish & chips, greasy hamburgers, greasy meat pies. . .You get the picture. It's frequented mostly by the under-18 crowd in Nuku'alofa due to the low prices.

Miki's, just a few doors up the street from John's, is owned by a friendly couple, Mike and 'Iki, who have tried to fill a fast-food gap in Nuku'alofa. They actually serve brewed coffee (one of only three places in Tonga that do – two of them are in the capital) and their chicken subs, which go for T$3.50, are extremely popular. They have a great decor, too – from tasteful prints of works by famous European artists to pictures of Donald Duck and Marilyn Monroe. Lunches range from T$3 to T$5.

The *Arcade Takeaway* in the Tungi Arcade has more greasy fish & chips, but also curried mutton, crumbed chicken, corned beef omelettes (yes, really) and a host of other items which certainly won't tickle your palate but are nonetheless life-sustaining.

The *Falekai*, downstairs from the Fakalato on Wellington Rd, has Tongan food, chop suey, chicken, mutton curry, steak, barbecue, fish, sausage and the like. It's similar to the Arcade Takeaway but generally better, and has the added advantage of not being in the middle of a shopping mall. The word *falekai*, by the way, means restaurant.

In the opinion of nearly all the travellers in Nuku'alofa, the best ice cream in town can be found on the east side of Taufa'ahau Rd, not far from John's Place, inside a small convenience store. Try hokey-pokey and boysenberry!

There are numerous greasy-spoon joints around the Talamahu Market; those on the barest of budgets will be happy to find them.

Restaurants The cheapest dinners can be found at *Akiko's Japanese Restaurant*, which is described in the Budget Eats section.

There are two Chinese restaurants in town, the Hua-Hua and the Tong Hua, but only the latter is really worth the effort. The *Hua-Hua*, near the Dateline

Hotel, is too expensive, portions are small and you must pay extra for steamed rice.

Also near the Dateline is the *Tong Hua*, just across from the Aussie High Commission. It is housed in a former Mormon church that the king reckoned was too near the centre of town (there was no love lost between the king and the Mormons!). You enter past the bathtublike baptismal font. The bar and dining hall are in the chapel. Service in this place is extremely marginal and the waitresses are quite dense but the food, while not heavenly, is very good, and if you go with a group, one person can eat well for less than T$5.

The most elegant and certainly the most expensive restaurant in town is the *Seaview* (tel 21799), a cosy German-run place near the British High Commission on the waterfront. This is the other of the two places in Nuku'alofa which serve brewed coffee. In fact, they have a coffee garden which is open in the afternoon for those who'd like to relax in the shade for an hour or two.

Both their format and their prices are continental. Expect to spend at least T$20 per person for what is indisputably the best fare available in Nuku'alofa. Dinner is served from 6 to 10 pm and advance bookings are necessary.

Slightly down-market but still very good is *Chez Alisi & André* on Wellington Rd, some blocks west of Taufa'ahau Rd. Jean the chef does excellent French cuisine – filet mignon, crayfish crepes, and the like. A meal with wine, salad and French onion soup will cost T$15 to T$20.

The *Fakalato* is also on Wellington Rd, upstairs from the Falekai. It offers very good pizza and pasta dishes as well as other international fare. They're open for dinner only on Thursday and Friday from 7 to 10 pm. The rest of the week they serve only breakfast, lunch and snacks.

In the Tungi Arcade is the *Arcade Restaurant*, not to be confused with the Arcade Takeaway. They serve fairly good seafood and European fare from 6 to 10 pm Monday to Saturday. Wine is also available.

Fred's Restaurant, near the Cable & Wireless, is German-run and can be good. It seems that the quality is variable depending on Fred's moods. He specialises, of course, in German cuisine but has pretty nice seafood dishes as well. It's open from 6 to 11 pm Monday to Saturday. The average price of a meal is T$10.

The *Dateline Restaurant* at the International Dateline Hotel is the only place in Nuku'alofa open on Sunday. There's a dress code, but don't expect the Ritz. Travellers are not admitted wearing thongs (although the waiters all do!), singlets, or shorts. Men must wear a shirt with a collar on it.

The *Friendly Islander Hotel* on Vuna Rd has a T$11 Saturday night smorgasbord which consistently gets favourable reports.

Self-Catering If you're cooking for yourself, the *Talamahu Market* is the cheapest place to find fresh produce from root vegetables to tropical fruits and salad ingredients. Onions, however, are only available at the supermarkets.

Cowley's owns two bakeries in town, one on the main street and the other on Salote Rd called *The Bread Bin*. The latter is open on Sunday after 4 pm. They have a variety of cakes and sweets as well as white, whole wheat and seven-grain breads (delicious!) for 45 to 80 seniti per loaf.

The *Gold Crust Bakery* (a pole in front of the sign makes it look like 'old Crust') is on Taufa'ahau Rd, a few blocks south of the basilica. It has the same Sunday hours as The Bread Bin, and for those staying at Sela's it's closer.

The *Fale 'Ika* fish shop is next door to the Cowley's bakery in the centre. They have daily specials, but the best and cheapest place to buy fresh fish is at the market on Queen Salote Wharf, about a

15-minute walk east from the Dateline Hotel.

Cakes and other baked sweets can be found across Salote Rd from the police station. Mince and packaged meats are available from the cold storage near Burns Philp. *Vuna Government Market*, across from the Treasury building on the waterfront, has fresh chicken, fish and pork when it's available.

Burns Philp and Morris Hedstrom have branches of their supermarket chains just south of the Talamahu Market on Salote Rd, and 10 minutes to the east there is a new supermarket in the Kilikilihau Shopping Centre.

The supermarket with the widest variety seems to be Burns Philp. They even have taco shells, refried beans and jalapeno peppers! The new supermarket at the Kilikilihau Shopping Centre, however, threatens to give it a good run. Upstairs at the latter is a small takeaway that sells Aussie meat pies and chocolate eclairs. Morris Hedstrom is generally the least expensive of the three but it also has the least variety. Very few Tongans can afford to shop in any of these supermarkets.

Alcohol There is a liquor store at the shopping centre on Salote Rd, and Morris Hedstrom has a bottle shop just inside the main entrance. As well, there's a Royal beer shop at Fakafonua Centre near Queen Salote Wharf. Expect to pay a nominal liquor tax on top of the price that's shown. Technically, an alcohol licence is required to buy booze, wine, or beer in Tonga and there are limits to the amount each person can buy, but foreigners are in practice excluded from this rule. If you'd like an alcohol licence for novelty value, however, they are available for T$1 at the police station.

Entertainment
The most popular night spot is the *'Ofa 'Atu Disco* at the Friendly Islander Hotel. For men it can be a lot of fun but foreign

women will definitely have a cultural experience.

Public dancing among Tongans is limited to the arm's length thank-you-very-much-for-the-dance type of thing. For Tongan men, dancing with foreign women is like Christmas morning. If you don't want to be fondled by complete strangers, never go to a disco without a date, but even this isn't a 100% guarantee that there won't be problems. Some Tongan men will assume (thanks to videos!) that you're so promiscuous, you'd only welcome their attention whether you're there with a man or not.

The males/members only *Nuku'alofa Club*, behind the palace, is a stuffy upper-crust pub and billiards hall where you can rub elbows with ex-pats and Tongan yuppie politicians and businessmen. Technically, you must be the guest of a 'member', but male foreigners who are dressed 'properly' are normally allowed in. The cheapest place to buy a beer (Royal, of course!) is the *Tonga Club*, the historic pub a couple of blocks behind the Dateline Hotel. Another good place to buy a few drinks and play pool is the *Yacht Club* on Vuna Rd. The sign says 'members only' but visitors can get by for three months or so before they're expected to join. Shorts and thongs are not allowed and women should wear skirts.

If you're looking for sleaze, drunken violence and obnoxious behaviour, try *Joe's Tropicana Bar* on Salote Rd. The shenanigans there can be plainly heard by those staying at the Beach House, several blocks away! Women should probably avoid this place altogether unless they're keen on slobbering drunk Tongan men, fakaleiti prostitutes and thugs.

There is one movie house in town, *Loni's Cinema*, which shows two trashy movies nightly. The sprung seats, 1940s-style sound system and the sellotaped screen don't make for much film enjoyment, but you can have an entertaining experience watching the locals make out. Admission is 50 seniti. As you

enter, notice the Elvis Presley shrine at the top of the stairs. There's another one in the video store next door, where all manner of Elvis kitsch may be purchased. Don't miss it!

On Tuesday and Thursday nights around 6.30 pm, the king goes rowing at Faua Jetty. He crosses the yacht basin in a tiny canoelike craft called *Milo* while an entourage of security people follow him in a motorised dory. He's already lost close on 90 kg but, for health reasons, he hopes to lose more. Visitors are welcome to come have a look.

Things to Buy

Handicrafts Nuku'alofa has undoubtedly the best selection, quality and prices in the South Pacific. There are several shops specialising in handicrafts in the central area. They're all very close in quality, but since minor variations occur and prices are not uniform, it's best to do some shopping around before buying anything.

The Langa Fonua shop, which is in the same building as Friendly Islands Airways, was started by Queen Salote to promote continuing interest in indigenous arts.

The Friendly Islands Marketing Cooperative on Taufa'ahau Rd has a wide selection of items, including some lovely paintings on tapa.

In the grounds beside the basilica is the Manulua Handicraft Shop, which tends to have the lowest prices and some of the best work available.

Carvings in coral and wood can be bought directly from the artists who set up stands in Fa'onelua Tropical Gardens.

All handicraft shops will wrap and post your purchases home for a nominal fee, but if you choose to send them by airmail, be sure you get airmail. A lot of the clerks are only hazily aware of the distinction between air and surface mail.

An expatriate woman told me a story of another problem she'd had with one of the shops. It seems she bought a large basket and paid for airmail shipment to a friend at home. When the basket failed to arrive, she went back to the shop to see what had happened. There was the basket for sale on the shelf, still bearing her friend's name and address! One can only hope that this was an honest (if stupid) mistake, but take care that it doesn't happen to you!

Small Industries Centre In 1977, the Asian Development Bank loaned the government T$350,000 for the construction of the Small Industries Centre on a five-hectare block in the suburb of Ma'fuanga (near Queen Salote Wharf). Several small, labour-intensive industries have opened up there and tourists will find high-quality locally produced clothing, especially knitwear, for disproportionately low prices.

Getting There & Away
Air For details of flights and fares between Tongatapu and other islands, refer to the Air section in the Getting Around chapter.

Boat For details of inter-island ferries, including fares and schedules, refer to the Ferry section in the Getting Around chapter.

The yachtie route through Tonga begins in Niuatoputapu and runs southward to and through Vava'u, to Ha'apai and thence to Nuku'alofa. October and November are the best months to go yacht hitchhiking in Tonga. Details about crewing onto a yacht are covered in the Getting There chapter.

Getting Around
Airport Transport Taxis from the airport to town usually cost T$10, though the government sanctions fares of up to T$12. If you're booked into either the Ramanlal or the International Dateline hotels, you could take one of the airport buses they run; the trip between Nuku'alofa and the airport costs T$4. Friendly Islands Airways provides a T$3 bus service to the airport for those booked onto their flights.

Those arriving during daylight hours should have pretty good luck hitching into town in the back of a truck.

Taxi Within Nuku'alofa, taxis charge a standard T$1 fare for up to four passengers. If you're going to the outskirts, expect to pay double that.

Offshore Islands & Reefs

To the north of Tongatapu Island is a maze of islands, reefs and shoals which are full of all sorts of colourful marine life, coral and white beaches. Three of the islands, Pangai, Fafa and 'Atata, contain resorts, and a couple of them have local inhabitants.

DIVING
It goes without saying that the diving is very good in the shallows to the north of Tongatapu. The water temperature reaches 29°C in November and falls as low as 21°C in mid-winter. Underwater visibility near the main island averages 15 metres, increasing as one moves toward the barrier reefs where it averages 30 to 50 metres.

Just about anything that would be of interest to a diver is available – wrecks, coral, walls, caves, chasms and sand.

Coralhead Diving (tel 22176), the only diving charter on Tongatapu, suggests 10 major sites in the reefs area and they do trips to all of them.

'Atata Reef The shipwreck of the *Atropos* may be found in very shallow water on the reef near 'Atata Island. Large fish and painted crayfish may be seen in deeper water nearby.

Breakers Reef Since this is near the deep water beyond the reef system, sharks and other large fish may be observed here as well as over 100 other species of fish.

Fafa Island Turtles may be seen in this area and fortunate divers may be able to hitch a ride with

Tropical fish

one. Common species of marine life include blue damselfish, snappers, orange and white clownfish, octopi, groupers, giant clams and myriad shellfish.

Ha'atafu Beach This one is actually on the mainland and can be dived from the shore, but it must be done at high tide when it's easiest to swim across the reef. The reef goes from a depth of three to 15 metres at the first drop-off and then down to 30. Shellfish, groupers, tuna and barracudas are normally seen and there is a large cave to explore. From there, the reef drops off into a deep and formidable abyss.

Hakaumama'o Reef The 'reef faraway' is so called because it is about 20 km from the mainland. It is more exposed to strong wave action than other reefs in the area and, therefore, different species may be observed. The relatively shallow reef drops off abruptly into deep and unprotected waters. Look for brilliant parrotfish in this reef, which is protected from local fishing by its status as a National Marine Reserve.

King's Reef This is the best place to see black coral in the Tongatapu area and is only half a km from the main island. At a depth of 30 metres the coral flourishes on the sandy bottom in a tidal current, and lionfish and butterflyfish live among the trees. Unfortunately, visibility is relatively low in this area.

Makaha'a Reef Very large coralheads and very small fish are rife here, the coralheads serving as a breeding ground and nursery for the marine life.

Malinoa Reef This one is also a protected National Marine Reserve, which precludes collection of shells or spearing of fish. The reefs run between depths of 13 and 20 metres. Large coralheads rise from the sandy bottom to the surface at low tide and reef fish are found throughout them. Divers will also find the beautiful white egg cowries and sea anemones full of clownfish.

Pangai Island Near the landing site is the wreck of *My Lady Lata II* in 13 metres of water. There's a grouper that lives in the engine room, and the stern is full of butterfly fish, angelfish and moorish idols. Between the hull and the sand live a colony of eels. It's more or less like a segregated apartment complex for fish.

'Ualanga 'Uta Reef This is the home of the fire scallops, which have a blue light that constantly moves from port to starboard and back. For this reason, Coralhead Diving has nicknamed them 'flying saucer scallops'!

For those with transport to the reefs, Coralhead Diving rents all equipment necessary – full tanks, belts, buoyancy compensators, gloves, knives and so on – for a few pa'anga each plus a deposit.

They also do boat dives for T$40 to T$75 depending on the number of participants. The price includes equipment rental, transportation and two full tanks. Divers must be certified and proof of certification is required.

Certification is available after five to

eight days of instruction. Classes cost T$400 per student if there are fewer than five participants or T$300 if there are five or more.

For further information or booking, contact Coralhead Diving, PO Box 211, Nuku'alofa, Kingdom of Tonga (see Nuku'alofa map for their location).

NATIONAL MARINE RESERVES

In 1976 the government of Tonga created five marine parks and reserves, four of which included reefs immediately north of Tongatapu, under the National Parks & Reserves Act. The government hoped that the protection of specific areas of reef would foster the full development of certain reef species, which would in turn reproduce and replenish adjacent overfished and overcollected areas.

Entry to the reserves is free. Visitors are asked not to capture, collect, or destroy any form of marine life or natural aspect of the areas, and to carry rubbish away with them.

Those who want to do a lot of snorkelling and avoid the equipment rental fees can purchase inexpensive gear at the store called Sanft's on Taufa'ahau Rd in Nuku'alofa.

Hakaumama'o Reef

This is the 'reef faraway', the last reef north of Tongatapu before open seas. It is therefore subject to more battering by waves than the more protected reefs closer in. The reserve contains an area of 126 hectares and was created primarily for the protection of the parrotfish.

Monuafe Reef

This reserve and island park encompasses 32 hectares. It was created to preserve beach vegetation, butterfly fish and marine snails.

Pangai Island Reef Reserve

This most accessible of all the reserves covers 48 hectares. It includes stands of mangrove and eelgrass. There are shellfish

and other invertebrates, including sea cucumbers, sea urchins and marine snails, and numerous species of reef fish that inhabit the island's perimeter.

Malinoa Reef & Island Park

In addition to supporting octopi, groupers, damselfish, clownfish and various species of shellfish, this reserve contains the graves of six assassins who attempted to kill prime minister Shirley Baker; there's a nonfunctioning lighthouse as well. The reserve has an area of 73 hectares. Malinoa Island Trips (tel 23973) runs a Sunday charter to the island at 10.30 am from Faua Jetty. The per person cost with snorkelling gear and lunch included is T$30; without lunch it's T$25.

RESORTS

There are three island resorts in the reefs north of Tongatapu. They're all a bit dear for the average budget traveller but they may be more economically visited on day trips.

Pangai Island Resort

Ten minutes by launch from Faua Jetty, *Pangai Island Resort* (tel 22588) is the closest of the three to Nuku'alofa and also the most popular. On Sunday afternoons, while Tongatapu slumbers, Pangai becomes a crowded and noisy getaway for tourists and not-so-pious locals alike. Even the crown prince spends his Sundays here incognito!

Pangai Island (or Pangaimotu) can be circumnavigated on foot in about 20 minutes. Part of it is in a marine reserve and there are a variety of natural habitats in the surrounding area as well as some of the best beach shelling in the Tongatapu Group. Near the landing site is the wreck of *My Lady Lata II*, which serves not only as a diving site but also as a diving board – after a few beers, the locals and the more intrepid tourists get pretty daring.

The resort offers snorkelling, sailboarding, catamaran sailing, surf skiing, billiards and a bar. On Sunday they serve a pseudo-Tongan lunch for T$10 which should be given a miss. Gear rental is available on site. Snorkel gear (mask, fins, snorkel) rents for T$3 per hour, a *popao* (outrigger) for T$6, a catamaran for T$20 per hour (but you can take it for fractions of hours), sailboards for T$6 and a surfski for T$2. A deposit is required on all rented items.

From Tuesday to Saturday they have a sunset happy hour, with drinks, desserts, biscuits, cheese and fruit. If you'd like dinner as well, book it in advance.

Accommodation on the island is in the form of beach fales (thatched huts). Single occupancy costs T$20, doubles are T$28 and triples are T$45. You can pre-book them by writing to Pangai Island Resort, PO Box 740, Nuku'alofa.

Getting There & Away Sunday trips to Pangai leave from Faua Jetty at 10.30 and 11.30 am and 12.30 pm, and return at 4 and 5 pm. Return fare is T$10. Quite a few private boats also go out, so you shouldn't have any difficulty hitching a ride for less. The happy hour return fare is only T$4. Make arrangements at the Pangai Island Office near the Dateline Hotel in Nuku'alofa.

Fafa Island Resort
Fafa Island Resort (tel 22800) is a little further out and not as popular as Pangai, but that is one of its attractions. They offer fale accommodation, some of which is on the beach, for up to 24 people. According to their brochure, they 'offer true island living. Don't expect air-conditioning or other overdeveloped luxuries'. Snorkelling equipment, sailboards, volleyballs, surf skis and a catamaran are available for hire. The catamaran rents for T$15 per hour and sailboards for T$10.

Beach fales cost T$70 for a single and T$80 for a double without meals (includes transport and accommodation only), or T$108 single and T$156 double with full board. An extra person will pay T$25

without meals and T$63 with. Inland fales run to T$78 single and T$126 double with meals, or T$40 single and T$50 double without meals. The extra person charge is T$53 with meals and T$15 without. Airport transfers are T$6.

Advance bookings can be made by writing to Fafa Island Resort, PO Box 1444, Nuku'alofa, Kingdom of Tonga.

Getting There & Away The resort does a day trip on Sundays which costs T$20 including transport and lunch, but you'll have to check with them for departure times, as there is no set schedule.

'Atata Island Resort
Royal Sunset Island Resort (tel 21254) is the most up-market of the three. Located on 'Atata Island, 10 km from Nuku'alofa, it is also the most remote. It is New Zealand-run with new, clean fale rooms, but prices are steep and budget travellers probably won't want to do more than a day trip to the island. Although this island has the same spectacular beaches, reefs and shelling as the other two, the real attraction here is the Tongan village that shares 'Atata with the resort. The island is larger than the others and has 200 permanent inhabitants.

The usual gamut of equipment is available for hire here. Food, accommodation and transport costs T$60 per double unit per day. On Sundays and Thursdays, they run a day trip which includes transport and a barbecue lunch for T$28 per person.

Around Tongatapu Island

Those who will be spending some time in Nuku'alofa would do well to have a look around the main island of Tongatapu. It has a variety of natural wonders – beaches, caves, blowholes, a natural archway and coral reefs – as well as some

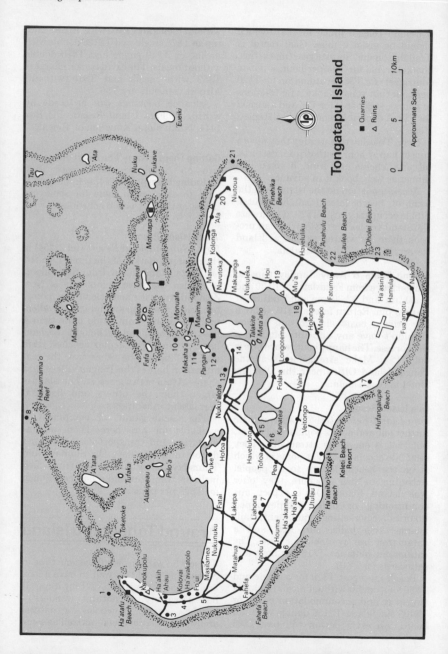

EASTERN TONGATAPU

Tonga National Centre

The Tonga National Centre in the village of Vaiola was constructed in 1988 with international assistance. It serves as a sort of cultural centre, where visitors can see displays dealing with Tongan history, paintings of its monarchs and a museum of historical artefacts as well as demonstrations of Tongan arts. Mat and basket weaving, tapa making, wood, bone and black coral carving, painting, kava preparation and serving and 'umu construction are all included. Visitors can of course purchase any of the articles being made but, in general, prices will be higher than at the handicraft outlets in town.

Tours are conducted on Tuesdays and Thursdays between 2 and 4.30 pm. Admission charge for the tours is T$5 per person, but to have a look around at any other time costs only T$1.

There is an amphitheatre at the centre which is sometimes used for local entertainment events such as theatre and music shows and even coconut husking contests!

To get there, take the Vaiola bus from town and ask to be let off at the hospital. The National Centre is right across the road.

Captain Cook's Tree

Captain Cook's tree isn't really a tree; it isn't even much of a stump. This nonattraction is actually a memorial near Holonga village. It marks the site where Captain Cook supposedly first landed on Tongatapu in 1777 and took a nap under a banyan tree before moving on to Mu'a to visit the Tu'i Tonga.

Lapaha & Mu'a

Sometime around the year 1200, the Tongan capital was moved from Niutoua to Lapaha (which is a km from Mu'a), by the 11th Tu'i Tonga, Tu'itatui. The area around Mu'a therefore contains the

of the most extensive and well-excavated archaeological sites in the Pacific.

The landscape is nearly dead flat, and most of the island's interior is taken up in agricultural land and rural villages. In the south are a few vanilla plantations, but the majority of the food crops produced here are consumed by the family of the plantation owner.

Getting around cheaply isn't really a problem for those prepared to walk several km to points of interest from public bus stops or for those hiring bicycles, but a fair amount of time will be necessary to cover the island's sights. To see it quickly will cost a bit more. If you're in a hurry, guided sightseeing tours and taxi tours are available, or you could hire a motorbike or car.

richest concentration of archaeological remnants in Tonga.

Lapaha Archaeological Site Just outside the archaeological site, you will see the moat which once surrounded the *kolo*, or royal capital. These days it appears to be little more than a shallow ditch where it crosses the road and those who aren't watching for it will miss it.

By far the most imposing ancient burial tomb in Tonga is the Paepae'o Tele'a or the 'platform of Tele'a', a monumental pyramidlike stone structure. It was long thought to have been constructed to house the remains of Tele'a, or 'Ulukimata I, a Tu'i Tonga who reigned during the 16th century. Actually, his body may not be inside the 'tomb' at all, since legend has it that he was drowned and his body lost. Traditional burial sites were topped by a vault, or a *fonualoto*, which was dug into the sand on top of the platforms and lined with stones in preparation for the body.

This platform, however, contains no such vault, which supports the theory that the Paepae'o Tele'a is not a tomb at all but in fact just a monument.

With the exception of the vault, this structure contains the best and most massive examples of all the early Tongan burial tomb construction styles. The stones used in building it are enormous. The corner stones of the bottom tier on the eastern side of the monument are L-shaped. The upper surfaces of all the stones are bevelled; their bases are firmly embedded in the earth, stabilised by the use of stone protrusions jutting out under the surface.

These and all the Lapaha construction stones are made of quarried limestone taken from dead coral reefs probably on Tongatapu and nearby Motutapu and Pangai Island; they were transported using cradles slung between two seafaring canoes called kalia. (Some maintain that the stones were carried from the Ha'apai

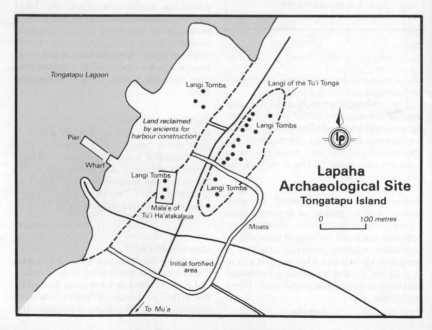

Tongatapu Lagoon

Langi Tombs

Langi of the Tu'i Tonga

Langi Tombs

Land reclaimed by ancients for harbour construction

Pier

Wharf

Langi Tombs

Langi Tombs

Lapaha Archaeological Site
Tongatapu Island

Mala'e of Tu'i Ha'atakalaua

Moats

0   100 metres

Initial fortified area

To Mu'a

Group or from 'Uvea Island far to the north-west.) Oral history preserves tales of the wooden rollers, sennit ropes and incredible leverage (and of course slave labour) required in moving the enormous blocks to the construction sites once they'd been landed. The fitting together of the massive blocks was done after they were in place.

These days, the Paepae'o Tele'a is suffering from age and weathering, but it remains obvious that it was built in memory of an individual who carried a lot of weight in the society that created it.

The langi or pyramidal stone tombs constructed in ancient Tonga were traditionally used for the burial of royalty. Commoners were interred in much simpler heaps of sand lined with volcanic stones, much as they are today. Around the vicinity of Mu'a there are 28 royal stone tombs and 17 others scattered around the islands. Some are monumental and some are merely conical mounds of stone and sand.

As mentioned before, the fonualoto is missing from the Paepae'o Tele'a. The Namoala tomb, also at the Lapaha site, has a fine example of a fonualoto but it is empty. Typical of such structures, it was covered with a stone slab first and then with *kilikili* or pumicelike volcanic gravel collected from Kao and Tofua in the Ha'apai Group. These stones are still valuable as grave decorations in Tonga.

If the Namoala tomb was typical, it would have once had a shelter of tapa, coconut fronds and fine mats on top of it. This housed the matapule, or talking chief, who would live on the langi and from there attend to the extensive funeral arrangements and ceremonies that followed a burial.

The Namoala langi is said to have been the burial site of a female chief but tradition supplies no further details. On the southern side there is a stairway leading to the top. The stones used in this construction are much narrower than those in adjacent pyramids.

To the north-east of the principle mounds is found the 'Esi'aikona, an elevated platform used as a rest area by the chief and his family, a sort of way station for travelling VIPs,

Near the Namoala tomb is the Hehea mound, which was originally believed to be a rubbish tip created during the construction of the langi. Recently, however, it was cleared of vegetation to reveal two fonualoto amid haphazardly placed earth and rock. Unlike the other structures the Hehea was built on artificial landfill, but it's not known who engineered this incredible reclamation project or when it was done.

The langi with the cross on top of it, across the street from the others in the modern cemetery, is the grave of the last Tu'i Tonga, who was deposed by King George Tupou I.

Mu'a In the village of Mu'a is a large old stone church which is of interest in itself. It contains lovely stained glass work and an impressive traditional Polynesian podium.

Just outside the gate of the church you'll find a rather ordinary half-metre-high boulder. Tradition has it that this *makatolo* stone was hurled by the demigod Maui from the island of 'Eua at a noisy rooster that had been keeping him awake at night. Visitors to Tonga will be particularly sympathetic to his reaction to such a situation.

Near the village is a cinema that is housed in an old barnlike structure. Attending a film here will be another of those proverbial 'cultural experiences'. Bring a mat to sit on, as there are no seats, and don't forget some munchies. Most of the locals chat through the entire picture, catching only bits of the English dialogue. They only break the conversation, it seems, during chase scenes or violence on the screen.

It's easy to get to Mu'a on public transport. A bus leaves from the eastern terminal in Nuku'alofa every few minutes,

Ha'amonga 'a Maui Trilithon

but be sure to head back to town before about 2 pm or you may be stuck.

Ha'amonga 'a Maui Trilithon

Near the village of Niutoua, at the eastern end of Tongatapu, is one of ancient Polynesia's most intriguing monuments. Although its name means 'Maui's burden' and legend has it being carried by Maui from distant 'Uvea on a carrying yoke, archaeologists and oral history credit its construction to the 11th Tu'i Tonga, Tu'itatui, who reigned around the year 1200.

The structure consists of three large coraline stones, each weighing about 40 tonnes, arranged into a trilithic gate. The uprights are about five metres high and just over four metres wide at their bases. The lintel, which rests in notched grooves in the uprights, is nearly six metres long, 1½ metres wide and just over half a metre thick.

It seems that Tu'itatui was more than a little paranoid. His name means 'leader who hits the knees', indicating that he employed the knee-striking method of warding off potential assassins. Seaward of the gate is a large boulder called the Makafakinanga, which was supposedly used by Tu'itatui as a backrest during the construction in order to shield his back from surprise attack while directing the work.

Some suggest that the uprights were to represent the Tu'i's two sons, whom he feared would be at odds over succession of the title upon his death. Another theory has it that the uprights formed the entrance to the royal compound in the days when Niutoua was the capital of Tonga. These days, however, it is becoming more or less accepted that the structure was used as a sort of Stonehenge, which it slightly resembles.

King Taufa'ahau Tupou IV theorised that an odd design on the lintel may have had something to do with determining seasons. Swathes were cleared from the trilithon to the sea nearby in line with the arms of the double-V design. On 21 June 1967, the winter solstice, the sun was observed to rise and set in perfect alignment with the clearings. It was also noted that it rose and set along the other two arms on the longest day of the year.

The Ha'amonga Trilithon is located in a National Historic Reserve encompassing 23 hectares. In addition to the gate, several langi and 'esi (resting mounds) are included.

If you're going to see the trilithon, try to get the first bus out in the morning or you may have some problems returning to Nuku'alofa that same day due to infrequency of departures.

Muihopohoponga Reserve

Near Niutoua is a two-km stretch of white sandy beach at the easternmost extreme

Design on Trilithon

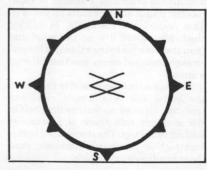

of Tongatapu. It has been set aside as a nature reserve to protect several species of native trees and some of the type of natural bushland that once covered the entire island. It is accessible by walking two km along a track leading eastward from Niutoua.

'Anahulu Cave & Haveluliku

Along a dirt track south of Niutoua, you'll come to the village of Haveluliku. Turn left at the road and ask the children playing there to get someone to open the entrance to the cave and turn on the lights. Admission is T$2 per person payable to the man with the key.

The cave, which is full of stalactites and stalagmites, hasn't been well cared for and the natural decorations have been subjected to decades of handling and vandalising. It's still a beautiful other-worldly place, however, under the coloured lights that have been installed inside.

Upon entering, you'll notice a strong smell of ammonia due to decomposing bird shit. The culprits, hundreds of cave swallows or *peka peka*, nest in the rock walls; the sound of their screeching as well as the constant dripping of water creates an eerie atmosphere.

As you approach the rear wall of the cave, descend the stairway on your left to the freshwater pool. Local children use it as a swimming hole, and the more intrepid of them climb the surrounding stalagmites and dive into the cold water. Visitors, of course, are welcome to join them.

Remember to carry a torch if you plan to explore the deeper recesses of the cavern, since the lights only illuminate a relatively small area.

More of Maui's projectile stones may be seen in Haveluliku. By public transport, the village is best accessed by walking three km from the village of Mu'a, the site of the langi tombs.

Oscar's Hideaway

On the beach about four km south of Haveluliku is 'Oholei Beach, where a local named Oscar Kami operates what is probably the best tourist feast in the country at 7 pm on Wednesday and Friday nights. The coastline at this point is riddled with limestone caves and the deserted white beach goes on and on.

The feast includes a traditional 'umu, shellfish, chicken, and roasted suckling pig. Afterwards Tongan dancers perform the lakalaka, tau'olunga, kailao and fire dance inside Hina Cave. Even those normally put off by events staged for 'tourists' cannot fail to be impressed with this presentation.

The cost per person is T$12 not including drinks (yes, there's a bar). Return transport from Nuku'alofa is T$8 per person. You can book the feast at the Dateline Hotel, Sela's Guest House, or Beach House.

Those who would like to camp on this lovely beach can negotiate permission with Oscar, who always attends his feasts. Expect to pay about T$5 for the privilege.

Fua'amotu International Airport

Tonga's international airport is near the village of Fua'amotu, at the extreme southern end of the island. There is a duty-free shop and a coffee shop, both of which are open only during the arrival and departure of international flights. Between the parking lot and the runway is a large not-so-flattering statue of King Taufa'ahau Tupou IV.

Hufangalupe

Five km south of the village of Vaini is Hufangalupe, which means 'the pigeon's gate'. This large natural archway in the coraline limestone is flanked on the south by 30-metre cliffs and on the north by plantation lands. The sea pounds through the opening and tears at the walls of the bridge and adjacent pit.

If you want to see Hufangalupe in one

day you'll have to get an early start, as nearly 10 km of walking is required. To get there, walk south from Vaini – buses go there many times daily from Talamahu Market – almost to the coast, a distance of nearly five km. If you reach the cliffs, you're on top of the bridge. Turn around and go back until you see a very faint track leading away to the right (as you're heading inland). Follow this track for a few metres and you'll see the archway. It's possible to climb all the way down to the sea in the gully but it's very steep and the coral rocks are razor sharp.

A good view into the pit can be had from the span itself. Following the road eastward from the span, you'll see numerous dramatic 30-metre cliffs and the turbulent sea below – quite a contrast to the calm and lazy northern shore of the island.

WESTERN TONGATAPU
Vanilla Plantations

On the southern coast of Tongatapu, west of Hufangalupe, are found the vanilla plantations that produce Tonga's primary export crop. Although the Vava'u Group is actually the centre of production in the country, this is the primary area of production on the main island.

Vanilla is produced from an orchid plant whose vine grows up to 25 metres in length. In Tonga, the young vines are supported by a treelike shrub called *fiki*, which provides shade for the brittle orchid plant. It takes three or four years after planting before the vine produces flowers and 10 years before it reaches maturity. If it is hand pollinated the flowers will develop into beans, but only about half the flowers receive this treatment in order to avoid placing too much stress on the vine.

Once the bean is matured, it is harvested and cured. The green bean is placed in hot water for a few minutes in order to arrest its growth process. It is then put in a sweat box for two full days where the enzyme which creates the alcoholic

Vanilla pods

vanilla is activated. Once this has begun, the bean is dried in the sun or in an oven. Sun-drying requires daily three-hour sunbaking sessions over a period of seven days for the pampered little beans. After this process, they are placed in a shady area for two months in order to complete the drying process. Finally, the beans are bundled and placed in trunks, where they spend another two months before they are ready to be graded and sold.

Beans which have undergone this entire curing process fetch T$85 per kg, while green vanilla beans are only worth about T$15.

Keleti Beach

The clean little *Keleti Beach Resort* (tel 21179) actually sits adjacent to a series of beaches divided by rocky outcroppings. They slope gently into clear pools which are excellent for swimming at high tide. The outer reef consists of a line of terraces and blowholes that shoot like Yellowstone geysers when the waves hit them at high tide. At low tide the blowholes turn into calm elevated tubs which are perfect for lazing in and observing the variety of life trapped there.

The managers, Marilyn and Roy Staines, are a very hospitable Canadian couple who will do anything in their power to provide you with information and particulars of travel around the islands. They have a library of reading material about Tonga and a book exchange.

The resort has an excellent restaurant, which is open on Sundays, and a number of Nuku'alofa people experiencing Sunday burnout end up here.

A single private fale with full board costs T$250 per week and a double costs T$460. Singles with shared facilities are T$220 per week and doubles are T$400. For a further breakdown of prices, including family and daily rates, or to make reservations, write to Keleti Beach Resort, PO Box 192, Nuku'alofa, Tonga Islands.

The resort operates a bus to and from town. The return fare is T$7. It leaves the resort at 9 or 10 am and returns in the afternoon. Taxis one way from town for up to four people will cost T$7 but keep in mind that they do not operate on Sundays.

Houma Blowholes

The Mapu'a 'a Vaca, or the 'chief's whistles', stretch for five km along the southern shore of Tongatapu, near the village of Houma. They are best viewed on a windy day at high tide, when the maximum amount of water possible is forced up through natural vents in the coraline limestone forming geyserlike fountains of seawater up to 30 metres in height. On an especially good day, hundreds of them will be active at once (but if the surf is too high, it will wash up over the terraces containing the vents and 'extinguish' the fountains). Next to the magnificent Taga Blowholes on the island of Savai'i, in Western Samoa, they are the most impressive in the South Pacific.

To get there, take a bus from the western terminal at Talamahu Market to Houma and walk one km south to the parking area above the blowholes.

'Umu Tangata

At the intersection of three roads, just south of the planned community of Fo'ui, is the 'Umu Tangata or 'man oven'. It seems that long ago a cannibalistic chef was preparing a feast, when he got distracted by an invasion of outsiders. He left the meal unattended for so long that a tree grew out of each person in the underground oven. Descendants of these original trees, of course, remain to this day.

Kolovai Flying Fox Sanctuary

The Flying Fox Sanctuary in the village of Kolovai is an impressive sight. Thousands of flying foxes, immense bats with wingspans of up to one metre, hang upside-down from the casuarina trees found around the town.

Although these nocturnal bats are found all over the South Pacific, Tonga is the one place where they are considered tapu, or sacred. While they are eaten unsparingly by gourmet islanders elsewhere, they remain protected in Tonga and only members of the royal family are permitted to hunt them for sport.

To get there, take the bus to Fahefa and either walk or try to hitch a ride northward to Kolovai.

Good Samaritan Beach

This fairly marginal beach is nothing to go out of your way for, but there is a secluded resort there, the Good Samaritan Inn. It isn't nearly as nice as Keleti Beach but it does provide an option for those who'd like to sample several beaches on a longer-term basis than would be possible in a day trip.

The resort is run by the same people who own Chez Alisi & André in Nuku'alofa and it also has a restaurant specialising in French cuisine (not as good as the one in town).

Grotty little fales here cost T$9 single or

T$18 double with shared facilities or T$24 single and double with private facilities. They charge T$4 per extra bed in either type of room. A seven-bed dormitory is available for T$40.

If you want to get there without paying the T$10 to T$20 taxi fare, go to Chez Alisi & André in Nuku'alofa and let them know you're looking for a ride. If someone from the establishment is in town, they'll take you out there.

A note of warning: some women have reported that they have had to deal with midnight intruders here. Especially if you're staying alone, take due precautions.

Ha'atafu Beach Reserve

The Ha'atafu Beach Reserve encompasses 8½ hectares of shallow reef and an area of deep water just outside the breakers. The area inside the barrier reef provides excellent snorkelling at high tide, but when the water is low, most of the reef lies just below the surface. Thanks to its location on the juncture of both habitats, more than 100 species of reef and deep-sea fish may be observed here.

Swimming is safe in the shallow areas, but beyond the barrier reef, strong currents, extensive coral beds and breaking surf make the prospect dangerous. The best surfing in Tongatapu is found here but only experienced surfers should attempt it, as those who are not careful will have to deal with being flung headlong into a shallow reef.

Other Attractions

At the extreme north-west 'horn' of Tongatapu is the traditional landing site of the first Christian missionaries in Tonga. About one km down the road toward Nuku'alofa is a plaque commemorating the first holy communion in the country.

In the village of Liahona in central Tongatapu is a large Mormon complex, including a high school and temple compound. The Seventh Day Adventist counterpart, Beulah College, is near the village of Vaini.

GETTING THERE & AWAY

Bus

Nuku'alofa has a bus system that is fairly useless for getting around town but quite effective in getting out and around the island. All 'long-distance' buses depart from the main terminal at Talamahu Market. The eastern terminal serves destinations to the east of Nuku'alofa and the western terminal serves the western half of the island. Fares cost between 20 and 40 seniti. Don't set off for anywhere after about 12 noon unless you're planning to stay the night or are willing to take your chances hitching back.

In the urban areas of Tongatapu, bus stops are marked with a sign that reads 'Pasi'. Elsewhere, you can flag down a bus by waving your hand and arm, palm down, as the bus approaches. In Tonga, unlike in other South Pacific countries, you pay as you board the bus.

Driving

Rental car rates and agencies are described in the Getting Around chapter. Currently, petrol sells for 70.9 seniti per litre on Tongatapu. Drinking and driving is highly illegal in Tonga, even though a lot of people don't take much note of that law. If there's an accident and you have alcohol on your breath, you're taken to gaol whether or not you were at fault.

Motorcycle

Motorbikes may be hired at two different locations in Nuku'alofa. Ian's Rentals (tel 23973) rents 80cc bikes for T$25 for 24 hours, 120cc bikes for T$30 and 180cc for T$35. Weekly rates are the daily rates times six. Kimiko's (tel 22170) also rents bikes. Considering that a motorbike holds two people and is quite fuel-efficient, this is an economical way to get around.

Bicycle

Bicycles may be rented from the Pangai

Island Office, which is on Vuna Rd next to the Tonga Visitors' Bureau in Nuku'alofa. Basic one-speed models rent for T$2 per hour, T$10 for 12 hours, or T$15 for 24 hours. It's important to note that many of the bikes that are available don't have brakes; although Tongatapu is flat, it may be necessary to stop now and again. Be warned!

The Tongatapu Group

As well as Tongatapu Island and its offshore motus, the Tongatapu Group contains several other islands. These include 'Eua, 'Eueiki and 'Ata, all of which will be described in this chapter. Minerva Reef, Tonga's southernmost extreme, will also be discussed.

The Tongatapu Group is the largest of the Tongan island groups.

'Eua Island

The island of 'Eua, in the Tongatapu Group, is ideal for bushwalking; in fact, anyone who wishes to see it properly will have to be willing to walk. It is the most naturally diverse island in the country,

with a variety of landscapes and the last significant stands of natural bushland south of the Niuas in the country. A Peace Corps volunteer posted there once observed that 'Eua had the cliffs of Normandy, the savannas of the Serengeti, the limestone sinks of the Yucatán, the rainforests of Costa Rica and the hospitality and serenity of the South Pacific all wrapped up on one small island.

With an area of about 87 square km, 'Eua is the third largest island in the country. Unlike Tongatapu it is hilly, with its highest point rising to 382 metres above its cliff-bound eastern coast.

'Eua's primary economic mainstay is its forest land. The Forestry Division of Tonga's Department of Agriculture has

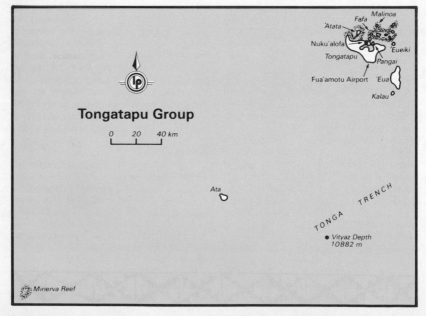

its headquarters there. The government oversees and controls cutting of native and seeded forests, and operates a sawmill at the island's southernmost village, Ha'atu'a. Currently there is an environmental battle brewing between those who would like to see the forests protected and those who would seek to escalate development on the island and exploitation of its forestry resources.

'Eua sees very few visitors who spend more than a morning talking business before hopping on the next plane back to 'civilisation' on Tongatapu. Those who are looking to get off the beaten track (inasmuch as Tonga has a beaten track) will be quite content with the place. The pace of life is slower than on Tongatapu and the atmosphere is rural. The pounding of tapa mallets slices through the tranquillity from dawn to dusk and the sweet smoke of cooking fires permeates the air and fills the valleys. A visitor will get the distinct impression that things haven't changed much here over the years.

Three days will be the minimum time required to see anything at all but plan on a week if you have it. 'Eua won't disappoint you!

History
Abel Tasman, the first European to land on 'Eua, arrived in 1643 and named the island Middleburgh. He got on well with the Tongans encountered there and he spent a few days trading. In October 1773, Captain Cook stopped for two days but he recorded little of the visit. In 1796, several deserters from the US ship *Otter* went ashore at 'Eua and became the first European residents of the Tonga Islands.

In September 1946, the island of Niuafo'ou erupted for the 10th time in 100 years. Although no one was killed, the government of Tonga became concerned about the potential danger of continued habitation of the island and decided to evacuate it in the interest of safety. The residents were first transplanted to

Tongatapu but the lack of agricultural land there necessitated another move, this time to 'Eua. The villages of central 'Eua – 'Angaha, Futu, 'Esia, Sapa'ata, Fata'ulua, Mu'a, Mata'aho, Tongamama'o and Petani– are all named for the home villages of their inhabitants on faraway Niuafo'ou. Many people have now resettled on their home island, but a good proportion of 'Eua's population is still composed of evacuees and their descendants.

Orientation
'Eua is shaped roughly like an isosceles triangle with its base on the eastern coast. The western third of the island is a low coastal plain which merges into an area of forested hills, with ridges which trend north and south forming the spine. The eastern edge consists of one and two-tier cliffs up to 100 metres high.

There is a road which extends the length of the island just inland from the west coast; most of the congestion is between the villages of 'Ohonua in the north and Ha'atu'a in the south. The extent of the island's public transport system includes this stretch. The airport is near the 'peak' of the triangle, west of the road, and the ferry wharf and harbour are found in the village of 'Ohonua.

Across the hills and ridges of the interior is a network of tracks and bush roads which are accessible only on foot, on horseback, or in a hardy vehicle.

Beaches
The one thing that 'Eua is not renowned for is its beaches, but there are a few worth mentioning. The best one is Ha'aluma Beach on the south coast. It is a lovely palm-fringed beach but it is not ideal for swimming due to extensive reefs just offshore. From here you can plainly see the small island of Kalau just a couple of km away.

If you are prepared to camp, Ha'aluma offers the best beach camping on the island. To get there, take the bus to the

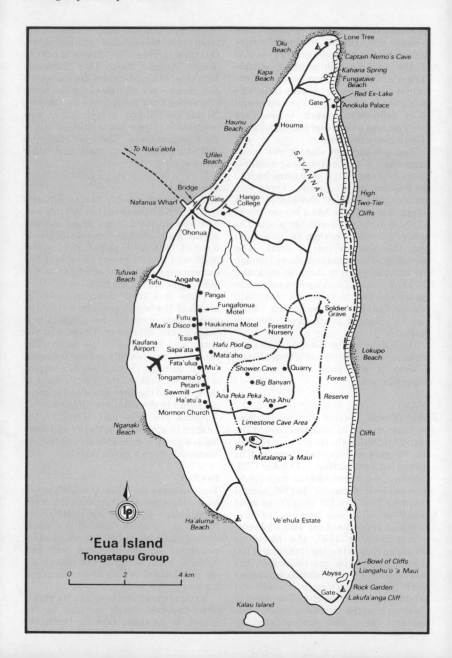

'Olu Beach
Lone Tree
Captain Nemo's Cave
Kapa Beach
Kahana Spring
Fungatave Beach
Red Ex-Lake
Gate
Anokula Palace
Haunu Beach
Houma
SAVANNAS
To Nuku'alofa
'Ufilei Beach
High Two-Tier Cliffs
Bridge
Gate
Nafanua Wharf
Hango College
'Ohonua
Tufuvai Beach
Tufu
'Angaha
Pangai
Fungafonua Motel
Futu
Soldier's Grave
Maxi's Disco
Haukinima Motel
Forestry Nursery
'Esia
Hafu Pool
Kaufana Airport
Sapa'ata
Mata'aho
Lokupo Beach
Fata'ulua
Mu'a
Shower Cave
Quarry
Tongamama'o
Big Banyan
Forest
Petani
Sawmill
'Ana Peka Peka
'Ana 'Ahu
Reserve
Ha'atu'a
Mormon Church
Limestone Cave Area
Cliffs
Nganaki Beach
Pit
Matalanga 'a Maui
Ha'aluma Beach
Ve'ehula Estate

'Eua Island
Tongatapu Group

0   2   4 km

Bowl of Cliffs
Liangahu'o 'a Maui
Abyss
Rock Garden
Gate
Lakufa'anga Cliff

Kalau Island

southern terminus of the line at Ha'atu'a and walk four km south along the road. Where the road makes a sharp bend to the left, a track leads off more or less straight ahead. The beach is a km down the track.

Tufuvai Beach, near the village of Tufu, can be reached from either Pangai or 'Ohonua with a flat, easy walk of a couple of km. The beach is nice but, due to an extreme undertow, it is very dangerous. There's a hole in the reef for swimming but it should only be attempted at the turn of low tide.

North of 'Ohonua there are a series of relaxing beaches but none of them are particularly suited to swimming. With quite a bit of scrambling over high rock outcroppings, the northern end of the island can be reached along the beaches in a day or so. The nearest beach to town and the most popular for picnics and afternoon lazing is 'Ufilei, just 20 minutes north of the ferry dock.

Fungatave and Lokupo beaches lie below spectacular cliffs on the eastern coast but, for all practical purposes, they are inaccessible without technical expertise.

The reefs surrounding the island are full of life – look in the tidal pools for marine snails, brittle stars, crabs and shellfish.

NORTHERN 'EUA

From 'Ohonua, cross the river bridge and walk the 4½ km to the village of Houma. Just less than two km north of the village, the road will split into four. The route on the far left leads down to the beach. The one which leads roughly straight ahead crosses a flattish open area to a place called Lone Tree. There is no village here, just a 'site', but it will be fairly obvious once you're there where the name came from.

The area of Lone Tree is a good place to camp and, once there, it can serve as a jumping-off point to other places of interest. North-westward, it's possible to climb down the two tiers of cliffs on the shafts of coral which protrude from the

surface at 80° angles. Extreme caution should be exercised if you opt to do this.

Walking eastward, you'll reach the cliffs of the east coast. Just below, in the side of the cliff, is the large limestone cave that the Peace Corps refers to as Captain Nemo's Cave; it's one of many which are found in this relatively inaccessible area.

Now return to the four-way intersection. The second road from the right as you face north will take you to the freshwater pool, Kahana Spring. The road at the far right goes for 1½ km, leading through a gate to a place called 'Anokula or 'red lake'.

'Anokula

'Anokula sits on top of windswept 120-metre cliffs and affords the most spectacular vista in Tonga. The rock outcrop just to the south looks out on a view encompassing all of 'Eua, 'Eueiki and part of Tongatapu.

What's left of the red lake for which the site was named can still be seen, although these days it looks more like a red sand trap. Beside the lake is 'Anokula Palace, a bit of royal real estate that looks like a WW I German helmet. Flying foxes ride thermals around the cliff below the palace.

Sometimes on nights of a full moon, the king comes to 'Anokula to watch the moon rise over the sea. The legend is that at such times, if all observers remain absolutely still, they can see people swimming in the incredibly turbulent water below – they're lost spirits on an outing.

If you walk southward from 'Anokula, you will pass through some virgin rainforest and into acacia-dotted savanna lands reminiscent of East Africa (minus the wildlife, of course). This area is also excellent for camping, but bring your own water, as no reliable supply is available and there are no coconut trees in the vicinity.

North-East Coast

If you keep following the road even further

south, it will swing to the left and drop down one tier of cliffs to a bench area below where there are numerous plantations and a few scattered habitations. The cliffs above this bench are pocked with limestone caves and the more intrepid can scramble up to some of them for a better look. When in doubt, ask farmers for the best routes.

The extremely game can bushwhack their way southward along the bench to the point above Lokupo Beach. It is surrounded by cliffs and swimming is impossible, but there's good rock climbing in the area. Very few people, not even locals, have ever seen this place. Be sure to take camping equipment and water.

Hango College

Those who are into agriculture may want to pay a visit to Hango College, Tonga's agricultural school, just up the hill from the river bridge near 'Ohonua. They are relatively progressive in their approach and offer a two-year certificate in animal husbandry/veterinary science. There is also a three-year course of study which leads to a diploma.

CENTRAL 'EUA

The central part of the island east of the road is an area of low hills covered with Tonga's greatest extent of natural forest. Much of the area is underlaid with eroded limestone, causing a Swiss cheese landscape of caves and sinkholes. Unfortunately, there are only limited trails and routes through the caves area and visitors will need the guide services of a local plantation owner if they want to be assured of finding something.

From Hango College, it's possible to follow the convoluted route along bush trails to the Soldier's Grave (see map), but it is far easier to access the central portion of the island from the main road near 'Esia. At the sign reading "Apitanga Polisi", turn inland and walk two km to the Forestry Reserve office. Just behind the building is beautiful Hafu Pool, a freshwater spring perfect for a swim on a hot day. Although it's been slightly marred by pipes and culverts, Hafu Pool is actually natural.

Following the same road further uphill you'll enter the actual forest reserve. While passing through the forested areas, look for Tonga's two native parrots, the blue-crowned lory and the musk parrot.

Soldier's Grave

About a km past the point where the road curves rather sharply northward, there will be a turn-off to the right leading uphill to 'Eua's highest point. On top of the nearest hill is the Soldier's Grave, which has a sappy and most likely well-embellished story associated with it. It seems that a New Zealand soldier and a Tongan got themselves good and drunk one evening and decided to play a bizarre game of hide-and-seek. They asked a friend to hide a gun for them. It was decided that the one who first found the gun was to kill the other. Unfortunately for the soldier, the Tongan won the game. The Tongans reportedly felt so bad about the incident that they erected a monument in the soldier's honour on the island's highest point.

Caves

In the never-never south of Soldier's Grave and Hafu Pool are numerous named and even more numerous unnamed caves and sinkholes. Probably the most easily located is Shower Cave. On the hillside you'll be able to pick out a huge banyan tree, the largest tree in Tonga. Within easy striking distance to the north of it is Shower Cave, a limestone sink with a steady stream of freshwater inside.

Near the bush road to the south are 'Ana Peka Peka (Swallows' Cave) and 'Ana 'Ahu, which can be found with some difficulty. It's best not to try swimming in the former because it is the source of part of 'Eua's water supply.

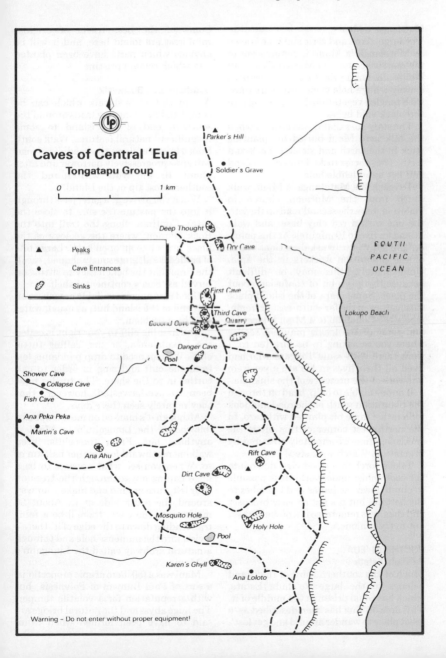

Caves of Central 'Eua
Tongatapu Group

0   1 km

▲   Peaks
●   Cave Entrances
🕳   Sinks

▲ Parker's Hill

● Soldier's Grave

Deep Thought

Dry Cave

SOUTH
PACIFIC
OCEAN

First Cave

Third Cave
Quarry

Second Cave

Danger Cave

Pool

Lokupo Beach

Shower Cave
● Collapse Cave
Fish Cave

Ana Peka Peka
● Martin's Cave

Ana Ahu

Rift Cave

Dirt Cave ▲

Mosquito Hole

Pool

Holy Hole

Karen's Ghyll

Ana Loloto

Warning – Do not enter without proper equipment!

Matalanga 'a Maui

The large, dank and eerie sinkhole known as Matalanga 'a Maui, is reminiscent of the massive *cenotes* of Mexico's Yucatán Peninsula. On a bright day it appears as simply a huge hole whose walls are lined with tangled vegetation disappearing into the black void below.

The story goes that it was created when the folk hero Maui buried his planting stick in the earth and shook it back and forth. The process rocked the entire island and left an indelible hole.

To reach the Matalanga 'a Maui, walk south from the Mormon church in Ha'atu'a, take the second road on the left, the one with a red clay base, and walk inland for five to 10 minutes. At this point, it's probably best to ask directions of one of the plantation workers in the area. Unfortunately, this may be difficult because there is a bit of confusion about the place. Some maps of the island place this feature in the far south-east extreme, where the Liangahu'o 'a Maui is located, and some of the locals may not realise where you're asking to be directed to. I went there with some Tongans who had lived all their lives in Ha'atu'a yet were unaware of the presence of the sinkhole.

If no one is able to help, head off through the plantation south of the road and look for a rather large pit planted with taro. In the north-west corner of this pit is the sinkhole, almost completely obscured by vegetation. Watch your step!

Take a torch for a good view down into the cool, moist underworld. It is possible to climb down the lianas and branches to the bottom, but it's not an easy prospect and the site is remote, so it's probably best not to try it alone.

SOUTHERN 'EUA
Ve'ehula Estate

Much of the southern third of the island belongs to the large Ve'ehula Estate, which has Sinai prison in the middle of it. This area of 'Eua has been described as 'a great place to wander around and get lost'.

Some of the best tracts of original rainforest are found here, and it will be obvious which parts have been planted and which remain pristine.

Southern 'Eua Bushwalk

An interesting bushwalk which can be completed in a long day leads around the southern end of the island to some magnificent natural features. Walk south from Ha'atu'a along the road. The road will grow progressively narrower and after about 10 km you will round the southernmost tip of the island.

When you arrive at a gate, pass through it into the pasture (be sure to close the gate). Continue along the trail into the Rock Garden, where the geology of the place reads like an open book. Large bits of eroded coral, grotesquely shaped, recall the time that the bench they're sitting on served as 'Eua's continental shelf.

Good camping is available anywhere on this end of the island but, as usual, water may be a problem.

The first big cliff to your right is called the Lakufa'anga, or the 'calling turtle cliff'. Women used to drop pandanus leis from the cliff and sing in order to call turtles in to the shore. The turtles have been so overharvested, however, that they're rarely seen these days.

Although it's marked on most maps as a 'blowhole', the Liangahu'o 'a Maui is anything but. From the cliffs, keep walking northward for another half km or so. When you see what appears to be a huge gaping abyss through the trees on your left, turn around and make your way around the south side of it. About 30 metres into the trees, there'll be a faint trail leading down to the edge of it; there's a view into the immense hole and through a natural archway called the Liangahu'o 'a Maui.

Maui was a folk hero of epic proportions, a sort of Paul Bunyan of Polynesia, but with a reputation for a volatile temper. The huge abyss and the natural bridge are said to have been formed when Maui

Top: Makahokovalu Ruin, 'Uiha Island, Ha'apai Group
Left: King Taufa'ahau Tupou IV, Lifuka Island, Ha'apai Group
Right: Reef between Lifuka and 'Uoleva Islands, Ha'apai Group

Top: View from 'Utula'aina Point, Vava'u Island
Left: Young Tongan offers snack, Longomapu, Vava'u Island
Right: Swallows' Cave, Kapa Island, Vava'u Group

angrily threw his spear across 'Eua and it lodged in the rock wall here.

This is a lovely spot. Haunting, intermittent insect choruses begin suddenly, crescendo and disappear. Pigeons call in the wood and the sea below roars and beats the remaining rocks beneath the bridge. No photo will ever do the place justice. . .

Beyond here, the track continues northward to an impressive bowl of cliffs and two km beyond that there is a good view of the coast northward. The track continues on indefinitely and, in some seasons, it will be possible to get through nearly to 'Anokula, but allow several days for such a trip.

PLACES TO STAY

As would be expected, your options on 'Eua are fairly limited. The most popular place is the *Fungafonua Motel* in the village of Pangai, as it is run by the agents for Friendly Islands Airways and they round up potential guests as soon as they arrive and offer free transport to the motel. The Fungafonua used to be called Leipua Lodge.

They have two types of room, Tongan and foreign. The Tongan rooms aren't too clean but they only cost T$5 single and T$10 double. Normally, they won't allow foreigners to occupy these rooms. Foreigners have to pay T$15 single and T$20 double, but you will be able to bargain them down by T$5 or so if they aren't full. All rooms available to foreigners have private baths. Water is available on an average of 10 minutes per day, although they'll try to convince you otherwise.

If you're staying there, try to get a mountain view room. Especially at dawn and dusk, the scene of everyday life outside your window will be better than a good film.

The other place offering formal accommodation is the *Haukinima*, just a km or so to the south. They don't seem to be too interested in their guests' comfort, so don't expect much. Facilities are basic

and unkempt, but they do have a kitchen which guests may use. A room here will set you back T$10 for a single and T$15 for a double.

The third option is probably the most pleasant. There are forestry cabins available for about T$1 per night but facilities are very basic, so you'll need to bring your own sleeping bag. Cooking will be 'Tongan-style' – over a campfire outside. Go to the sawmill in Ha'atu'a and tell the person in charge that you're interested in staying in one of the cabins; they'll send you in the right direction.

PLACES TO EAT

There are two bush stores near the boat harbour in 'Ohonua and one in Pangai, where you can purchase staples; they don't offer much variety so, if you plan to cook for yourself, you'd be wise to bring food from Tongatapu.

The *Jireh Restaurant* just below the church in 'Ohonua is a friendly little place, where many of the locals go to eat and socialise. They serve excellent meals. A fish curry with kumala, plantain and a sweet drink goes for T$2.

There is a pub in 'Ohonua three buildings up from the wharf but it's pretty sleazy.

Lilo and Vila Vaka'uta at the *Fungafonua* in Pangai also serve meals, but they're a bit overpriced for what you get. A breakfast of eggs, toast and coffee is T$3.50, a lunch of fish and root vegetables is T$4.50 and dinner, which includes a repeat of lunch and possibly some lu pulu, goes for T$6. Book in advance if you want to eat there.

ENTERTAINMENT

Maxi's Disco (named after the owners' cat) is the red, white and blue building across the street from the Haukinima. It is open for dancing only on Friday nights but the bar opens anytime there are construction crews on the island.

GETTING THERE & AWAY
Air
Friendly Islands Airways flies a nine-passenger Britten-Norman Islander between Fua'amotu Airport and 'Eua at least twice daily, but schedules are followed very casually. The first flight goes at 8 am, but if there are enough passengers for two flights, they'll do two runs. If there is sufficient interest, there is another flight in the afternoon, which leaves Tongatapu sometime between 2 and 4 pm. The flights take about 12 minutes and return to Tongatapu several minutes after landing at 'Eua.

Boat
The ferry MV *Ngaluta'ane* sails to and from Queen Salote Wharf in Nuku'alofa, Tuesday to Saturday. It departs at 5.30 am from Tongatapu and arrives at 'Ohonua Wharf at 9 am. At 11 am it departs 'Eua and arrives back in Nuku'alofa at 1.30 pm. The one-way fare is T$4.50 for adults, T$4 for students and T$3.50 for children aged four to 12.

From the ferry, watch for tuna, dolphins and flying fish, which often escort the ship across the strait.

GETTING AROUND
Bus
The public bus runs between 'Ohonua and Ha'atu'a every half-hour until the driver gets tired, usually about 1 pm.

Driving
The Fungafonua Motel rents out a 4WD vehicle for T$45 per day, but rental must be arranged in advance.

Horse
The Fungafonua also hires out horses for T$5 per day if you arrange a day in advance; note that you will have to ride bareback.

Tours
The Fungafonua does informal 'tours', which in reality are just a shuttle service to the more interesting sights. The southern tour consists of a ride to the gate

at the southern end of the island and an afternoon pick-up from Ha'aluma Beach. Where you walk in between is up to you.

Another trip drops you at the Soldier's Grave so that you can spend the day exploring the central area of the island. You'll have to walk back to town, but it's pleasant enough and all downhill.

The northern tour goes to 'Anokula Palace for a quick look and then drops you at 'Ufilei Beach, just north of 'Ohonua, from where they'll pick you up at a pre-specified time.

Each of these options cost T$8 per person for one or two people, but three or more pay only T$5 each.

Other Islands & Reefs

'EUEIKI ISLAND

The island of 'Eueiki lies north-east of Tongatapu, just outside the barrier reef that shelters that island's lagoon. Its name means 'little 'Eua', and it offers the best surfing in the kingdom.

This small island is also the legendary site of the origin of kava. Out of respect for his station, an 'inasi (agricultural show) was given for the Tu'i Tonga here somewhere in the dim dark Tongan past. Unfortunately, the harvest that year on 'Eueiki had been poor and so there was a shortage of food for the king when he arrived (Tongan kings have always been hearty eaters).

The family designated to provide a feast for the Tu'i Tonga had a daughter sick with leprosy. They considered her expendable, so they killed her and baked her in a 'umu to provide the main course. The king ate well but when he was told what he'd eaten, he got angry at the family for serving their own daughter. He ordered them to bury what remained of the feast.

After a little while, an odd-looking plant grew from the head of the grave. The family cared for it because they realised it

was a gift from their daughter. Another plant later grew out of her feet.

One day a rat came and nibbled on the first plant. It grew tipsy and staggered around until it encountered the second plant. When it took a nibble of that one, it returned to its senses. At this point, the family realised the properties of both plants, kava and sugar cane, and knew how to use them.

Several tamer and less gruesome versions of this tale have been contrived to recount to young children and squeamish tourists. The original, it is assumed, was introduced by the Tu'i Tonga as a form of convenient political coercion at a time when he was trying to stop the practice of cannibalism.

Getting There & Away

There is no scheduled public transport to 'Eueiki. If you'd like to visit the island, ask around Faua Jetty in Nuku'alofa for someone who may be going that way. Expect to pay a pa'anga or two for the ride.

'ATA ISLAND

In 1683, Abel Tasman sighted this volcanic island 136 km south-west of Tongatapu and named it Pylstaart. 'Ata has two volcanic peaks, but both are extinct; the higher one has an altitude of 382 metres.

The island has significant deposits of guano phosphates but they are rendered inaccessible by the lack of a harbour.

In late May 1863, the Tasmanian whaling ship *Grecian* landed at 'Ata after several rather unorthodox changes of crew under the command of Captain Thomas James McGrath. The details of what happened there are hazy but, in 1929, two Tongans who were 'Ata school children at the time reported that the ship was painted to resemble a man-of-war. The mayor of the island, Paul Vehi, went aboard and spoke with the visitors. When he returned to shore, he reported that they were interested in selling provisions and

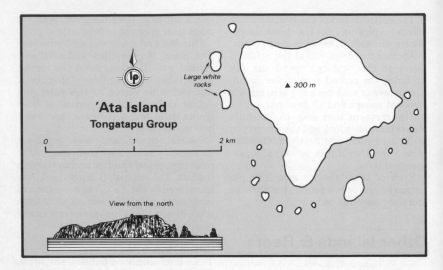

'Ata Island
Tongatapu Group

Large white rocks

▲ 300 m

0   1   2 km

View from the north

that the 'Ata people were invited to bring their wares below decks on the ship. Once their goods were accepted, they were sent into cabins ostensibly to select items they desired in exchange. The people remaining on shore never saw them again.

John Bryan, a former crew member on the *Grecian*, reported that about 130 'Ata Islanders had been taken on board. It is also likely that the *Grecian* had been responsible for the kidnapping of 30 residents of Niuafo'ou, who had willingly left that island with the promise of lucrative jobs in Fiji.

The islanders blamed the mayor for arranging the kidnapping but it is unlikely that he knew anything about it beforehand.

Since the *Grecian* was not licensed by Peru to land with slaves at Peruvian ports, where kidnapped Pacific Islanders were normally taken, it seems that the cargo (including the Tongans) was sold to the *General Prim*, a slaver which met the *Grecian* somewhere in the Cook Islands while searching for 'recruits' to carry back to Callao (Lima). When the *General Prim* arrived in South America, its captain

reported that he carried 174 slaves from the island of 'Frinately' – which was obviously a mistranscription of Friendly.

Shortly after this incident, in order to prevent further kidnappings, King George Tupou I ordered the remaining 200 residents of 'Ata to resettle on 'Eua and the island remains uninhabited to this day.

Getting There & Away

These days, 'Ata can only be accessed by private yacht. However, there is no good harbour, so finding a suitable safe anchorage would be quite difficult.

MINERVA REEF

Minerva Reef, which is awash most of the time, is Tonga's southernmost extreme. It lies 350 km south-west of Tongatapu and serves as little more than a rest point for yachts travelling from Tonga to New Zealand.

Australians Tom and Jan Ginder stopped there in their yacht *Seark* in late 1988 and described it this way:

After two days of fast sailing [from Nuku'alofa] we came to Minerva Reef and entered through a narrow pass in the circle of coral. Here in the Pacific hundreds of miles from any terra firma we dropped anchor and looking around saw breaking waves during high tide and two feet of intriguing brown reef at low tide. Imagine standing in the middle of a vast ocean on a few feet of exposed coral and no land in sight. While exploring for shells we found blocks of tarred pig-iron ballast, a wonderful huge anchor, and many copper nails, all that remained of some long-forgotten tragedy. For three days and nights [we] lay in quiet water, although wind whipped up the seas outside our saucer. However, the combination of full moon, spring tides and foul weather could make Minerva Reef anchorage dangerous. It was just two days to full moon so with regret we left.

The Ha'apai Group

The solitude of Ha'apai will assault your senses. This is the South Pacific of travel posters – scores of low coral islands, colourful lagoons and reefs, km of deserted white beaches fringed with coconut palms, towering volcanoes... All that, and tourists are so rare that each one is heartily welcomed by the friendliest folks in the kingdom.

The 12,000 people who live scattered around the islands' 109 square km are almost exclusively involved in agriculture. Many of Ha'apai's residents have opted for the faster pace of life offered by Tongatapu. Quite a few others have ventured as far afield as Australia and New Zealand, keeping the population of the group manageably low – many perfectly habitable islands lack people.

Not much has changed in Ha'apai over the last 100 years or so. There are a few modern contrivances available these days – telephone, radio, video – but life still moves on at a snail's pace and one lazy day melts into the next. Youngsters play in the sea, women weave fine mats and cook meals, men throw their fishing lines out on the reef and then spend a couple of hours on their plantations for good measure. On Fridays, men attend kava circles and teenagers watch videos or dance at the church halls. On Sundays, everyone turns out for church. In a nutshell, that pretty much sums up life in this quiet corner of Tonga.

It goes without saying that the presence of visitors is not taken lightly. Whether you're aware of it or not, the people will know where you are and what you're up to. You will be the topic of many conversations during your visit and, undoubtedly, you will be the recipient of the abundant hospitality of the locals.

As a general rule, the smaller the island, the more warmly visitors will be welcomed. Just try asking permission to camp on the more remote islands and you'll quickly learn that the locals will be offended that you would consider staying somewhere other than in their homes. These outer islands of Ha'apai are best reached through taking your time and being willing to wait for rides to the more out-of-the-way places.

History

The first European to visit the Ha'apai Group was Abel Tasman, who stopped at Nomuka in 1643 to take on freshwater. Nomuka's sweetwater lake was to be the focus of many visits to the group throughout the years of European Pacific exploration.

On his second and third voyages in 1773 and 1777, Captain James Cook landed at Nomuka. Finau, the chief of Ha'apai, sent him from there to Lifuka. It was on Lifuka that Cook and his men narrowly escaped becoming the guests of honour at a cannibalistic feast they had been invited to attend. Lavish entertainment was offered as well as abundant food and Cook was inspired to name the Ha'apai Group the 'Friendly Islands'. If it hadn't been for some childish squabbling among the chief and his nobles regarding the execution of their plot, the name would never have stuck.

It was in April 1789 that Ha'apai won its place in history, when the mutiny on the *Bounty* occurred near the island of Tofua. The mutineers, led by Fletcher Christian, set Captain William Bligh and 18 crewmen adrift in an open boat with only meagre supplies. When they landed at Tofua seeking provisions, they found the natives unfriendly and had to beat it fast. Even so, Quartermaster John Norton was killed in the scuffle.

Off the northern end of the island of Lifuka, on 1 December 1806, the British privateer *Port-au-Prince* was ransacked

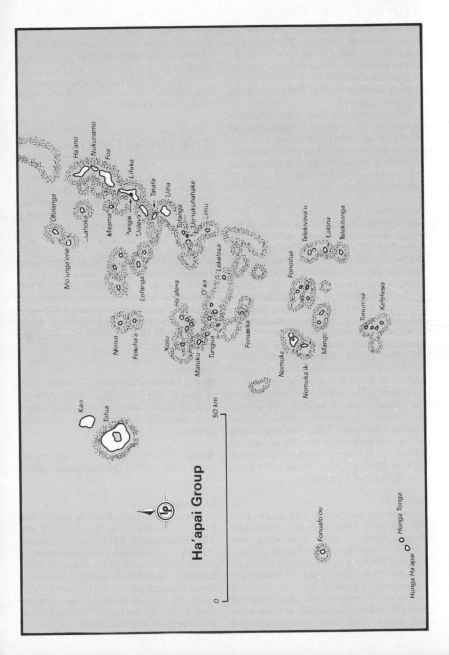

Ha'apai Group

and most of her crew was killed. The tale of one survivor, William Mariner, who remained as a guest of the chief Finau for four years, has become the classic account of pre-Christian life in Tonga. (See the History section in the Facts about the Country chapter.)

Ha'apai was the first island group to convert to Christianity, thanks to the efforts of convert Taufa'ahau, who was baptised King George I in 1831. He set the stage for a united Tonga and established the royal line which remains in power to this day.

Geography

Geologically, Ha'apai is the centre of the Tonga Islands, the place to which all the other main islands are leaning thanks to the great weight of the volcanoes Kao and Tofua in the north-western extreme of the group.

The main body of the archipelago is composed of two island clusters and one raised barrier reef. The Nomuka Group is furthest south, while the Lulunga Group lies to the north, centred on the island of Ha'afeva. To the north-east is the north-east/south-west trending line of raised reefs that forms most of Ha'apai's land area; this will be referred to in this book as the Lifuka Group. It includes the islands of Ha'ano, Nukunamo, Foa, Lifuka, 'Uoleva, Tatafa and 'Uiha. The population centre, the main wharf and the airport are all on Lifuka. Volcanic outliers to the west include Hunga Tonga, Hunga Ha'apai, Kao, Tofua and Fonuafo'ou.

Diving

Experienced snorkellers and divers who see Ha'apai from the air, especially divers, tend to gaze downward and salivate. The reefs and shallows of the Ha'apai Group would compete with any in the world for sheer colour, diversity and diveablity. At present, however, the only people who've been able to appreciate the group's underwater world are yachties who carry their own equipment and provide their own transportation. Quite simply, there is no commercial diving charter in operation in these paradisiacal islands.

Divers who like things that way should take heed before the entrepreneurial spirit takes hold of someone!

The Lifuka Group

The string of islands along the eastern barrier reef of Ha'apai will be referred to as the Lifuka Group, since Lifuka Island and its capital of Pangai are overwhelmingly the hub of all activity there.

PANGAI

Although Pangai is the largest settlement between Tongatapu and Vava'u, it is little more than a small village and you can walk across it in a matter of a few minutes. Since the only formal accommodation in Ha'apai is located in Pangai, it would serve as the best base for exploring the group.

Information

Post & Telecommunications The post office is beside the Friendly Islands Airways office and the Cable & Wireless is beneath the immense tower in the centre of Pangai.

Banks There is a Bank of Tonga on the main road, next to the Government Rest House.

Churches

In the village itself, there is really very little of interest. On the lawn of the Methodist church, you'll find the concrete outline of a cross which commemorates a 'miracle' that took place there in 1975. Residents report that one night they saw a flame falling from the sky to land in front of the church. In the morning, they say they found the outline of a cross burned into the grass. If it had happened in front

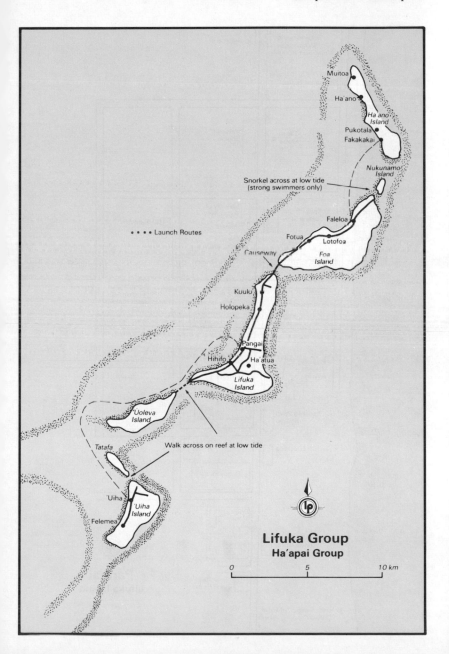

Muitoa

Ha'ano

*Ha'ano
Island*

Pukotala
Fakakakai

*Nukunamo
Island*

Snorkel across at low tide
(strong swimmers only)

Faleloa

Fotua

Lotofoa

*Foa
Island*

• • • • Launch Routes

Causeway

Kuulu

Holopeka

Pangai

Hihifo

Ha'atua

*Lifuka
Island*

*'Uoleva
Island*

Tatafa

Walk across on reef at low tide

'Uiha

*'Uiha
Island*

Felemea

Lifuka Group
Ha'apai Group

0   5   10 km

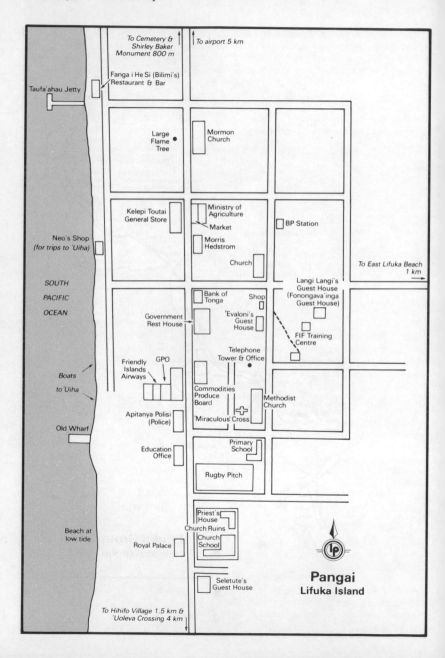

To Cemetery &
Shirley Baker
Monument 800 m

To airport 5 km

Taufa'ahau Jetty

Fanga i He Si (Bilimi's)
Restaurant & Bar

Large
Flame
Tree

Mormon
Church

Kelepi Toutai
General Store

Ministry of
Agriculture

Market

Morris
Hedstrom

Church

BP Station

Neo's Shop
(for trips to 'Uiha)

SOUTH
PACIFIC
OCEAN

To East Lifuka Beach
1 km

Bank of
Tonga

Shop

'Evaloni's
Guest
House

Langi Langi's
Guest House
(Fonongava'inga
Guest House)

Government
Rest House

FIF Training
Centre

Boats
to 'Uiha

Friendly
Islands
Airways

GPO

Telephone
Tower & Office

Old Wharf

Commodities
Produce
Board

Methodist
Church

Apitanya Polisi
(Police)

'Miraculous' Cross

Education
Office

Primary
School

Rugby Pitch

Priest's
House

Beach at
low tide

Church Ruins

Church
School

Royal Palace

Seletute's
Guest House

Pangai
Lifuka Island

To Hihifo Village 1.5 km &
'Uoleva Crossing 4 km

of the Catholic church, perhaps the site would have become an internationally famous shrine and the destination of pilgrims, but the low-key Methodists merely outlined the burned area with concrete and left it at that. Cynics in the village, most of them non-Methodists by the way, attribute the whole 'miracle' to mischievous teenagers with kero tins and cigarette lighters.

The Catholic church, at the southern end of the village, is nothing but a heap of rubble thanks to Typhoon Isaac, which struck Lifuka in March 1982. From the ruins, the church appears to have once been a very nice building.

Royal Palace

The Ha'apai Royal Palace is the gingerbread-style building across the street from the Catholic church. When the king is in residence there the street is often blocked, which necessitates a rather long detour around the rugby grounds.

Shirley Baker Monument

About 800 metres north of town is the grave of Shirley Baker, Tonga's first prime minister and adviser to King George Tupou I; there's a monument to him as well. Baker was nearly the victim of assassination, and was exiled from Tonga by the British 'advisors' sent to set up a protectorate and stabilise the government, which was suffering at the hands of squabbling religious factions. He later returned to Tonga with the permission of King George Tupou II and lived out his days in Ha'apai. He died in 1903, in the place where he seemed to be happiest.

Places to Stay

The least expensive place to stay is the *Government Rest House*, next to the Bank of Tonga on the main road. There's a rather grotty kitchen with equally grotty cooking pots, utensils, and kero burner, but it's still good value for only T$2 per person. Rooms are big and airy, and Paea, the caretaker, is very friendly. The

communal showers and toilets are clean but only cold water is available.

Equally friendly and very clean is *Langi Langi's Guest House* (shown as *Fonongava'inga* on some maps). There's no sign but it's just next door to the FIF Training Centre. The owner charges T$5 per person, and offers very nice meals for T$2.50 for breakfast or lunch and T$5 for dinner. Her showers have fairly bad pressure, but this is still the nicest place to stay in town.

'Evaloni's Guest House is also very nice and offers the best food available in Pangai, thanks to a wonderful cook named Lizzie. Ask her to make banana cakes for breakfast! For a single or double, the price is T$12. Breakfast or lunch costs T$3.50 and dinner (which is highly recommended) costs T$6.50.

'Evaloni also runs a beach resort on the east coast of Lifuka Island. Accommodation is in little fales, which cost T$7 per person. No meals are available and it's a bit of a walk out through the plantations from town, but the resulting solitude is worth it.

The only other place to stay is a rather run-down guest house called *Seletute's*. The owner is friendly enough, but if you plan to stay watch your valuables closely or carry them with you, as several travellers have reported money going missing here. Some other travellers who unwittingly stayed here while some nobles were visiting from Tongatapu told me that they were forced to stay in their room whenever the nobles were in the house and that they were forbidden to speak lest they disturb the VIPs!

Seletute's costs T$18 per person including three meals daily or T$16 without lunch. For nonresidents, breakfast and lunch are T$4 each and dinner is T$8.

Camping is possible anywhere along the empty eastern shore of Lifuka.

Places to Eat

As mentioned in the Places to Stay

section, *'Evaloni's* is the best place to eat on the island, followed by *Langi Langi's* and *Seletute's*. If you'd like to eat at any of these places, book several hours in advance. For prices, see the Places to Stay section.

The only restaurant in town is *Fanga 'i He Si*, also known as *Bilimi's*, in front of the main wharf. I repeatedly tried to eat there but each time I went in, they informed me that they weren't open and provided some excuse or other: 'The prince is coming', 'We're having a dance here tonight', 'There isn't any food', 'The cook isn't here', and so on. Given their record, I'd advise you not to rely on being able to get a meal here. They do have a pub that seems to be full to overflowing most of the time, however.

The market in Pangai is on the main street, appropriately placed in front of the Ministry of Agriculture office. Limited groceries, beer, ice cream and dry goods are available from Morris Hedstrom and Kelepi Toutai, but they close at 4 pm (sometimes earlier) on weekdays and at 12 noon on Saturdays. A host of small bush shops sell staples until 9 pm. The shop just south of the market and the one beside 'Evaloni's sell fresh bread.

Entertainment

Every Saturday morning there is church entertainment in the streets outside the snooker hall across from Morris Hedstrom. On Saturday nights the restaurant/pub at the ferry wharf holds a dance. Kava clubs meet in several halls around the village on Friday nights. In addition, there are often dances in church halls and the several video machines in Pangai are sometimes put into public service. If you're lucky, you may get to participate in a local bingo game, a big event in Pangai! The lucky winners take home chickens or fish. Ask around town for information regarding the Pangai social calendar.

Getting There & Away

Air Friendly Islands Airways has two flights daily between Tongatapu and Vava'u that will stop in Ha'apai if there are at least two people to be dropped off or picked up. The fare from Tongatapu is T$62 and from Vava'u, T$44. Five km north of Pangai, the runway of Salote Pilolevu Airport is bisected by the road.

Be sure to reconfirm your flight out of Ha'apai several times at the office near the police station or there may not be space when it comes time for you to leave. Or worse, they may not bother to stop for you.

Boat Both the MV *'Olovaha* and the *Fokololo 'oe Hau* call in at Pangai, the former twice weekly, once from Tongatapu and once from Vava'u, and the latter whenever the owner feels like going. For a fare breakdown and schedules, see the Ferry section in the Getting Around chapter.

Getting Around

Friendly Islands Airways will carry passengers between the airport and Pangai for T$1 per person each way. Taxis are scarce, but those that do run charge T$3 to or from the airport for up to four people. A bus from Pangai to the airport turn-off costs 20 seniti.

AROUND LIFUKA ISLAND

Outside of Pangai, the island of Lifuka is composed almost entirely of agricultural plantations. There's little for the visitor to do but explore these 'apis and wander along the empty white beaches that nearly encircle the island. The western shore offers calm blue water, excellent for snorkelling, while the eastern coast is more exposed. Although it is sheltered by a reef, the water action can be dramatic and the beautiful beach far more wild than its leeward counterpart.

There is a hospital in the village of Hihifo, less than two km south of Pangai. From Hihifo, walk along the dirt road to the lovely beach at the southern end of the island to see Tongan fishing and to watch

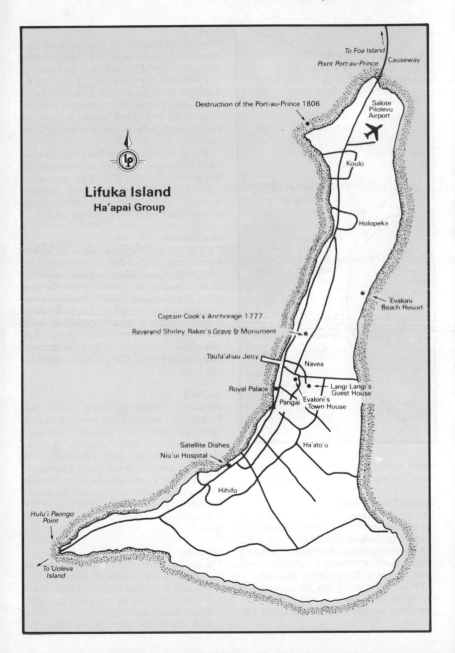

Lifuka Island
Ha'apai Group

To Foa Island
Point Port-au-Prince
Causeway

Destruction of the Port-au-Prince 1806

Salote
Pilolevu
Airport

Koulo

Holopeka

'Evaloni
Beach Resort

Captain Cook's Anchorage 1777

Reverend Shirley Baker's Grave & Monument

Taufa'ahau Jetty

Navea

Langi Langi's
Guest House

Royal Palace

Evaloni's
Town House

Pangai

Ha'ato'u

Satellite Dishes

Niu'ui Hospital

Hihifo

Hulu'i Paongo
Point

To'Uoleva
Island

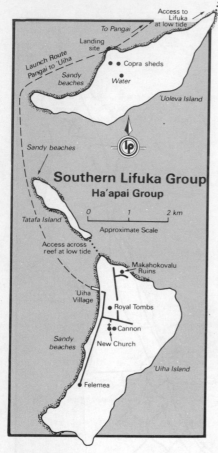

Southern Lifuka Group
Ha'apai Group

copra workers returning on horseback from 'Uoleva Island across the reef.

Getting There & Away

The bus service operates between Hihifo, in the southern half of Lifuka Island, and Faleloa, in the northern half of Foa Island. It begins operation at around 7 am and stops sometime between 2 and 4 pm. A bus from Pangai to Foa Island is 40 seniti.

Those who would like to do a bit of exploring on horseback can hire horses from Soni Kaifoto in Pangai for about T$5 per day.

FOA

The island directly to the north of and connected by causeway to Lifuka is called Foa. Its only real attraction is the beach at the extreme northern end. To get to it, take the twice-hourly bus from in front of the Kelepi Toutai general store in Pangai, ride to the end of the line at Faleloa (40 seniti) and walk northward for half an hour.

If you want to get a bus from Faleloa back to Pangai, be at the stop as early in the afternoon as possible. Your chances of finding transport of any kind decrease steadily after 2 pm and I know from experience that it's a very long walk.

NUKUNAMO

The small uninhabited island of Nuku-namo, just north of Foa, is surrounded by white beach and offers excellent shelling. It is accessible on foot or by snorkelling from the northern end of Foa; however, you can only cross at low tide, so if you're going, it might be wise to get a very early start. Currents through the pass here are powerful and only strong swimmers should attempt it. The island is owned by the king.

HA'ANO

Ha'ano is a strikingly clean, well-cared-for island. The people are proud of its new churches and four pleasant villages, which are, from north to south, Muitoa, Ha'ano, Pukotala and Fakakakai. Of course, it also has some lovely beaches.

To get to Ha'ano, take the bus to Faleloa on Foa Island and catch one of the water taxis that leave for Ha'ano whenever the bus arrives in Faleloa. The fare is 50 seniti.

'UOLEVA

The uninhabited island of 'Uoleva lies just less than a km south of Lifuka. It is composed mostly of coconut plantations and some of the nicest and most peaceful beaches imaginable.

The northern shore is suitable for

camping, especially at the north central cape of the island. Rainwater is available from filthy tanks just south of the copra sheds there, but it should be boiled for at least 20 minutes before drinking. Ask permission of the copra workers before drinking coconuts. At the time of writing, very basic fale-type guest accommodation was being planned for the northern coast of 'Uoleva.

In the centre of the coconut plantations are some 16th-century burial mounds but they are very difficult to find without a guide.

Getting There & Away

To get to 'Uoleva, you can walk across from Lifuka on the reef at low tide; however, beware of the current that passes between the two islands. Another option is to hitch a ride on a 'Uiha-bound boat and ask to be dropped at the northern point of 'Uoleva. For information ask at Neo's, the small shop on the waterfront in Pangai; the owner of the shop lives on 'Uiha.

'UIHA

'Uiha is a very clean and friendly island. It has two villages: 'Uiha, which has the main wharf, and Felemea, about 1½ km to the south.

On 26 January 1863, the Peruvian blackbirder *Margarita* left Callao (Lima) and was never seen again. According to a preacher who was on 'Uiha at the time, a ship called in there and lured some islanders aboard. When their families on shore realised what had happened they banged iron pots in order to lead the slavers to believe that they should return ashore and pick up more people who had decided they'd like to go along. The ploy worked and the ship was seized, the Tongans released and then the ship, which was probably the *Margarita*, was destroyed. As evidence of this event, the 'Uihans display two cannons, one planted in the ground outside the church in 'Uiha

village and the other in front of the altar inside. It's used as a baptismal font!

In the centre of 'Uiha village are royal tombs in a large elevated cemetery. In late 1988, the tombs of three relatively obscure members of the royal family were moved to 'Uiha, two from Pangai and one from Tongatapu, accompanied by much pomp and ceremony. Ostensibly the project was to consolidate the tombs of the royal family, but some think that a rumour of treasure in the cemetery compound at 'Uiha prompted the king to look for a popular excuse to excavate the otherwise tapu area.

Walking beyond the royal tombs, you won't be able to miss 'Uiha's absurd-looking new church. It strongly resembles something out of a fairy tale, a sticky peppermint Santa Claus castle!

At the northern end of 'Uiha, about a 10-minute walk from the village, are the Makahokovalu ruins. The name means 'eight joined stones', but there are actually nine laid vertically end to end in an L-shape. A few similar stones are found lying about the site, reportedly scattered by a hurricane. There hasn't been much theorising as to the purpose and origin of the complex, but if you're on 'Uiha anyway, it's a pleasant walk out there.

In late 1988, while the royal tombs were being relocated, the king's daughter Princess Pilolevu took a notion that she'd like to visit the site. In one day, a new road was cut through to the ruins and the stones were cleared of years of overgrowth.

Getting There & Away

The easiest way to get to 'Uiha is by launch or fishing boat from Pangai, which will cost about T$1 per person if they're going anyway. Arrange rides at Neo's shop not far from the small boat wharf in Pangai. There is as yet no formal accommodation on 'Uiha but if you'd like to stay the night, enquire at the shop whether anyone on the island is taking in guests. The MV *Fokololo 'oe Hau* calls in from time to time, also, but there is no timetable.

TATAFA

Uninhabited Tatafa is a short low-tide walk across the reef from northern 'Uiha. It is surrounded by a lovely beach and would be excellent for camping, but you'll have to carry water or ask permission to drink coconuts. Don't forget to take a bush knife to open them! There is also good snorkelling around Tatafa.

Other Islands

KAO

The immense volcanic cone visible from Lifuka and the other main islands on a clear day is Kao, the highest point in Tonga with an elevation of 1109 metres.

The island is uninhabited save by one eccentric hermit.

Landing on Kao is extremely difficult. Once ashore, you can get up and down the mountain, which looks formidable from the sea, in a couple of days depending on the weather, which can get quite nasty. Take camping gear and warm, rainproof clothing for this difficult climb if you're set upon doing it.

Marlin fishing around Kao is excellent but at present there is no one offering charters from Pangai, so all fishing has to be done from private yachts.

Getting There & Away

Getting to Kao will probably prove quite expensive. Your best bet would be to try to catch a ride with the Catholic hospital boat *Fa'amoeki* ('sail with God'), which does runs between Lifuka, Tofua, Kao (sometimes) and Ha'afeva. For more information contact Father Sione at the

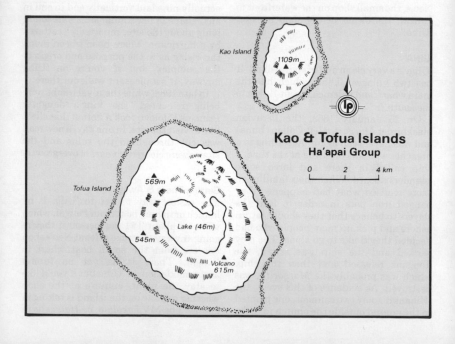

Kao Island

1109m

Kao & Tofua Islands
Ha'apai Group

0   2   4 km

Tofua Island

569m

Lake (46m)

545m

Volcano
615m

Catholic mission. If you'd like to charter this boat to any of these areas, plan on paying about T$300 per day for up to about 30 people. You may have to do some convincing to get them to land at Kao.

The Department of Education also has a boat, the MV *Pako*, which resembles the *African Queen*. It carries up to 60 people and charters for T$300 daily when it isn't needed for government business. Enquire at the Department of Education office in Pangai.

TOFUA

Tofua, near which the mutiny on the *Bounty* took place, is the most active volcano in the Tonga Islands – people on passing ships will see it constantly smoking away. The best and most extensive kava plantations in the country are on Tofua. There has been no permanent village since 1874, when the king evacuated the island due to excessive volcanic activity. Most of the island's current inhabitants live there part-time while they tend and harvest the kava crop.

Captain Bligh

The island also produces tamanu trees for canoes and toa, or ironwood, trees in small noncommercial quantities.

The island, 47 square km in area, is a circular crater, with a lake of seven square km which is four km across at the bottom. On the 558-metre-high northern rim of the crater is the smoking vent, which is called Lofia. Jungle-covered red and black lava cliffs, which rise directly out of the surf, make landing on Tofua difficult.

On the island is the tomb of John Norton, quartermaster of the HMS *Bounty*, who was clubbed to death by islanders when Captain Bligh and 18 loyals landed there to provision after the famous mutiny. Bligh and the rest of the men escaped and embarked on a 6500-km journey to Timor in an open boat and with minimal rations.

If you go to Tofua, be sure to take enough food for yourself and some provisions for the workers stuck there, especially tinned corned beef. It would be heartily welcomed!

Getting There & Away

Getting to Tofua is the same as getting to Kao, so refer to the previous section for details. The Catholic hospital ship stops at Tofua for one day at a time, sufficient to do the climb up to the crater.

HA'AFEVA

Ha'afeva lies about 40 km to the south-west of Lifuka. It is a very small island but upwards of 500 people live in its village and the rest of the land is taken up in plantations, making it a very crowded place. Although Ha'afeva is a friendly island, it's rather unkempt and there aren't any good beaches. There is, however, a sunken fishing boat, which makes for good diving on the reef north-west of the island.

Getting There & Away

Ha'afeva is accessed most easily on the MV *'Olovaha*, which sails from either Tongatapu or Lifuka once weekly. For fares and schedules, refer to the Ferry section in the Getting Around chapter. The Catholic mission hospital boat also travels frequently to Ha'afeva and it should be easy to hitch a ride.

From Ha'afeva, it's possible to find small local boats going to the outer islands of Matuku, Kotu and Tungua, which offer excellent snorkelling.

NOMUKA

Historically the island of Nomuka, only five square km in area, has been far more prominent than it is today, thanks to the presence of a sweetwater lake in its centre. Once again, Dutchman Abel Tasman was the first European to arrive. He named it Rotterdam while taking on water there. Later well-known visitors included James Cook, William Bligh and William Mariner.

This island has a reputation in Tonga for being a bit more aloof than the rest. Nomuka's companion island, Nomuka'iki,

Nomuka Island
Ha'apai Group

is used as a prison where indentured convict labourers serve their sentences on the plantations.

As on all the Ha'apai Group islands, camping in Nomuka is best on the lee shore. There are no guest houses or restaurants on the island.

Access is by small craft from either Lifuka or Ha'afeva or on Walter Line's MV 'Onga Ha'angana.

FONUAFO'OU

In 1781 Spaniard Francisco Antonio Mourelle and in 1787 Frenchman Jean de la Pérouse both reported a shoal 30 km west of Nomuka. In 1865, the passing ship HMS Falcon also noted it. Only 12 years later, smoke was seen rising from that spot by the warship Sappho and, in 1885, a cinder, scoria and pumice island 50 metres high and two km long rose from the sea, spewed up in a violent submarine eruption. Tonga planted its flag and claimed the island for the king. This has happened before in the Pacific and it will happen again, but. . .

In 1894, a few years after it was first identified and named – Falcon Island by Europeans and Fonuafo'ou or 'new land' by the Tongans – the island went missing; less than two years later there appeared an island 320 metres high which subsequently disappeared. In 1927 it emerged again, however, and by 1930, it had risen in a series of fiery eruptions to 130 metres in height and 2½ km in length. By 1949, there was again no trace of Fonuafo'ou. Researchers believe that it had probably eroded into the sea. When I sailed past, it was up again. In the plain words of one Tongan I discussed the matter with: 'Yes, it comes and it goes.' In the Vava'u Group, Late'iki Island/Metis Shoal seems to be up to the same game these days.

The only way to catch a glimpse of Fonuafo'ou (assuming you are there when it's around!) is to ride the ferry between Niuafo'ou and Tongatapu, which normally passes within a few km of it, or else to sail there on a private yacht.

HUNGA TONGA & HUNGA HA'APAI

These twin volcanic islands in the far south-western corner of the Ha'apai Group contain large guano deposits, but the lack of an anchorage makes exploitation of the resource impractical. Hunga Tonga has an altitude of 161 metres and Hunga Ha'apai is 131 metres. Both volcanoes have been dormant since European discovery.

The Vava'u Group

Vava'u's Port of Refuge, a long narrow channel between tussocklike limestone islands, is the best harbour between Pago Pago and New Zealand. This and the fact that the Vava'u Group boasts uniquely picturesque islands, myriad jumbled channels and waterways and scores of lovely secluded anchorages make it one of the yachting capitals of the world.

Between the months of August and November hundreds of cruising yachts descend on Vava'u to explore its wonders, and some are so entranced that they opt to risk a typhoon season in the harbour rather than leave so idyllic a setting. And this was the place Finau 'Ulukalala I warned Captain Cook not to approach because there was no good anchorage!

The tranquil islands have a population of about 20,000 scattered throughout the 50-odd thickly wooded islands of the group; a third of the people live in and around the capital, the village of Neiafu.

Yachties and other world travellers habitually compare Vava'u with the Bahamas, the Virgin Islands and the Rock Islands of Palau (which it very closely resembles), but such comparisons only serve to detract from the inspiring uniqueness of the place. Beyond the lush green hills, the turquoise waters, the beaches and the exquisite reefs are quiet villages, hidden caves, windy cliffs and a pleasant South Seas ambience that as yet manages to outdistance Vava'u's touristy tendencies.

History

The Vava'u Group islands were run across more or less accidentally by Spaniard Don Francisco Antonio Mourelle in 1781 while en route from the Philippines to Spanish America. Mourelle and the crew of his ship, the *Princesa*, had run frightfully short of supplies when they spotted a Vava'u outlier, volcanic Fonualei, on the horizon. Upon discovering that it had nothing to offer in the way of food or water they sailed on, nursing the ship along on a feeble wind.

When they finally sighted the main island on 4 March 1781, they sailed up the 11-km channel to the harbour at Neiafu, which they named Puerto de Refugio, or 'port of refuge', a body of water the Tongans knew as Lolo 'a Halaevalu, or 'oil of the Princess Halaevalu', because of the smooth natural oily sheen it bears on a calm day. It goes without saying that the luxuriant island was a welcome sight to the desperate Spaniards; they claimed the new-found paradise for Spain and named it Islas de Don Martin de Mayorga after the viceroy of Mexico. The visitors received a hearty welcome by the islanders and their ship was well provisioned before again setting sail shortly thereafter.

In 1793, the Spanish sent Captain Alessandro Malaspina to Vava'u to survey the new Spanish territory and formally make their claim known to the inhabitants of the islands. He buried a decree of Spanish sovereignty somewhere on the main island and quickly hurried on to attend to the myriad other tasks laid out for him in the Pacific by the home government.

William Mariner, who was adopted by Finau 'Ulukalala I, the reigning chief of Ha'apai, when his ship, the privateer *Port-au-Prince*, was sacked and most of its crew killed, also spent a great deal of time in Vava'u (he had actually been involved in the Tongan conquest of this northern group). It was from Vava'u that he finally left Tonga. The king of Vava'u, the son of the late Finau 'Ulukalala, realised that the young man had been long enough away from his own country. When the English brig the *Favourite* landed at

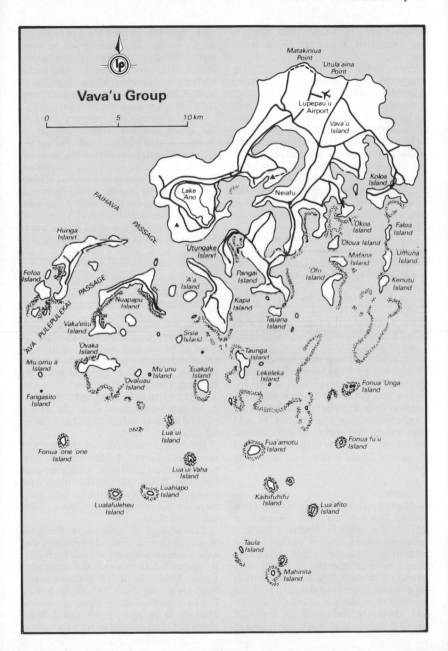

Vava'u in early November 1810, Mariner was permitted to return with it to Britain.

Upon seeing the marvels that lay aboard the ship, the Tongan king begged to be permitted to accompany Mariner; he was willing to forsake his princely life in the islands for even a very low station in the land of Papalangi (the Tongan name for Europe, meaning 'country of the white people'). He wanted to learn to read, write and operate the mechanical wonders wrought by the foreigners. In one anecdote, Mariner recounts that the Tongan even refused to drink kava, being disgusted with it after having tasted wine aboard the ship!

Captain Fisk of the *Favourite* refused young Finau's entreaties, whereupon the Tongan extracted from Mariner an oath that he would someday return to Tonga on another ship and carry the king back to England. Unfortunately for him, William Mariner never returned to Tonga and Finau 'Ulukalala II's tomb can be seen today in the village of Feletoa, on the main island of Vava'u.

'Ulukalala II's son was converted to Christianity by King George Tupou I of Ha'apai. Upon the death of 'Ulukalala III, George was entrusted to look after the throne of Vava'u for the boy 'Ulukalala IV. George seized the opportunity to add Vava'u to his own realm; by 1833, he was already well on his way to the formation of the united Tonga which he achieved in 1845.

Geography

Geologically, the main body of the Vava'u Group, 275 km north of Tongatapu, consists of a single landmass, a block of limestone tilted toward Ha'apai. The northern extreme ends in high cliffs which plunge straight into the surf with very little coral offshore. The southern part of the group is a submerged zone where the summits of numerous islands and islets peek above the surface of the water in rounded masses that reach elevations of

up to only 186 metres. Most of these are wholly or partially surrounded by coral reefs. Volcanic outliers of the group include Toku and Fonualei to the north, and Late and Late'iki (Metis Shoal) to the west. A line of coral reefs runs southward from Vava'u toward the Ha'apai Group.

With 2000 mm of precipitation annually, the group has the wettest climate in Tonga. Most of the rain falls during the typhoon season (late November to April) but gentle warm rains and occasional downpours may occur at any time of year. The average temperature at Neiafu is about 24°C, that is 18°C to 25°C between May and September and 24°C to 32°C during the typhoon season. Trade winds blow at an average of 15 knots all year round.

Neiafu

Neiafu sits smack in the centre of just about everything that's happening in Vava'u. As the administrative capital of the island group, it has all the government agencies, the police headquarters, the hospital, the communications office and most of the tourist facilities and restaurants to be found in Vava'u. Over 25% of the population lives in Neiafu and associated villages.

Before European contact, Neiafu was considered sacred burial ground, and political unrest and tribal skirmishes were forbidden. Those entering the village were required to wear a ta'ovala, or waist mat, as a symbol of esteem for those chiefs entombed there.

The waterfront area below the Free Wesleyan church is called Matangimalie, which means 'pleasant winds'. Formerly, it was called Loto'alahi; the conqueror Finau 'Ulukalala II (of Mariner fame) built his palace there. In 1808 he built a fortification on slightly higher ground at Pouono, as he was apparently dubious about any tapu associated with the area in earlier times. The fort was called Vaha'akeli, which means 'between trenches', a reference to the moats that surrounded it.

The central area of Neiafu lies between several low hills. To the north-west lies flat topped Mt Talau (131 metres). Over the hill to the north is Vaipua ('two waters') Inlet. Eastward is Neiafu Tahi, and to the south is the road to Pangai Island, along which you'll find the principal yacht anchorage and the Paradise International tourist complex.

Information

Tourist Offices The best information about current events, activities, feasts, vehicle rentals and so on is available to guests of the Hilltop Guest House from the proprietor Hans, who keeps track of such things. During the right season, the yachties who frequent the pub at the Paradise International Hotel are also friendly sources of up-to-date information and good conversation.

Next best is the Tonga Visitors' Bureau, located next to the Bank of Tonga on the main drag. Sione, the man in charge there, is the person to contact for solid and reliable information. The other employees merely keep his seat warm while he's off on official business and they cheerfully admit that they don't know the first thing about anything you might be inclined to ask.

The travel agents at the Hawaiian Airlines/Teta's Tours office are equally hopeless; unless you are looking for a bus tour of Vava'u Island, give them a miss. Regarding airline tickets and confirmations, guests of the Hilltop Guest House are again at an advantage. They will sort out your travel arrangements for just the price of the telephone calls necessary to do so.

Post & Telecommunications The GPO, police station and telecommunications offices are all located in the complex just above the main wharf area. In the days when cruise ships called in at Vava'u, this place served as a vibrant handicraft market as well.

Fax services are available at the Cable & Wireless for an outrageous fee, but the Paradise International Hotel will allow guests and yachties to use theirs for only T$4 per page.

Banks The Bank of Tonga is next to the Tonga Visitors' Bureau, on the main street.

Travel Guides Most of the sights of Neiafu are described thoroughly in an interesting little book called *Walking Tour of Neiafu, Vava'u* by Pesi & Mary Fonua (Vava'u Press, 1981). When I was last in Tonga, however, the book wasn't available anywhere.

Miscellaneous Photocopies can be made at the shop/snack bar beside the tourist office as well as at the Hand Craft Centre between the high school and the Paradise International Hotel. Both places charge 15 seniti per copy.

Film is available in limited varieties at Burns Philp and Morris Hedstrom on the main street.

Watersports

The only establishment that hires out snorkelling and watersports gear to the general public is Vava'u Watersports on Fatafehi Rd, just down the hill from their sign. Hoby cats rent for T$30 for 24 hours, sailboards for T$20 and snorkel, mask and fins for T$5 (be sure to get a mask that fits properly!). Vava'u Watersports also does jet boat tours for T$40 per hour with up to 12 people – a quick way to zip around the archipelago if you're in a hurry!

Guests of the Hilltop Guest House can hire kayaks for T$5 per day including transport to the waterfront. Kayakers who would like an easy time of it should remember to ride out of the harbour on an outgoing tide and return on an incoming tide (there are two of each daily in the Port of Refuge).

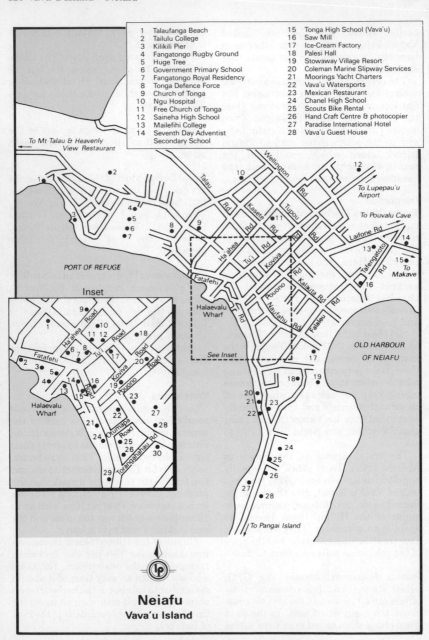

1	Talaufanga Beach
2	Tailulu College
3	Kilikili Pier
4	Fangatongo Rugby Ground
5	Huge Tree
6	Government Primary School
7	Fangatongo Royal Residency
8	Tonga Defence Force
9	Church of Tonga
10	Ngu Hospital
11	Free Church of Tonga
12	Saineha High School
13	Mailefihi College
14	Seventh Day Adventist Secondary School
15	Tonga High School (Vava'u)
16	Saw Mill
17	Ice-Cream Factory
18	Palesi Hall
19	Stowaway Village Resort
20	Coleman Marine Slipway Services
21	Moorings Yacht Charters
22	Vava'u Watersports
23	Mexican Restaurant
24	Chanel High School
25	Scouts Bike Rental
26	Hand Craft Centre & photocopier
27	Paradise International Hotel
28	Vava'u Guest House

To Mt Talau & Heavenly View Restaurant

PORT OF REFUGE

Inset

Halaevalu Wharf

See Inset

To Lupepau'u Airport

To Pouvalu Cave

Laifone Rd

Tafengatoto Rd

To Makave

OLD HARBOUR OF NEIAFU

To Pangai Island

Neiafu

Vava'u Island

Inset key

1	George's Bakery
2	Vava'u Club
3	Fisheries Department
4	Shipping Cooperation of Polynesia
5	Customs Department
6	GPO, Land & Survey Office (Maps)
7	Tonga Telecommunications Commission
8	Police Station
9	Pota 'Uaine Guest House
10	Mohetaha Guest House
11	Sailoame Market
12	Bus Station
13	Anglican Church
14	Burns Philp
15	Friendly Islands Airways
16	Morris Hedstrom
17	Free Wesleyan Church of Tonga
18	Siu'ilikutapu College
19	Police Magistrate
20	Foeata Guest House
21	Fungalelea Theatre
22	La Mer Restaurant
23	Cemetery
24	Si'i Kae Ha Handicraft Centre
25	Tonga Visitors' Bureau, Duty-Free Shop & Handicraft Centre
26	Photocopies & Breakfast Bar
27	Quarry
28	Hilltop Guest House & Cafe
29	Nasaleti Hall
30	Langahake Kava Club

Fishing charters are offered by Bigfoot Fishing Charters, (tel 70212) in a 12-metre motor sailer for T$30 per day including lunch and equipment hire. Book through the Paradise International or at the Tonga Visitors' Bureau. A much more basic way to get in a little fishing is to turn up at the wharf at 8 am on a Friday morning and arrange a day with an incoming local fisherman; he will doubtlessly know the best local fishing holes and will happily negotiate a reasonable price for his transportation and expertise. As usual, you will probably be able to arrange transport with yachties but you'll have to provide your own fishing equipment.

Yacht Charters Moorings, Ltd offers bareboat yacht charters by the day or week from their office on Fatafehi Rd. Those with a great deal of money and dreams of independently exploring the outer limits of the Vava'u Group will find this an appealing option. At the time of writing, chartering a yacht for a day cost between US$225 and US$475, depending on the size of the boat. Weekly rates work out slightly cheaper. You pay extra for provisions, crew, tax and insurance.

For pre-booking information contact Moorings, Ltd, 1305 US-19 South £402, Clearwater, FL 34624, USA; or Atlantic & Pacific Travel, 480 Lake Rd, PO Box 330259, Takapuna, Auckland, New Zealand.

Private charters to outer islands can be arranged with yachties who may like to pick up some extra cash or a spare set of hands while cruising around the islands. If you'd like to do some diving in Vava'u, this is also the best way to go. To make arrangements, either put up a notice on the bulletin board at the Paradise International or make your presence and your wishes conspicuous around the resort or the anchorage.

Free Wesleyan Church
The new Free Wesleyan church was dedicated on 29 August 1970. It's built on the site of the old church, which was destroyed by the devastating typhoon of 16 and 17 March 1961. The new church is of interest for its stained-glass work. Windows depict such diverse characters as John and Susan Wesley, Queen Salote Tupou III and Jesus Christ himself. All that remains of the old church is a hall, which is used as a classroom of the Siu'ilikutapu College by day and a kava club by night.

Hala Tafengatoto
The name means 'the road where blood flows'. Tradition has it that this sunken trail, the route to the village of Feletoa, ran with the blood of warriors killed

during the conquest of Vava'u by Finau 'Ulukalala II.

This trail is one of a network of sunken clay pathways found around the main island of Vava'u. This one meets the Old Harbour in the extreme eastern environs of Neiafu. Although the scene isn't as morbid these days as it once was, the ruddy clay base of the path is reminiscent of the source of its name. Today, the clay is collected and used as a shampoo by the Tongans.

Pouono & Pouono Cemetery

The name Pouono means 'six posts' and refers to the traditional six posts of a meeting fale. This village green contains the courthouse and the *lali* drums used to mark the beginning of a court session.

In the cemetery (across the street) is an ancient langi tomb where Ta'emoemimi, the daughter of the 35th Tu'i Tonga, Tu'ipulotu'ilangi Tu'oteau, is buried. There are also a couple of early-19th-century graves containing the remains of Wesleyan missionaries David Cargill and Reverend Francis Wilson.

Neiafu Tahi

The Old Harbour of Neiafu is much shallower then the Port of Refuge but it served as the main landing site on the island until the arrival of relatively large European ships required a deepwater port. Around the year 1808 Finau 'Ulukalala II, in the midst of the conquest of Vava'u, bound several resisting chiefs into decomposing canoes and left them adrift in Neiafu Tahi to sink and drown.

Near the entrance to Hala Tafengatoto are several freshwater springs bubbling into the Neiafu Tahi. The most reliable is Matalave, around the harbour to the east. Nearby is the rocky outcrop that is said to have been the primary Vava'u landing site of the kalia, the double-hulled canoes used in ancient times.

The wreck of the copra steamer *Glen McWilliam* lies in 30 metres of water in the Old Harbour. The ship caught fire at the dock in 1917 and, in the interest of safety, it was shoved out into the harbour and allowed to sink. The legend has it that the captain and first mate refused to abandon ship during the crisis and went down with it. Today, it's a popular dive site.

Hala Lupe

The Hala Lupe, the 'way of doves', is the name given to the stretch of road along the waterfront between the Catholic church and the Moorings office. It is so called because the road was constructed by women prisoners convicted of adultery by the church and their singing while they worked reminded listeners of the mournful cooing of doves.

Fangatongo Rugby Ground

On the road westward to Mt Talau is the Fangatongo Rugby Ground where matches are played on Saturdays from April to July. The large tree at the southern end of the field is reputedly able to provide shelter for up to 500 spectators!

Kilikili Pier

Kilikili is the name given to the black volcanic slag pebbles which are used to decorate grave mounds throughout the islands. Those used today come mostly from the islands of Kao and Tofua in the Ha'apai Group. This pier, at the far western end of town, used to serve as a British coaling station; it was so named because the Tongans thought the coal loaded by the foreigners there resembled those familiar little pebbles. It now serves as a popular swimming area.

Mt Talau

The flat-topped mountain that dominates the Port of Refuge is called Mo'unga Talau. It is actually only 131 metres high and is easily climbed in an afternoon.

The Tongans tell an interesting tale of how it came to lose the peak which of course it once supported. A mischievous *tevolo*, or devil spirit, from Samoa happened by one day and decided to nick the attractive peak and carry it away to his homeland. There is some disagreement as to what happened next. Some say that a patriotic Tongan tevolo caught the offender and forced him to drop the peak by convincing him that daylight, the time for all devils to be back under cover, was near. Another source claims that the mountain simply became too heavy for him and he dropped it of his own free will. Whichever the case, the mountaintop splash-landed in the middle of the Port of Refuge. It is now called Lotuma Island and is used as the Vava'u naval base of the Tongan Defence Forces.

To climb the mountain, continue out along Tupueluelu Rd, going past the rugby ground. Follow the road up past the Heavenly View Restaurant (aptly named!) and through a residential area, until it narrows into a bush track. When the track begins to descend, a side track will turn off to the right and lead steeply up over slippery rock surfaces to the summit.

The view from the three viewpoints at the top encompasses the town of Neiafu and the Port of Refuge, Vaipua Inlet and the 128-metre-high Sia Ko Kafoa on the other side of it. Across the Old Harbour are Pangai and 'Utungake islands. The other truncated mountain (no one knows where the top of this one ended up) in the distance is 186-metre-high Mo'ungalafa, which rises above the freshwater Lake 'Ano at the western extreme of Vava'u Island.

Places to Stay – bottom end

Thanks to its tourist appeal, there are quite a few nice places to stay in or near Neiafu. The most popular these days is *Hilltop Guest House*, which is on top of Holopeka ('place of gathering bats') Hill. This is a magical place, which boasts a 180° view over both harbours, the surrounding hills and the neighbouring islands, not to mention the whole of Neiafu.

It's run by Hans and Sela Schmeiser, an Austrian and Tongan couple who will do anything they can to help you make the most of your stay on Vava'u, including sorting out your travel bookings and arranging hire cars, feasts, barbecues, outer island tours, and the like. They hire out kayaks for T$5 per day, including transport to the water, and bicycles for T$6 per day or T$3 per half day. Laundry facilities are available for T$1.50 per load, soap included.

From 1 November to 30 November and 15 February to 1 April, they charge T$10 per double room (T$14 for a room with a view). The rest of the year the rooms go for T$15 and T$18 with a 20% discount for single occupancy and a 20% surcharge for stays of under three days. Those staying longer than a fortnight receive 20% discount on a double room.

If you'd like to stay, it's best to book in advance or you may be out of luck. If you're booked in, Hans will fetch you at the airport or wharf free of charge and deliver you back when it's time to go. They also provide mosquito nets and cooking facilities. Hans is still doing his best to iron out wrinkles but this is unquestionably the nicest, cleanest and most informative place to stay on Vava'u Island.

If the Hilltop is full, *Vava'u Guest House*, across the street from the Paradise International, is nearly as nice. Single rooms rent for T$6, doubles for T$9, single fales for T$12 and double fales for T$15. If you're staying here ask for one of the old rooms, as the new rooms are painted bilious green (unless, of course, you happen to like bilious green!).

Excellent family-style dinners are available for T$5 extra per person but you must book before 4.30 pm on the day you'd like to eat there. Nonresidents pay T$6 and it's well worth the money – Virginia from Vermont is a superb chef!

They'll do laundry for T$1 per kilo, 50 seniti extra for soap. You can use the Paradise International pool for T$1.50 if you ask but most people don't ask and therefore don't pay anything.

The *Tufumolau Guest House*, near the Old Harbour, is very clean and has a new sterile-looking dormitory-type building with cooking facilities. The staff are very friendly and it's close to town. The nightly charge is T$7 per person and they'll do Tongan-style meals for you if you book in advance.

Near the market is the *Pota 'Uaine Guest House*. It's under friendly Tongan management but it's a bit grimy around the edges. At T$5 per person, it's about the cheapest place in town if you're alone. Cooking facilities are available or they'll prepare meals for a few pa'anga.

The *Foeata Guest House* is owned and operated by a man who designs tanks, which should be fairly obvious when you see it; it has been occupied more or less permanently by foreign aid volunteers since 1984 and isn't currently available to travellers.

The *Stowaway Village Resort* (tel 70137) beside the Old Harbour is a rather grotty but pleasant place 1½ km east of the centre. Single rooms go for T$7, doubles for T$13.50.

Places to Stay – middle & top end

The *Paradise International Hotel* (tel 70121) is Vava'u's answer to the ritzy resort and is by far the poshest place to stay in all of Tonga. Although service is abysmal the rooms are clean, hot water is available at all hours and there's a pleasant bar area beside the refreshing (albeit scummy) pool. Check out the bit of airplane near the bar – it belongs to the hotel's owner, Carter Johnson, who crashed it several years ago. The other bit is in the Pouono area of central Neiafu.

There is a Friday night disco and videos are available (see the Entertainment section). An ordinary single room costs T$24, doubles are T$31. More deluxe rooms range from T$35 to T$85 per night.

The main Vava'u yacht anchorage is in the Port of Refuge in front of the Paradise International. The hotel charges yachts T$2 per day, T$10 per week and T$30 per month to anchor there. One day at the wharf costs T$10 and one night T$6. Electric hookups are available for T$5 per day. Wharf usage while you fill tanks or clean boats for part of a day is T$5. You may not run generators or entertain loudly in the anchorage on Sundays.

On the island of 'Utungake, two causeways removed from Neiafu, is the German-run *Tongan Beach Resort* (tel 70380), which offers secluded and clean fale accommodation. Each unit has private baths and hot water. For a single they charge T$32 and a double unit costs T$38 per night. They have a restaurant and bar as well as a reasonable beach.

Places to Eat

Snacks The German-run *Ice-Cream Factory*, near the Stowaway Village Resort, is a site of potential weight gain. It makes delicious ice-cream, ice blocks and choco-dips. Try some of their addictive Kiwi hokey-pokey ice-cream and you'll keep coming back for more. If you're with another person or two, buy it in bulk and pig out – it's the best in the South Pacific!

Those who know Vava'u and Tonga well will also know that Robyn's Coffee Shop had become an institution among yachties, ex-pats and travellers in Neiafu. In late 1988, however, Robyn closed down the operation, married the yacht club director in Pago Pago and went off to live happily ever after in American Samoa. In doing so, she's left quite a void. If you want good coffee in Vava'u these days, you'll have to see Hans at the *Hilltop Guest House*; but there is no longer any place to just hang out and shoot the breeze for a few hours.

Restaurants Most travellers eat at the *Vava'u Guest House*, which offers excellent food and variety for only T$6 per dinner (T$5 for guests). For that, you'll get twice as much as one person can possibly eat but it's so good you'll want to try.

Again, weight gain could be a serious problem for those staying too long here! I can't recommend it enough. If you're having dinner with them, book before 4.30 pm the same day so they can prepare an appropriate amount.

Another excellent place to eat is the *Hilltop Guest House*, which has a cosy dining room and a view out across the harbour and islands. It's slightly up-market, but the atmosphere, the quantity and the quality warrant the T$9 per person price. The owner, Hans, is an Austrian chef and he does European wonders with Tongan foodstuffs – book in the early afternoon to reserve a meal.

Hans makes unbelievable banana curry soup and chocolate coconut crepes! A complete meal will consist of salad, soup, bread, a main course, vegetable, dessert, candlelight and classical music above the twinkling lights of Neiafu. For a slightly higher charge you can have lobster, but you'll have to book it the previous day. Coffee lovers will be happy to know that this is one of the three places in Tonga that serve real brewed coffee.

Compared to these options the dining room at the *Paradise International Hotel* is pretty pathetic, but if you're staying there it will be convenient. The food is ho-hum and the prices high. I went in one afternoon for lunch and ordered from the menu, and the cook told me that she couldn't be bothered to prepare that particular item. Give it a miss unless you're craving boring North American-style fare.

La Mer, just up from the Bank of Tonga, reportedly does some very nice seafood dishes – 'ota 'ika and fresh local fish in particular – for T$3 to T$6.

Another excellent and friendly establishment is the small place known simply as *The Mexican Restaurant*. It's run by a delightful American-Samoan man at the moment, but he's planning to head off to the USA and train someone local to make the tacos. He offers good fish and chicken dishes with soup, salad and vegetables for

T$7. The restaurant is located on Fatafehi Rd, across from Vava'u Watersports.

The *Heavenly View Restaurant* on the slopes of Mt Talau lives up to its name and also serves very nice European-style fare. Book in advance if you'd like to give it a try.

The restaurant at the *Tongan Beach Resort* over on 'Utungake Island is also rather nice, but it is a little inconvenient if you're not staying there. The best time to go over is on Sunday, when you can swim at the beach while the rest of the island goes to church. They also make a mean apple strudel which shouldn't be missed.

Tongan Feasts Those interested in a Tongan feast will find a variety to choose from in Vava'u. The most popular is the weekly affair at 'Ano and Lisa beaches on Pangai Island. It costs T$11 including transport. Bookings for this and other feasts can be made at *Vava'u Guest House* or at the *Paradise International Hotel*.

Self-Catering For those putting together their own meals, imported grocery products are available at Burns Philp and Morris Hedstrom in the centre. The freshest fish can be found at 8 am on Friday mornings at the wharf, which is when the fishing boats arrive with their catches.

The bakery in Neiafu is a nondescript little white building west of the centre. It's called *George's Bakery* but there's no sign identifying it as such, so you may have to ask a local to point it out to you. On Saturdays you'll have to be early buying bread, as they're normally sold out before 9 am. As usual, they close on Saturday at 12 noon and reopen at 4 pm on Sunday.

For fresh produce, go to *Sailoame Market* just above the government complex in the centre. You'll find papaya, bananas, watermelons, pineapples, coconuts, custard apples, passion fruit, and taro as well as a variety of locally produced vegetables – tomatoes, cabbage, carrots, capsicum and aubergine. Onions, garlic and herbs are imported from New Zealand, and can only be purchased at the department stores on the main street.

Entertainment

The most popular disco in Neiafu is the one at the *Paradise International Hotel*, but unaccompanied foreign women shouldn't attend unless they want a great deal of physical attention from Tongan boys. Things get started at about 8 pm and close down at 11.30 pm. Admission charge is T$1 for nonresidents, but yachties and Vava'u Guest House people are admitted free. The music is typically horrid but it's good fun nonetheless.

The bar at the Paradise is a good place to meet yachties, especially if you're hoping to crew on with someone. The only real local drinking spot is the *Vava'u Club* west of the centre, a western-style saloon with pool and snooker options.

The *Nasaleti Hall*, near the Moorings

Painting tapa

office, offers socialising, talking, card playing, kava drinking and the like, but unaccompanied women should stay clear. There are other Friday night kava clubs to be found all over Neiafu. Ask any local man and he'll be able to steer you in the right direction.

On the main street there is a cinema that shows reject foreign films on weekends. The Paradise International Hotel has a video machine and they show videos nightly at 8.30 pm. Make enquiries at the front desk and state your preference of videos if someone else hasn't already done so. Admission is free for yachties and resort guests and T$1.20 for everyone else.

Things to Buy

There are several handicraft shops around Neiafu. The most expensive is in the lobby of the Paradise International Hotel. Both the Hand Craft Centre, which is near the Paradise, and the shop beside the Tonga Visitors' Bureau have a variety of reasonably priced items, but you'd do better to ask around at the market for the names of local artisans. They will not only give you a better deal but they will also earn more themselves by selling directly to you than by selling to the shops. The outlets, however, accept major credit cards and offer the option of wrapping and posting your purchases home.

Tailor-made clothing is available at Olga's, near the harbour. She can complete something for you in just a couple of days.

Getting There & Away

Air Friendly Islands Airways flies between Vava'u's Lupepau'u Airport and Tongatapu at least twice daily, more often if demand dictates. To or from Ha'apai you will have to confirm and reconfirm at the FIA office in either Neiafu or Pangai (Ha'apai). The fare to Tongatapu is T$88; to Ha'apai it's T$44.

Boat The MV *'Olovaha* does the run

between Nuku'alofa and Neiafu once a week, leaving the former on Tuesdays at 6 pm and arriving in Neiafu at 1 pm on Wednesdays. It departs Neiafu Thursday evenings at 10 pm, arriving in Nuku'alofa at 6 pm Friday. The MV *Fohololo 'oe Hau* also does the run. For fare breakdowns, see the Ferry section in the Getting Around chapter.

Tours There is a package tour to Vava'u run by Vital Travel in Nuku'alofa. It operates in the low season (which is all November and from 15 February to 1 April). The price includes return transport from Nuku'alofa, a five-day stay at Hilltop Guest House, bike rental for five days, a boat tour, airport or wharf transfers and a kava ceremony. The tour costs T$248 if you opt to travel by plane or T$148 if you travel on the MV *'Olovaha*.

Getting Around

Airport Transport Those booked into the Hilltop Guest House will be picked up at the airport free of charge. The Paradise International Hotel also operates a bus to and from the airport; it costs T$4 per person. The standard taxi fare between the airport and town is currently T$6.

Around Vava'u Island

Vava'u Island is a different world once you're away from Neiafu. Not that Neiafu is bustling, but the rest of the island is just a tranquil jumble of small villages, plantations and true bush.

In most of the villages a passing vehicle is noteworthy, and the visit of a foreigner is the event of the week. Travellers will find that the Vava'u people become warmer and more welcoming in direct proportion to their distance from the tourist centre of Neiafu, and that Vava'u Island is full of beautiful and interesting features, most of them quite different

from the outer islands of the Vava'u Group.

The easiest way to get around is by hire car or motorbike but, with a bit of effort, individuals can get a fairly good idea of what there is to see on bicycle, by public transport, or on foot.

If you're travelling around the island (especially by hire car), it might prove helpful to divide it into two parts, east and west, because the road system lends itself well to this and because a full day is required to 'do' each half.

WESTERN VAVA'U ISLAND
Sia Ko Kafoa

Vaipua Inlet, which nearly bisects the island, separates the Neiafu area from western Vava'u. The inlet was used as a way inland for ancient Polynesian canoes en route to the fort complex at the village of Feletoa, which means 'many brave warriors'.

On the western shore are the twin hills of Lei'ulu and Sia Ko Kafoa. This is an area which, historically, has served as a burial ground, an 'esi or resting site, a lookout and a fortification. The points of interest here can be comfortably visited from Neiafu in a morning or afternoon or as part of a road tour of the western end of the island.

From Neiafu, follow the road up past the hospital to Mata'ihoi Landing. Numerous small boats make the crossing from here across Vaipua Inlet to Ha'akalua Inlet daily, and you can ride along for a token fee of about 50 seniti. From the landing, climb up to the village of Taoa. The name, which was given to the village by the 14th Tu'i Kanokupolu, the cruel Tuku'aho, in the late 1700s, means 'spear'. Tuku'aho sought refuge here from a murder conspiracy plotted by Finau 'Ulukalala II. In 1799, he returned to Tongatapu, where he was executed by the Vava'u assassins.

The hill behind Taoa, Lei'ulu, is used as a burial ground. Walk downhill along the coral road behind this hill. When the road

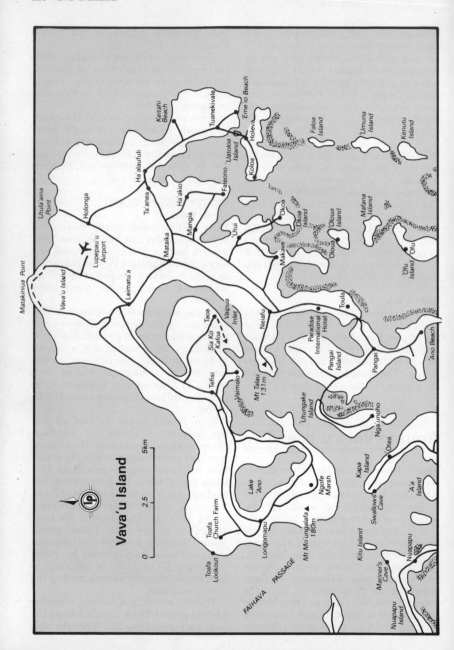

Vava'u Island

Top: Idyllic beach on Nuku Island, Vava'u Group
Left: Tapa & traditional home, Falehau, Niuatoputapu Island
Right: Wharf at Falehau, Niuatoputapu Island

Top: Kids on Niuatoputapu Island
Left: Policeman on patrol, Niuafo'ou Island
Right: Vai Lahi crater lake, Niuafo'ou Island

begins to turn to the right on an uphill slope, about 10 minutes from town, the track to the summit of 128-metre-high Sia Ko Kafoa turns off uphill to the left.

On the summit is an 'esi, a mound used as a rest area by chiefs and nobles as they passed through and a place where young virgins were presented to amorous chiefs. Originally, this particular 'esi, which measures three metres in height and 30 metres or so in diameter at its base, was known as Matangavaka, or 'sight of boats'.

After climbing the mound, turn left along the ridge at the base and follow the track downward to the shore at the village of Vaimalo, which means 'thank you for water', before catching a boat back to Mata'ihoi Landing.

Lake 'Ano

This freshwater lake at the extreme western end of the island is an eerie sort of place, and is accessed only by a very steep and muddy climb down into its crater from the friendly village of Longomapu. If approaching it via the main road from the north, turn left at the intersection in the village and follow that road for several hundred metres. Look carefully for a track that turns off to the right and leads away downhill. Under optimum conditions, the track will lead you to the shore of the lake in about 10 minutes, but recent rains will render it a bit more difficult. The lake is good for a refreshing swim or a bit of fishing for edible *lapila*.

Ngofe Marsh

Although Ngofe Marsh isn't a must-see, it is a beautiful expanse of reeds and wetlands in a bowl of surrounding hills. Travel south-eastward on the main road from Longomapu and turn right at the first opportunity. This rough road, which leads around the marsh before rejoining the circuit around Lake 'Ano, should only be attempted in a 4WD vehicle.

Toafa Lookout

From this cliff, near the church farm to the north-west of Longomapu, you can see volcanic Late Island on a clear day. The view is a beautiful contrast to the more subtle vistas on the southern coast of the island.

'Utula'aina Point

'Utula'aina Point provides perhaps the most spectacular view on the island of Vava'u and should not be missed. From the village of Holonga, continue northward until the point where a track cuts off sharply to the right and heads off downhill, while another track leads off into the scrub straight ahead (a few metres beyond on the right is a parking spot). At this point, you have three options, all of which can be completed in an hour or two. Be sure to carry water along on all these short walks. The sun is intense and there are no shops nearby that sell liquid refreshment.

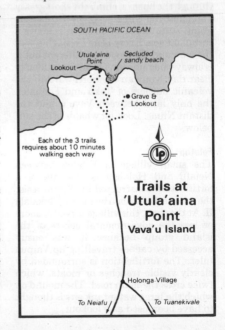

SOUTH PACIFIC OCEAN

'Utula'aina Point

Secluded sandy beach

Lookout

Grave & Lookout

Each of the 3 trails requires about 10 minutes walking each way

Trails at 'Utula'aina Point
Vava'u Island

Holonga Village

To Neiafu

To Tuanekivale

The track to the right leads down into a small gully and back up the other side. After a walk of less than 10 minutes you'll see a stone burial mound on your left and an interesting tree beyond. The view from here of the north coast is fairly good, better if you're game enough to climb the tree.

If you follow the track straight ahead for 50 metres or so from the intersection, past the parking site, you'll notice a very faint and very steep trail cutting off to the right. Follow it downhill for about 10 minutes until it issues out onto Vava'u Island's loveliest beach. More than likely, you'll have it all to yourself. A shallow shelf of coral in the area makes it of little interest for swimming or snorkelling, but the beach serves well as a sunning and picnicking spot.

The third option is to follow the track straight ahead from the intersection. It will curve around to the left a bit and, after a 10 to 15-minute walk, will emerge into a grassy open area. Bear towards the right through the bushes, climb the short grassy knoll and you will emerge on 'Utula'aina Point, surrounded by steep cliffs above a turbulent sea. Every time I visit this spot the view and the mood are different but it is always magnificent. On an exceptionally clear day, you can see northward to the volcanic outliers of Toku and Fonualei, the only land between Vava'u and the distant Niuas. Look for whales in the surf below.

Feletoa

The small village of Feletoa between Neiafu and Holonga is the site of a fortification constructed in 1808 to resist the conquest of Vava'u by Finau 'Ulukalala II. At the time, this village served as more or less the governmental centre of the island group because it was easily accessed by canoes travelling up Vaipua Inlet. The fortification is surrounded by clearly visible trenches or moats, which twice cross the main road. The mound on which the large water tank sits is thought to have been used as a lookout.

Between nearby Mata'ika village and Feletoa, on the south side of the road, is a burial site that contains the langi tomb of the ubiquitous Finau 'Ulukalala II. Finau died of what appears to be internal haemorrhaging after an animated wrestling contest in Neiafu, despite the sacrifice of a young Neiafu child in an attempt to appease the greater powers of the day. The body was carried by mourners to Feletoa and buried there.

Matakiniua Point

This beautiful area of high cliffs north of the airport is best accessed on foot in dry weather; extremely high grasses and mud obscure the road, although it could be negotiated in dry weather in a sturdy 4WD vehicle. The loop trip from Leimatua village to the coast, westward along the cliffs and back to Leimatua would take a full day on foot.

Check out the old airport, which was deemed too dangerous to accommodate aircraft due to updrafts and odd air currents around the cliffs.

EASTERN VAVA'U ISLAND

Makave

Most of your touring on the eastern half of Vava'u Island will involve beach-hopping, and this beach, easily walkable from Neiafu along the shore of the old harbour, is one of the most interesting. Walk past the entrance to Hala Tafengatoto (see the Neiafu section) and follow the shore eastward towards the village of Makave. Along the shore you'll find the ancient canoe mooring site in the form of an obtrusive rock and a cave. Further east are the springs of Matalave, which are ideal for a freshwater bathe. An hour's walk from Neiafu you'll come to the beach below Makave village.

Makave means 'take a stone', which refers to the ancient custom of piling a stone on Kilikilitefua Wall near the town upon the birth of a child. To visit this wall, follow the faint track from the end of the beach, which leads to the road. Turn southward and continue along the peninsula until a small rise. At this point the remains of the stone wall, now less than a metre high, can be seen stretching nearly 100 metres across the peninsula. It once reached a height of 1½ metres, but bits of it were removed for use in a concrete water tank scheme.

Makave village is the legendary home of a mysterious dark, giant people, who were said to have been seen by early Tongans.

Legend also has it that the peninsula which stretches southward from Makave was once the island of 'Utuatea. It is said that the village and the island were tired of being responsible for two separate tax assessments, so they decided to join forces. Under the direction of a clever chief named Tu'i'afitu, the villagers constructed a 150-metre-wide isthmus to connect the two areas in a single night. As yet, archaeologists have not confirmed this story.

Toula

Near the southern point of Vava'u Island is the village of Toula, which is most easily accessed along the road south from the Paradise International Hotel. Heading south, turn left at the village and follow the path uphill and past a cemetery. As you begin to descend to the beach, you'll see the Cave of Veimumuni in the bluff. Inside is a wonderful freshwater spring and swimming hole, normally full of local children.

There are several similar legends associated with this place, all of which have as their central character a beautiful spirit maiden, who appeared on the rock before the cave and teased mortal men with her beauty and everyone with the contents of the mysterious cave which she guarded. One version has her finally being outwitted by a tea (albino) woman, who became the first mortal to taste the water inside the cave before being tickled into submission by a pair of tevolo, or devil spirits. Another has her being tricked into the clutches of an amorous young gardener. All the stories end in universal access to the clear and refreshing waters of the cave. In reference to the first story, wells around Toula are called vai 'ene or 'tickling water'.

From this cave, walk north along the shore to a series of inviting caves, where Toula villagers used to bury enemies from other villages. There is good shelling in the tidal pools at low tide, and this pleasant stretch of shoreline is a good place to lie back and read a book on a hot afternoon.

Other Beaches

At the easternmost end of the island, near the village of Tu'anekivale, are a couple of reasonable beaches which are pleasant for strolling or sunbaking but are less than optimum for swimming or snorkelling. The nicest of these is Keitahi Beach, a couple of km east of the road between Ha'alaufili and Tu'anekivale. Currents are rather dangerous there at high tide, but strong snorkellers can find some interest in the large tidepools about 100 metres offshore. At low tide, anyone with proper footwear can wander out across the reef.

'Eme'io Beach is reached by taking the left fork from Tu'anekivale, from where it's about two km to the shore. It's a peaceful and scenic area to explore on foot but swimming is hopeless.

Further south across the causeways to 'Uataloa and Koloa islands are a few scattered beaches, but of greater interest is the mangrove that grows in the waterways around this swampy area.

GETTING THERE & AWAY
Bus

Buses leave from the Sailoame Market terminal in Neiafu for all parts of Vava'u accessible by road. The Pangai/'Utungake bus is red and white. The one to Tu'anekivale, at the far eastern end of Vava'u Island, is pink and white. Other buses connect Neiafu with Longomapu, Holonga, Leimatua and Tefisi. The drivers of all these vehicles go when they feel like it and quit when they feel like it, so don't depend too heavily on them, especially in the mid to late afternoon.

Boat

It's possible to charter a fishing boat by agreement and negotiation with its owner. Yachties also offer charters from time to time, so it might pay to check the bulletin board at the Paradise International reception desk (in Neiafu).

Driving

Automobiles may be hired from Neiafu Tahi Rentals (tel 70229). If you plan any real exploration, ask for their Suzuki 4WD. They charge T$20 for 12 hours and T$40 for 24. Drivers are responsible for petrol and the first T$250 damage to the vehicle. No insurance is available. There's a lot of red tape involved in vindicating yourself in the case of an accident, so don't have one. All vehicles hired out are left-hand drive; since Tonga drives on the left side of the road, you're provided with an added measure of insecurity.

Motorcycle

For those not energetic enough for push bikes, motorbike rentals are available at Vava'u Watersports. For 24 hours, the 80cc models go for T$18 and the 120cc for T$25.

Bicycle

Although the hilly nature of Vava'u doesn't exactly lend itself to exploration by bicycle, those on a budget who'd like to see a bit of the main island and islands connected to it by causeway should consider this option. The boy scouts hire out bikes for T$6 for a full day, T$3 for a half day and T$30 weekly. They've got a variety of models – three 12-speeds, one mountain bike, BMX trail bikes, kids' bikes and quite a few balloon-tyred one-speeds. They provide a rather basic leaflet and map, which can be used as a rough itinerary around Vava'u and its connected

islands. Their kiosk, which is open only in the mornings, is on Fatafehi Rd in Neiafu, near the end of the high school athletic field. Just walk toward Vava'u Guest House from town and you can't miss it.

Guests of the Hilltop Guest House in Neiafu can hire bikes from Hans and Sela for the same prices.

Horse

Horses may also be hired on a private basis. Gunter at the Tongan Beach Resort on 'Utungake Island should be able to help you make arrangements. Expect to pay about T$5 per day, but be warned that beginners shouldn't even consider this option. There are no saddles available and most of the horses are barely gentled. They seem to have minds of their own and they do know what low-hanging branches are for!

Tours

Road tours around Vava'u and adjoining islands may be booked through the Paradise International Hotel in Neiafu. On Mondays they offer a day tour which covers sights at the eastern end of the island, and on Wednesdays they visit the western half. Both tours cost T$10 per person; half-price for children under 12. A town tour is offered on Fridays for T$8.

Other Islands

PANGAI

Just across the scenic causeway from Toula village is Pangai Island (or Pangaimotu), so called because the word *pangai* refers to anything royal and the island belongs to the royal estate. The main village of Pangai was the home of the chief Vuna, whom Will Mariner discusses in his book in some detail. Vuna was one of the infamous 'handsome men' of Tonga, whose insatiable lust for young virgins and irresistibility to all women seriously disrupted many lives.

Beaches

'Ano and Lisa beaches near the southern end of the island are the sites of weekly Tongan feasts put on for tourists. Transport to the sites is included in the T$11 price. If you'd like to attend one of the feasts, enquire at the Paradise International Hotel or the Vava'u Guest House.

Near 'Ano Beach is what appears to be an abandoned resort scheme, where it is possible to camp. Coconuts are available for drinking. Look for the large old whale oil pot at the extreme southern end of the island. Some yachties I met laughingly referred to it as a 'missionary cooking pot', and it's not difficult to imagine why!

'Utulei

The village of 'Utulei, across the Port of Refuge from Kilikili Pier in Neiafu, is of interest because it is the setting of the books *Friendly Isles* and *'Utulei, My Tongan Home*. These are widely read autobiographical accounts of island life by Patricia Ledyard Matheson, a long-time palangi resident of the village. 'Utulei is inaccessible by motor vehicle, so you'll either have to kayak across the harbour from town, or park at the top of the hill behind the village and walk down.

Near the turn-off to 'Utulei is a quarry, a massive gash in the hillside, from above which there's a very nice view across the Port of Refuge.

Getting There & Away

Buses to Pangai leave from the Sailoame Market terminal in Neiafu. Pangai buses, which go on to 'Utungake Island, are red and white.

LOTUMA

The tiny island of Lotuma is a Tongan Defence Forces naval base. Some Tongans believe that it used to serve as the summit of truncated Mt Talau across the harbour before it was unfortunately stolen and dumped into the water by a thieving Samoan devil. Once you've seen this island you'll be able to understand why the story surfaced; however, all viewing will have to be done from elsewhere, since Lotuma is currently off limits to nonmilitary personnel.

'UTUNGAKE

The main attraction of 'Utungake Island is the Tongan Beach Resort, which is described in the Neiafu Places to Stay section. It is connected by causeway to Pangai Island and is a good place to laze on a Sunday afternoon. The Hilltop Guest House in Neiafu arranges transportation for a few pa'anga if enough guests are interested. There is another nice beach at the far southern end of 'Utungake, for those interested in going out there.

The small island of Mala, just to the south, has a good swimming and snorkelling beach, but there is a significant current that passes between these two islands and Kapa further south. Beware also of a legendary cannibal god reputedly living on Mala, who is said to capture and eat passing boaters.

'OFU

This friendly island south-east of the main island offers good shelling and is the primary habitat of the prized *'ofu* shell. Locals trying to sell them will tell you that they are found on no other island but, in fact, they survive in limited quantities throughout the Vava'u Group. Expect to pay about T$5 for a shell in good condition.

The school at 'Ofu has a visitors' register and the hospitality of the people is legendary. They are all too prepared to pass out food and shell necklaces to visitors, so go to 'Ofu prepared with some simple reciprocal gifts or you'll end up feeling bad.

KENUTU

Kenutu is an uninhabited small island east of 'Ofu. The coral patches to the south offer magnificent snorkelling and

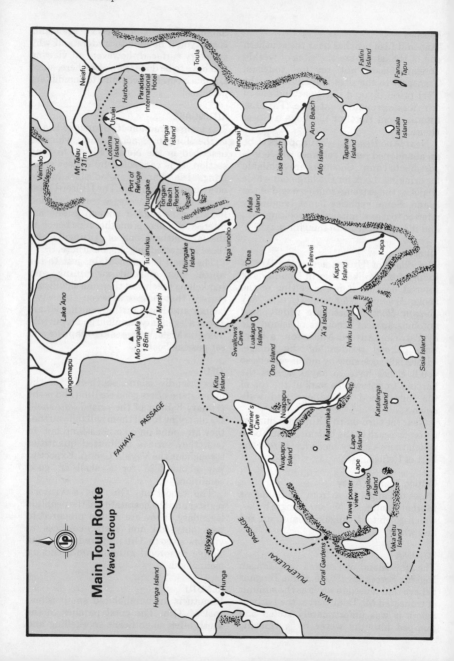

Main Tour Route
Vava'u Group

diving and the beaches are superb. The land itself is heavily wooded but there's a well-defined trail across it to steep cliffs on the eastern coast. Since there is no village, it is possible to camp just about anywhere and drink coconuts.

The reef between Kenutu and Lolo Island, which is just to the south, is very dramatic and shouldn't be missed. On the eastern side the waves crash and boil, pounding violently on the coral, while on the western side, the waters are crystal calm.

In the centre of the uninhabited island of 'Umuna, just to the north of Kenutu, is a large cave which contains a freshwater pool. Both Lolo and 'Umuna are accessible from Kenutu by crossing the reef on foot at low tide.

HUNGA

The westernmost major island of the Vava'u Group, Hunga offers excellent snorkelling opportunities. Its placid lagoon is formed by Hunga and the neighbouring islands of Kalau and Fofoa; it makes an excellent anchorage for cruising yachts, although the entrance is rather tricky. There is a peaceful village and some nice cliffs on Fofoa.

NUAPAPU

Mariner's Cave

Nuapapu is best known for the hidden cave, called Mariner's Cave after Will Mariner, at its northern end; Mariner was apparently the first European to see it. It is interesting to note, however, that in his book he mistakenly placed the cave on Hunga Island.

Mariner writes that he was taken to the cave by Finau 'Ulukalala II. Finau had gone to inspect some plantations in the area and, having extra time, decided to pay a visit to the legendary cavern. Mariner was puzzled when he saw several chiefs dive into the water and not return to the surface. He was then instructed to follow their example and was guided into a three-metre-long channel just a metre or

so below the surface of the water. When he emerged in a dim cathedrallike cavern, he decided that more illumination was necessary and returned to the canoe to procure a torch. With such illumination, he was able to determine the dimensions of the room to be about 14 metres high and 14 metres wide, with narrow channels branching off into darkness all around.

While they drank kava on a rock platform inside, one of the chiefs related the history of the cave's discovery.

A tyrannical governor of Vava'u learned of a conspiracy against him and ordered the primary conspirator drowned and all his family killed. The conspirator's beautiful daughter, who was betrothed to a young chief, was rescued by another chief, who also had amorous intentions towards her. He spirited her away into a secret cavern he had discovered in order to prevent her imminent demise. He visited her daily bringing gifts of food, clothing, coconuts and oils for her skin. His ministrations were so sincere that, eventually, he won her heart as well as her gratitude.

He formulated a plan to bring her out of the cavern, the primary point of which involved a secret voyage to Fiji with some underling chiefs and their wives. When they enquired why he would attempt such a trip without a Tongan wife, he replied that he would probably find one along the way. True to his word, he stopped the canoes before the bare rock above the cave entrance, dived into the water and emerged a few minutes later with the girl, whom his companions surmised to be a goddess until they recognised her as the daughter of the condemned conspirator. They all went off to Fiji, but returned to Vava'u after hearing of the death of the tyrant governor two years later and lived happily ever after.

The cave is today one of the primary tourist attractions of Vava'u and virtually every boat tour of the island includes it on the itinerary. On windy days, however, access to the cave may be difficult, due to

surf that could potentially beat swimmers senseless as it pounded against the rock.

Once you get into the cave, you will experience the strange atmospheric phenomenon that occurs there. Pacific swells surging through the entrance compress trapped air. When the sea recedes every few seconds, the moisture condenses into a heavy fog, the result of water vapour cooling as it expands; as soon as another wave enters the opening, the fog instantaneously vanishes.

Coral Gardens

Between the southern end of Nuapapu and the adjoining island of Vaka'eitu are beautiful coral gardens, another obligatory stop on the Vava'u tour circuit; they offer some of the best snorkelling opportunities in the island group. At low tide, you can cross on foot between the two islands.

VAKA'EITU

For anyone who may be wondering where that ubiquitous photo on all the Vava'u travel posters and brochures was taken, wonder no longer. The photograph was made looking south-westward at the bight of Vaka'eitu.

The island itself is home to a number of animals, including a famous pig named Otto, who gets on well with cats but doesn't associate much with his own kind – he's become a bit of a legend among yachties.

There is no village on the island and that magnificent beach on the travel poster is available for camping. However, if the plantations (which are owned by the Wolfgramm family, some of Vava'u's earliest German settlers) are being worked, you'll need to ask permission before settling in. Either arrange pick-up at the time you're dropped off or make your way across the reef to Nuapapu and try to catch a ride from there. Don't go to Vaka'eitu on any kind of a tight schedule because return transport to Neiafu may be a long time coming.

FOEATA

The island of Foeata, just south of Hunga, offers glorious white beaches and lots of good snorkelling in a secluded atmosphere.

KAPA
Swallows' Cave

The main attraction of Kapa Island is beautiful Swallows' Cave in a cliff at its northern end. The cave is in fact inhabited not · by swallows but by hundreds of starlings that flit about in the dim light and nest in the darkness of the cave's upper reaches. To get in you'll either need to be on a boat tour or have a dinghy or canoe, since the floor of the cave is up to 80 metres below the surface of the water.

Despite its depth, visibility in the cave is an incredible 50 metres and snorkellers will be amazed at the colour and clarity of the water there. Swimming there and gazing into the depths will give you the sensation of being weightless, suspended in mid-air. Those on a tour should stipulate in advance that they want to snorkel in the cave during the tour or they'll just get a quick trip through.

After you enter the cave, Bell Rock will be on your left. You can strike it with a solid object and listen to the melodic vibrations it emits. Keep moving on until you see a shaft of light shining through a hole in the ceiling and follow the rocky trail there into the adjoining dry cave. At the rear of the cave is a trail-like deposit of guano, which you can walk on.

Port Mourelle

Port Mourelle, on the protected western bight of Kapa Island, was the original landing site of the Spaniard Don Francisco Antonio Mourelle, the first European to visit Vava'u. It was here that he took on water from the springs of the swamp near Falevai (which means 'house of water'). There is a track from Port Mourelle down the spine of the island and another along the coast. Ask permission in either of the island's two villages if you'd like to camp.

NUKU

The tiny but lovely island of Nuku serves as the lunch stop on nearly all the boat tours of Vava'u. Thanks to its magnificent white beach, it also serves as the site of numerous official functions, celebrations and private parties. Excellent snorkelling is available south and east of the island; there the current is negligible, so marginal swimmers shouldn't have problems.

Those who would like a similarly idyllic beach, but without the touristy well-trodden feel to it, should go instead to Ngau and Taunga islands just to the south of Kapa. They offer good snorkelling and one of the nicest beaches imaginable.

MAHINITA

A tiny wooded island in the extreme south of the Vava'u Group, Mahinita is just about as secluded as it's possible to get. The coral reef on the approach is terraced and forms lovely pools which trap marine life at low tide. The forests of the centre of the island are pristine and peaceful, and snorkelling is optimum.

'EUAKAFA

The small island of 'Euakafa reaches an altitude of about 100 metres on its plateau and offers hiking as well as swimming and snorkelling opportunities.

Once, a Tongan king called Tele'a came to live on 'Euakafa because he considered

Tropical fish

Vava'u the most beautiful part of the kingdom. He took a lovely girl, Talafaiva, as his third wife and also accepted her dowry, which consisted of 100 other attractive girls. The whole big family set up housekeeping on the plateau of little 'Euakafa.

Outside the royal residence grew a *fo'ui* tree, which Talafaiva wanted chopped down; however, Tele'a refused to do so. One day, while Tele'a was out fishing, Lepuha, one of Tonga's irresistible 'handsome men', arrived to 'conquer' the bride of the king. By climbing the fo'ui tree, he was able to avoid the royal guard and enter the castle in order to seduce the queen. All would have been well if he hadn't tattooed her on the belly with his signature mark.

When Tele'a saw the mark he was outraged, but all the queen could do was blame the tree that she'd wanted to destroy in the first place. 'The fo'ui did it,' she said, and the fo'ui has served as a Tongan scapegoat ever since. Incidentally, Tele'a ordered his wife beaten for her indiscretion, but in doing so his servant inadvertently killed her. The king built her a tomb on the summit of 'Euakafa, which can still be visited, although there has never been a body found anywhere around it. Some claim that it was stolen by Lepuha. The fo'ui, by the way, is gone, too.

'OVALAU, MU'UNU, & 'OVAKA

Just a bit to the south-east of Vaka'eitu are the islands of Mu'unu and 'Ovalau, two more of those idyllic sunning, snorkelling, swimming and lazing-on-the-beach sort of places that travel brochures set travellers dreaming about. Nearby 'Ovaka is also pleasant, but can't hold a candle to its neighbours just to the east!

GETTING THERE & AWAY

Several companies based in Neiafu do the classic Vava'u water tour, which includes all the obligatory sights and activities:

Swallows' and Mariner's caves, picnicking at Nuku Island and snorkelling at the coral gardens (see the map called Main Tour Route, Vava'u Group). Soki's Tours charges T$15 per person for three people or more. Niva's Tours (tel 70101) leaves between 6 and 7 am and charges only T$10 (or less if you have a large group) for a full-day tour. If you'd like to visit more out-of-the-way places, boat charters are available from either company for T$40 for one or two people. Each extra person up to six people will be charged T$5 extra and each person beyond that will be charged T$10 extra.

If you're not booked on a tour but would still like to visit the most popular attractions, turn up between 8 and 9 am in front of Vava'u Watersports in Neiafu and see who's going.

OUTLYING VOLCANIC ISLANDS
Late

The island of Late was one of those evacuated by King George I when he realised that some of the outer areas of his kingdom were being ravaged by blackbirders (South American slave traders). The people of this island were resettled in Hunga beside its ideal lagoon.

Late consists of a volcanic crater 555 metres high which has lain dormant since 1854. Its wooded 15 square km are now uninhabited. On clear days it may be seen from the mainland.

Late'iki

This is another of those up and down, come and go sort of islands made famous by Fonuafo'ou in the Ha'apai Group. When this one is down it's called Metis Shoal.

In May 1979 Metis Shoal, which lies between the immense cone of Kao (Ha'apai) and Late, began spewing and erupting; for the third time in the past 100 years, a volcanic island broke the surface on the site. It had first emerged in 1858 but was gone by 1898. The island was next seen on 12 December 1967, when it made a

Late Island
Vava'u Group

0   2   4 km

View of Late

'pulsing glow on the horizon' during a particularly violent eruption. Within a week, it had reached an altitude of 18 metres.

On 7 July 1979, the king decided to take action. He sailed to the site and looked on as his son planted the Tongan flag on the new land and christened it Late'iki (pronounced lah-tay-EE-kee, if you're interested), which means 'little Late'. Who knows how long it will stick around this time...

Fonualei
This is the island that Mourelle named Amargura or 'bitterness', upon discovering it was barren and wouldn't provide him with much-needed and long-awaited supplies. It is situated 64 km north-west of

the main island of Vava'u and can be seen from the northern cliffs of that island on a clear day. In 1846 the island erupted, covering parts of the main island with volcanic ash.

The best way to have a good look at Fonualei is to sail to the Niuas from Neiafu. The ships pass within a couple of km of its eastern coast.

Toku
This is an old worn volcanic island near Fonualei whose inhabitants were also evacuated during the blackbirding scare of the 1860s. They resettled in 'Utulei village on Pangai Island, across from Neiafu. Toku remains uninhabited to this day.

The Niuas

The remote Niuas consist of three small volcanic islands in the extreme northern reaches of Tonga. With a population of less than 3000, all told they occupy only about 70 square km.

On 9 May 1616, the Dutchmen Schouten and Lemaire, in search of suitable trading partners to compete with the despised Dutch East India Company, had a disastrous confrontation with a Tongan sailing canoe. Disastrous, that is, for the canoe. Thanks to the hasty assumption on the part of the Europeans that the locals were hostile, shots were fired and several Tongans were drowned. Two were taken aboard the ship for observation and then released. After trading some trinkets for a meal and some weavings, Schouten and Lemaire went on their way. This was, by the way, the first recorded contact between Tongans and Europeans and the relationship hadn't gotten off to a good start.

The following day, the Dutchmen sighted Tafahi and went on to 'discover' Niuatoputapu and Niuafo'ou, but they never landed. After naming the islands Coconut, Traitor's and Good Hope, they moved on.

The next name-happy explorer to happen upon the Niuas was Captain Samuel Wallis, who passed through in 1767 in search of a fabled southern continent which was believed to balance the immense continents of the northern hemisphere. He stopped for a couple of days in Niuatoputapu and named it Keppel Island. The nearby volcanic cone of Tafahi Island he called Boscawen.

Tongan tradition remains alive here; the majority of the people still live in thatched Tongan fales, instead of the square European box houses ubiquitous elsewhere in the archipelago. As in the Ha'apai Group, the solitude of their surroundings has given the people a decidedly mellow attitude towards their world and their visitors. At the present time access is quite difficult but it is highly unlikely that anyone who goes to the trouble of visiting the Niuas will feel that the effort went unrewarded.

NIUATOPUTAPU ISLAND

Most visitors to Niuatoputapu ('New Potatoes' to tongue-tied yachties) arrive on private yachts. Since it is a port of entry into the country, many stopover here en route from the Samoas to the Vava'u Group between the months of September and November. During the rest of the year this island and its three small villages, one of which is the 'capital' of the Niuas, see very little activity.

The island, 240 km north of Vava'u, is shaped like a shoe with the toe pointed north-east. Topographically, it resembles a squashed sombrero, with a steep and narrow 130-metre-high ridge in the centre surrounded by a coastal plain, most of which is plantation land. Niuatoputapu produces nearly all the limes used in Tonga.

The northern coast is bound by a series of reefs but there is a passage through to Falehau Wharf near the 'toe' of the island. Yachts anchor just north-west of the wharf.

At the island's 'heel' is Mata'aho Airstrip, but at present it is used only for flights chartered by members of the royal family. There are no scheduled flights to any of the Niuas islands.

All three villages, Falehau, Vaipoa and the administrative capital, Hihifo, lie in a three-km line along the northern coast. They are all sleepy little places with scarcely a whisper of activity, and the presence of visitors creates an excitement that can scarcely be contained, especially during the months when there are no yachts at anchor there. Wherever you

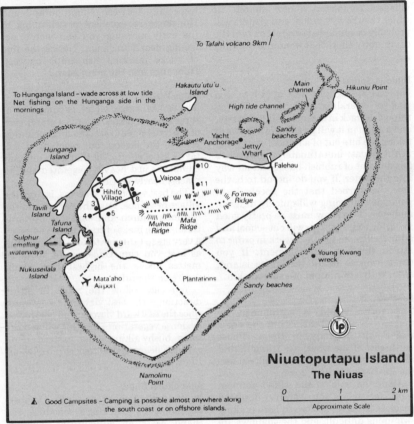

Niuatoputapu Island
The Niuas

0   1   2 km
Approximate Scale

⚓ Good Campsites – Camping is possible almost anywhere along
the south coast or on offshore islands.

1	Commodities Board & Shop
2	Police Station & GPO
3	Royal Palace
4	Niutoua Spring
5	New Church
6	Small Bush Shop
7	Bank
8	Carolyn's Guest House
9	Forestry Office
10	Bakery
11	Mormon Church

wander on this island, you will be greeted
with a smile. Every child you encounter

will demand to know your name,
exhausting the sum total of his or her
English vocabulary (however charming,
this does get a bit old hat after a
while!).

The island is ideal for walking and most
of its interesting sights can be covered in
just two days.

Hihifo

The sleepy village of Hihifo, on the north-
west corner of the island, contains the
police station, the Bank of Tonga, the post
office and a small cooperative store, which
is near the lagoon. In late 1988 the

villagers completed a new church, of which they're very proud, and visitors will probably be reminded several times of the community effort that went into building it.

Niutoua Spring

Niutoua Spring, just west of Hihifo, is a pool of sparkling cool water flowing through a crack in the rock. It is full of fish, and a swim in it will go a long way toward taking the bite out of a typical sticky day in the Niuas; unfortunately, however, a fair amount of rubbish has found its way into the water. If you do intend to bathe here, be warned that the spectacle of palangis swimming will quickly draw an audience. This show must be pretty good value for Tongans: kids will cut school and adults will abandon their work in order to attend the free entertainment. If you don't want to derail the entire island, swim with a minimum of exposed skin.

Beaches

The entire island is surrounded by magnificent white beaches but there is a remarkable diversity in them. Those north-east of the wharf are tranquil and ideal for cool early morning walks before the sun begins to beat down.

Along the 'sole' of the island you can walk for hours on sandy, deserted beaches. The reef is close in here making swimming difficult, and the shallows are full of marine life, including thousands of sea cucumbers. Near the eastern end of the island is the wreck of the Korean fishing boat *Young Kwang*, which ran aground in the mid-1980s.

Western Waterways

Near the village of Hihifo is a maze of sulphur-smelling waterways that wind between the intermittent islets of Nukuseilala, Tafuna, Tavili and Hunganga. At low tide, they form vast expanses of sand and leaning palms, and you can walk anywhere in the area by wading through a few cm of water. At high tide, the passages (especially between Niuatoputapu and Hunganga) are excellent for swimming. In the early morning you can watch net fishing near Hunganga. Notice the line of sticks marking fish traps between Hunganga and the main island.

Ridge Walk

The central ridge, which is composed of three smaller ridges, affords a grand view of the coastal plain and the multicoloured reefs of the lagoon, but reaching it will take a bit of effort. Not that it's a difficult climb: it's just heavily vegetated and, in places, nearly vertical.

The best way to go, it seems, is from the village of Vaipoa. Pass the bakery and the Mormon church and continue upwards through the maze of trails until you reach a very steep taro plantation. Scramble up as best you can. Once you're about 20 metres above the highest taro plant, you're on the ridge.

You can follow the ridge in either direction – the best views are westward, since the eastward views are all obstructed by dense vegetation – but this will require some bushwalking. The eastern route entails a near-vertical rock climb of about 10 metres.

Agricultural Show

In early September or early October, depending on the king's schedule, the island hosts an agricultural show. It culminates in a megafeast completely disproportional to the number of guests involved, and visitors are welcome.

Places to Stay & Eat

If you're after formal accommodation the choice is easy because there's only one. *Carolyn's Guest House*, at the southern end of Hihifo, is very friendly, clean and homelike. It's run by the sister of Queen Mata'aho. There's no sign, but everyone in town will know where it is.

Carolyn charges T$16 for a single and T$18 for a double room without meals. If you want to eat there (Carolyn is an

Traditional home

excellent cook!) book in advance. Breakfast costs T$4, lunch is T$5 and dinner is T$6. Coffee and a snack goes for about T$2.50.

Limited supplies are available at the cooperative in Hihifo. Bread is available at the bakery in Vaipoa after about 9 am every day, except Sundays.

Those who are prepared to camp will find numerous beautiful sites around the convoluted waterways near Hihifo and on the beach along the southern coast. Due to excessive wildlife of the buzzing variety, camping on the ridge is completely out of the question.

Getting There & Away

This can be tricky. The MV *'Olovaha* calls in from Vava'u on an average of every six weeks, and when they go, the *Fokololo 'oe Hau* is sure to follow. Your best option is to try going up on one and returning on the other, allowing you more than a few hours on the island. The problem lies with the *Fokololo*, which doesn't operate on a consistent schedule. Even when they have a basic plan there are no guarantees that their actual route will coincide with it, and an unplanned six-week stay on Niuatoputapu could get a bit tedious.

During the cruising season it should be quite easy to crew on for Niuatoputapu from Pago Pago (American Samoa), or 'Apia (Western Samoa). There are few yachts going to Niuatoputapu from other Tongan islands, however, because such a route would normally entail days of beating.

As mentioned before, flights to the island are limited to royal charters.

TAFAHI ISLAND

From the north cost of Niuatoputapu, the perfect cone of Tafahi Island dominates the view. If there were ever a search for an island that fits the description of the mythical Bali Hai, Tafahi would be a contender. One can't help gazing out across the lagoon and wondering what it's like over there. . .

Tafahi, nine km north of Niuatoputapu, is an extinct volcanic cone 656 metres high, with an base area of 3½ square km. Vanilla and kava are grown there only in

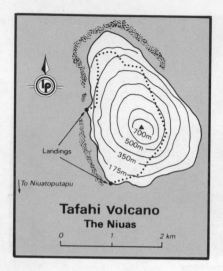

Landings

To Niuatoputapu

Tafahi Volcano
The Niuas

0   1   2 km

small quantities but the island does support a permanent population of several hundred.

If you get a very early start, you can climb to the crater and down in a day. There is an intermittent trail connecting the two landing sites on the western and southern sides of the island which leads up the relatively gradual northern slope to within striking distance of the summit. At the crater on a clear day you can see the peak of Savaii's Mt Silisili (Western Samoa), which is 1850 metres high and over 200 km distant. Don't forget to carry water!

Expect to pay between T$2.50 and T$5 for transport between Niuatoputapu and Tafahi. Be sure to arrange return transport in advance, especially if your conveyance away from Niuatoputapu is departing anytime in the near future.

NIUAFO'OU ISLAND

Niuafo'ou, which is also known as Tin Can Island, lies 640 km north and slightly west of Tongatapu; it's the remotest island in Tonga. The name Tin Can Island was coined by a pre-WW II palangi resident,

C S Ramsey, because of the island's unusual postal service. Since there was no anchorage or landing site on the island, mail and supplies for its residents were sealed up in a biscuit tin and tossed overboard from a passing supply ship. Strong swimmers would retrieve the parcels. Outbound mail was tied to the end of one-metre-long sticks, and swimmers would carry it thus, balanced overhead, to the waiting ship.

To most Tongans, Niuafo'ou is an enigma. Most of them have a vague idea where it is but psychologically it is unimaginably far, like a Timbuktu or a Shangri-La, and they are more familiar with such distant countries as Britain or Canada than they are with this remote corner of their homeland. Its inhabitants are credited with fortitude and regarded with reverence. In 1852 Walter Lawry, an early missionary, wrote of them:

. . .they prefer a land vitrified and comparatively sterile, without water and having no harbour or landing-place and where the sea is generally very turbulent, because, they say, their fathers lived there before them and there they are buried.

Although the situation isn't as bleak as all that these days, a full third of the island consists of barren and impassable lava flows. Most of the water supply is contained in its large crater lake or in sulphur springs.

History

During the past 150 years, the island has experienced 10 major eruptions, which have destroyed three villages. The village of 'Ahau on the south-west corner of the island was flattened by a lava flow during the eruption of 1853 and the former site of 'Ahau is today the most desolate part of the island.

In the devastating eruption of 1929, the village of Futu was buried beneath lava. Today, a few people live on the site of Futu, which serves as a very marginal

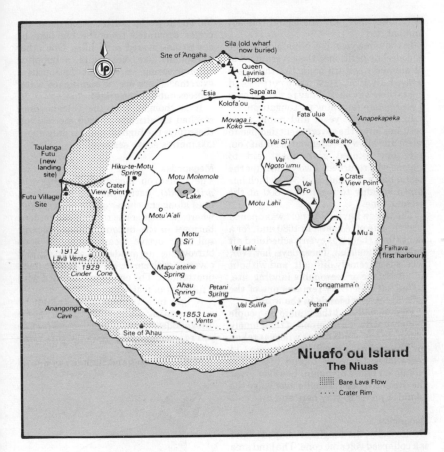

Niuafo'ou Island
The Niuas

::::: Bare Lava Flow
···· Crater Rim

landing area. A particularly violent eruption in 1943 destroyed plantations and decimated natural vegetation, causing a general famine on the island.

The most significant eruption, however, certainly wasn't the worst. In September 1946, earthquakes and lava flows on the northern slope buried the marginal wharf and capital village of 'Angaha. Although there were no injuries due to the quick evacuation of the area and although eight other villages escaped unscathed, the village of 'Angaha was destroyed and officials' homes were levelled or damaged.

The government debated whether 'Angaha, the seat of government, should be rebuilt or whether the entire island should be abandoned. Assuming that the island could not continue without local government and that future eruptions could render the place uninhabitable anyway, Queen Salote decided to evacuate the island. Beginning in late October the reluctant islanders were shuttled by boat to Tongatapu and then sent to 'Eua. The few recalcitrant inhabitants, 22 in number, who refused to leave during the general evacuation were forcefully collected in October 1947, and the island was left uninhabited.

In the same year, 608 Niuafo'ou people had already petitioned the government to be allowed to return home but they were refused. By 1950, a few copra cutters had made their way back. They remained only a year before returning to Tongatapu.

In 1958, eight years and many more petitions later, the government decided to relent and allow resettlement of Niuafo'ou, but they refused government aid to anyone who returned. Two years later the island had a population of 345, which has grown steadily to reach over 800 at the present time.

The Queen Lavinia Airport was opened near the site of 'Angaha in 1980 and, for a short time, there was even a scheduled air service to Niuafo'ou. These days, however, access is extremely difficult, and without an anchorage or reasonable landing site, Niuafo'ou effectively remains one of the least accessible islands in the world.

Visitors will find the Niuafo'ou people fiercely patriotic and proud of their lonely island. In the words of one who was taken to 'Eua against his will and returned 14 years later: 'Here we intend to stay. If Niuafo'ou blows up again, however great the fire and danger, I shall never leave the island. I prefer to stay here and die.'

Geography

Geologically, the doughnut-shaped island is a collapsed volcanic cone. The land area of the island consists of a caldera five km in diameter encircled by new lava flows. The crater is occupied almost completely by Vai Lahi ('big lake', an appropriate name), a freshwater lake which contains four major islands: Motu Lahi ('big island'), Motu Si'i ('small island') and Motu Molemole ('smooth island'), which has a crater lake of its own; the fourth island, Motu 'A'ali, appears above the surface when the water level is low.

Three smaller lakes, Vai Si'i ('small lake', also known as Vai Mata'aho after the nearby village), Vai Ngoto'umu and

Vai Fo, lie in the north-east corner of the crater separated from the big lake by casuarina-covered sand hills. One other significant lake, Vai Sulifa, a bubbling sulphur spring, is found at the southern extreme. There are no significant water sources outside the crater.

It is thought that the volcano once reached an altitude of 1300 metres, but these days the highest point is only about 200 metres above sea level.

Megapodes

The Niuafo'ou megapode (*megapodius pritchardi*), native only to this island, lives along the shores of the crater lakes, where it digs one to two-metre-deep burrows in the unconsolidated volcanic soil near active steam vents. In each burrow, the megapode deposits an egg and covers it with earth, leaving it to incubate unattended. The chicks are hatched with a full coat of feathers.

A line in a popular song written by a lamenting Niuafo'ou exile goes: 'Megapodes, speak your mind while you're near to your burrows else turn away without looking back. . .'

Megapode eggs and flesh are preferred

Megapode

by the islanders to domestic chickens due to the superior rich taste of the former. The lapila fish of the crater lakes are also eaten by the locals.

Things to See & Do

There is really no single thing that must be seen except, perhaps, for Vai Lahi, the crater lake. Those fortunate enough to reach Niuafo'ou will undoubtedly just want to explore. There is a track going right around and the island can be circumambulated in a single day, but Niuafo'ou is certainly worth more time. It's the sort of place that you'd like to settle into for a month or two (if you go, you may have to!) and try to grasp its essence.

On the southern and western shores is a vast and barren moonscape of lava flows. In the late 19th and early 20th centuries they oozed over the villages of 'Ahau and Futu, burying them completely. On the north shore, near the airport, are mounds of volcanic slag, lava tubes, vents and craters, which are easily accessible from the main road. Beneath them is the village of 'Angaha and its wharf, the pre-1946 centre of activity on Niuafo'ou.

Between the villages of Mu'a and Mata'aho, a trail leads up to a magnificent view of Vai Si'i, Vai Lahi and the islands. Between Futu and 'Esia, another trail affords a view of the entire expanse of Vai Lahi. From Mu'a, there is a rough road which crosses the sandy isthmus between the two major lakes and leads down to the shore of Vai Lahi. All around the crater, small trails will take you to numerous sulphur springs and lava vents.

The bubbling sulphur lake, Vai Sulifa, is best reached from Petani village.

Places to Stay & Eat

There aren't any, but it shouldn't be too difficult to arrange a stay with locals if you'll be on the island for awhile. There are numerous excellent campsites in the crater, especially on the lake shores, where drinking water is available. In other areas, locals will normally be happy to let you fill your water bottles from their rainwater tanks.

There is a bush store in the village of 'Esia, but it rarely has anything of interest unless the boat has recently come in. You'd get better variety and value purchasing produce directly from the locals.

Getting There & Away

This is the tricky part. Once in a blue moon, the MV 'Olovaha makes a run to Niuafo'ou, but if the weather isn't optimum, which it isn't about 70% of the time, the boat has to turn around and leave without stopping. The MV Fokololo 'oe Hau goes every five or six weeks, it is able to stop in slightly rougher weather, but surf much higher than half a metre renders unloading very tricky indeed.

There is no anchorage and no wharf and the entire island is exposed to the full wrath of the sea. Ships stop about 150 metres offshore. They drop two lines in the water which are retrieved by swimmers and carried to the cement platform that serves as the landing site. Passengers, luggage and cargo are literally dropped or thrown into a wooden dory at an opportune moment and ferried to shore, where hulking Tongans wait to pluck them out of the rolling and pitching craft and deposit them on shore.

Returning craft are filled nearly to the gunwales with copra. Oil drums and pens of squealing pigs are thrown (again, literally) on top of the sacks, then stalks of taro, yams, bananas, and other agricultural produce are fitted in wherever possible. Passengers are heaped and balanced on top of all this paraphernalia!

When there are only a few cm of freeboard remaining, water is pouring into the boat and the centre of gravity of the whole mess is at least a metre above the gunwales, the boats are shoved off through the surf. Passengers are constantly having to lean in one direction or another to prevent what seems to be the imminent capsize of the vessel. Upon arrival at the ship, passengers, cargo, pigs, etc are rolled, herded and pitched aboard.

If you come through this entire procedure without injury or distress of some sort, then count yourself lucky. In all fairness, though, the folks involved in this seemingly haphazard process have been at it for many years and they seem to know what they're doing, so you're in pretty good hands.

The trip back to Nuku'alofa takes up to 3½ days on the MV *Fokololo* and about two days on the MV *'Olovaha*. Since sailings to the Niuas are unscheduled, you'll have to enquire at the boats' respective Nuku'alofa offices for information regarding sailings.

By the way, as on Niuatoputapu, the only aircraft calling in to Niuafo'ou are those chartered by royals; a traveller wouldn't have much hope of reaching the island by air.

Index

149

MAPS

Temperature

To convert °C to °F multiply by 1.8 and add 32

To convert °F to °C subtract 32 and multiply by ·55

Length, Distance & Area

	multiply by
inches to centimetres	2.54
centimetres to inches	0.39
feet to metres	0.30
metres to feet	3.28
yards to metres	0.91
metres to yards	1.09
miles to kilometres	1.61
kilometres to miles	0.62
acres to hectares	0.40
hectares to acres	2.47

Weight

	multiply by
ounces to grams	28.35
grams to ounces	0.035
pounds to kilograms	0.45
kilograms to pounds	2.21
British tons to kilograms	1016
US tons to kilograms	907

A British ton is 2240 lbs, a US ton is 2000 lbs

Volume

	multiply by
Imperial gallons to litres	4.55
litres to imperial gallons	0.22
US gallons to litres	3.79
litres to US gallons	0.26

5 imperial gallons equals 6 US gallons
a litre is slightly more than a US quart, slightly less
than a British one

Guides to The Pacific

Australia – a travel survival kit
Australia is Lonely Planet's home territory so this guide
gives you the complete low-down on Down Under, from
the red centre to the coast, from cosmopolitan cities to
country towns.

Bushwalking in Australia
Australia offers opportunities for walking in many different
climates and terrains – from the tropical north, to the rocky
gorges of the centre, to the mountains of the south-east.
Two experienced and respected walkers give details of the
best walks in every state, plus notes on many more.

New Zealand – a travel survival kit
Visitors to New Zealand find a land of fairytale beauty
and scenic contrasts – a natural wonderland. This book
has information about the places you won't want to miss,
including ski-resorts and famous walks.

Tramping in New Zealand
Call it tramping, hiking, walking, bushwalking, or
trekking – travelling on your feet is the best way to come to
grips with New Zealand's natural beauty. This guide
gives detailed descriptions for 20 walks of various length
and difficulty.

Fiji – a travel survival kit
This is a comprehensive guide to the Fijian archipelago.
On a number of these beautiful islands accommodation
ranges from camping grounds to international hotels –
whichever you prefer this book will help you to enjoy the
South Seas.

Solomon Islands – a travel survival kit
The Solomon Islands are the Pacific's best kept secret. If
you want to discover remote tropical islands, jungle-
covered volcanoes and traditional Melanesian villages,
this book will show you how.

Tahiti & French Polynesia – a travel survival kit

The image of palm-fringed beaches and friendly people continues to lure travellers to Polynesia. This book gives you all the facts on paradise, and will be useful whether you plan a package holiday, or to travel the islands independently.

Rarotonga & the Cook Is – a travel survival kit

Rarotonga has history, beauty and magic to rival Hawaii, Tahiti or Bora Bora. Unlike those better known islands, however, the world has virtually passed it by. The Cook Islands range from mountainous islands to remote and untouched coral atolls.

Micronesia – a travel survival kit

Amongst these 2100 islands are beaches, lagoons and reefs that will dazzle the most jaded traveller. This guide is packed with all you need to know about island hopping across the north Pacific.

Papua New Guinea – a travel survival kit

Papua New Guinea is truly 'the last unknown' – the last inhabited place on earth to be explored by Europeans. This guide has the latest information for travellers who want to find just how rewarding a trip to this remote and amazing country can be.

Samoa – a travel survival kit

Two remarkably different countries, Western Samoa and American Samoa offer Polynesian culture at its best and some wonderful island escapes.

Also Available:
Papua New Guinea phrasebook

Lonely Planet Guidebooks

Lonely Planet guidebooks cover virtually every accessible part of Asia as well as Australia, the Pacific, Central and South America, Africa, the Middle East and parts of North America. There are four main series: 'travel survival kits', covering a single country for a range of budgets; 'shoestring' guides with compact information for low-budget travel in a major region; trekking guides; and 'phrasebooks'.

Australia & the Pacific
Australia
Bushwalking in Australia
Papua New Guinea
Papua New Guinea phrasebook
New Zealand
Tramping in New Zealand
Rarotonga & the Cook Islands
Solomon Islands
Tahiti & French Polynesia
Fiji
Micronesia
Tonga
Samoa

South-East Asia
South-East Asia on a shoestring
Malaysia, Singapore & Brunei
Indonesia
Bali & Lombok
Indonesia phrasebook
Burma
Burmese phrasebook
Thailand
Thai phrasebook
Philippines
Pilipino phrasebook

North-East Asia
North-East Asia on a shoestring
China
China phrasebook
Tibet
Tibet phrasebook
Japan
Japanese phrasebook
Korea
Korean phrasebook
Hong Kong, Macau & Canton
Taiwan

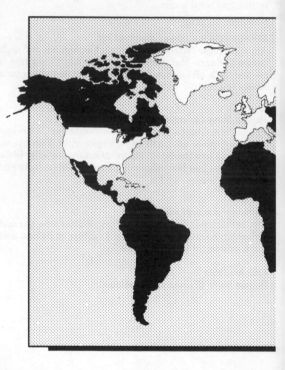

West Asia
West Asia on a shoestring
Trekking in Turkey
Turkey

Indian Ocean
Madagascar & Comoros
Mauritius, Réunion & Seychelles
Maldives & Islands of the East Indian Ocean

Mail Order

Lonely Planet guidebooks are distributed worldwide and are sold by good bookshops everywhere. They are also available by mail order from Lonely Planet, so if you have difficulty finding a title please write to us. US and Canadian residents should write to Embarcadero West, 112 Linden St, Oakland CA 94607, USA and residents of other countries to PO Box 617, Hawthorn, Victoria 3122, Australia.

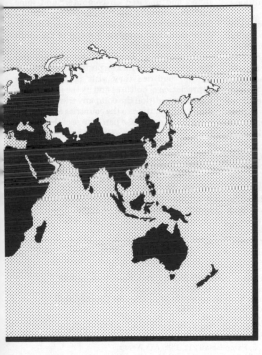

Eastern Europe
Eastern Europe

Indian Subcontinent
India
Hindi/Urdu phrasebook
Kashmir, Ladakh & Zanskar
Trekking in the Indian Himalaya
Pakistan
Kathmandu & the Kingdom of Nepal
Trekking in the Nepal Himalaya
Nepal phrasebook
Sri Lanka
Sri Lanka phrasebook
Bangladesh
Karakoram Highway

Africa
Africa on a shoestring
East Africa
Swahili phrasebook
West Africa
Central Africa
Morocco, Algeria & Tunisia

North America
Canada
Alaska

Mexico
Mexico
Baja California

South America
South America on a shoestring
Ecuador & the Galapagos Islands
Colombia
Chile & Easter Island
Bolivia
Brazil
Peru
Argentina
Quechua phrasebook

Middle East
Israel
Egypt & the Sudan
Jordan & Syria
Yemen

Lonely Planet

Lonely Planet published its first book in 1973. Tony and Maureen Wheeler had made a lengthy overland trip from England to Australia and, in response to numerous 'how do you do it?' questions, Tony wrote and they published *Across Asia on the Cheap*. It became an instant local best-seller and inspired thoughts of a second travel guide. A year and a half in South-East Asia resulted in their second book, *South-East Asia on a Shoestring*, which they put together in a backstreet Chinese hotel in Singapore in 1975. The 'yellow book', as it quickly became known, soon became *the* guide to the region and has gone through five editions, always with its familiar yellow cover.

Soon other writers came to them with ideas for similar books – books that went off the beaten track with an adventurous approach to travel, books that 'assumed you knew how to get your luggage off the carousel,' as one reviewer put it. Lonely Planet grew from a kitchen table operation to a spare room and then to its own office. Its international reputation began to grow as the Lonely Planet logo began to appear in more and more countries. In 1982 *India – a travel survival kit* won the Thomas Cook award for the best guidebook of the year.

These days there are over 70 Lonely Planet titles. Over 40 people work at our office in Melbourne, Australia and another half dozen at our US office in Oakland, California.

At first Lonely Planet specialised in the Asia region but these days we are also developing major ranges of guidebooks to the Pacific region, to South America and to Africa. The list of walking guides is growing and Lonely Planet now has a unique series of phrasebooks to 'unusual' languages. The emphasis continues to be on travel for travellers and Tony and Maureen still manage to fit in a number of trips each year and play a very active part in the writing and updating of Lonely Planet's guides.

Keeping guidebooks up to date is a constant battle which requires an ear to the ground and lots of walking, but technology also plays its part. All Lonely Planet guidebooks are now stored and updated on computer, and some authors even take lap-top computers into the field. Lonely Planet is also using computers to draw maps and eventually many of the maps will be stored on disk.

The people at Lonely Planet strongly feel that travellers can make a positive contribution to the countries they visit both by better appreciation of cultures and by the money they spend. In addition the company tries to make a direct contribution to the countries and regions it covers. Since 1986 a percentage of the income from each book has gone to aid groups and associations. This has included donations to famine relief in Africa, to aid projects in India, to agricultural projects in Central America, to Greenpeace's efforts to halt French nuclear testing in the Pacific and to Amnesty International. In 1989 $41,000 was donated by Lonely Planet to these projects.

Lonely Planet Distributors

Australia & Papua New Guinea Lonely Planet Publications, PO Box 617, Hawthorn, Victoria 3122.
Canada Raincoast Books, 112 East 3rd Avenue, Vancouver, British Columbia V5T 1C8.
Denmark, Finland & Norway Scanvik Books aps, Store Kongensgade 59 A, DK-1264 Copenhagen K.
India & Nepal UBS Distributors, 5 Ansari Rd, New Delhi – 110002
Israel Geographical Tours Ltd, 8 Tverya St, Tel Aviv 63144.
Japan Intercontinental Marketing Corp, IPO Box 5056, Tokyo 100-31.
Kenya Westland Sundries Ltd, PO Box 14107, Nairobi, Kenya.
Netherlands Nilsson & Lamm bv, Postbus 195, Pampuslaan 212, 1380 AD Weesp.
New Zealand Transworld Publishers, PO Box 83-094, Edmonton PO, Auckland.
Singapore & Malaysia MPH Distributors, 601 Sims Drive, #03-21, Singapore 1438.
Spain Altair, Balmes 69, 08007 Barcelona.
Sweden Esselte Kartcentrum AB, Vasagatan 16, S-111 20 Stockholm.
Thailand Chalermnit, 108 Sukhumvit 53, Bangkok 10110.
Turkey Yab-Yay Dagitim, Alay Koshu Caddesi 12/A, Kat 4 no. 11-12, Cagaloglu, Istanbul.
UK Roger Lascelles, 47 York Rd, Brentford, Middlesex, TW8 0QP
USA Lonely Planet Publications, PO Box 2001A, Berkeley, CA 94702.
West Germany Buchvertrieb Gerda Schettler, Postfach 64, D3415 Hattorf a H.
All Other Countries refer to Australia address.